Ethnographies in Sport and Exercise Research

Ethnography has become an important method for researching and interpreting the social world, not least in the field of sport and exercise studies. *Ethnographies in Sport and Exercise Research* is the first book to provide a contemporary overview of the current state of ethnographic research and its application within sport and exercise, introducing and explaining a range of well-established and emerging ethnographic approaches.

Featuring a heavyweight line-up of sport and exercise researchers, the book is divided into three parts. After an introduction to the book and to the history of ethnography in sport and exercise research, the first considers:

- the definition of the ethnographic field
- methods of gathering ethnographic data
- methods of representing ethnographic research.

In the second part of the book, a series of chapter-length case studies, spanning sports from boxing to fell running and themes from gender to fandom, demonstrates the challenges and rewards of ethnographic research in the context of sport and exercise, helping students and researchers to develop a solid understanding of qualitative research at both a theoretical and a practical level. The final part of the book considers future directions for ethnographic research, including an evaluation of its place in the expanding field of study in sport management.

A comprehensive assessment of the state of ethnographic research in sport, *Ethnographies in Sport and Exercise Research* is invaluable reading for any research methods course taken as part of a degree programme in sport and exercise, and a useful reference for all active researchers.

Gyozo Molnar is Senior Lecturer in Sport and Exercise Science at the University of Worcester, UK. His current publications and research revolve around national identity, the Olympics and sport-related international migration, and, with Dr Yoko Kanemasu, has focused on rugby.

He is co-editor (with Prof. Alan Bairner) of *The Politics of the Olympics* (2010, Routledge) and co-writer (with Dr John Kelly) of *Sport, Exercise and Social Theory: An introduction* (2012, Routledge).

Laura G. Purdy is Senior Lecturer in the Department of Sport and Physical Activity at Edge Hill University, UK. Her research interests lie in delving deeper into high performance/elite sporting cultures, focusing on the everyday realities of coaches and athletes/players. In doing so, she has utilised ethnographic methodologies and methods to explore the lived experiences of coaches and athletes/players in relation to the concepts of identity, power and interaction. In addition to disseminating her work via *Sport, Education and Society* and the *Sociology of Sport Journal*, she has contributed to rugby and basketball coaches' CPD in a number of international settings.

Ethnographies in Sport and Exercise Research

Edited by Gyozo Molnar and Laura G. Purdy

Routledge
Taylor & Francis Group

LONDON AND NEW YORK

First published 2016 by Routledge

2 Park Square, Milton Park, Abingdon, Oxon OX14 4RN
711 Third Avenue, New York, NY 10017, USA

Routledge is an imprint of the Taylor & Francis Group, an informa business

First issued in paperback 2017

British Library Cataloguing-in-Publication Data
A catalogue record for this book is available from the British Library

Library of Congress Cataloging in Publication Data
Ethnographies in sport and exercise research / edited by Gyozo Molnar and Laura Purdy.
    pages cm
  Includes bibliographical references and index.
  1. Sports – Anthropological aspects. 2. Sports – Research. 3. Sports – Anthropological aspects – Case studies. 4. Sports – Research – Case studies. I. Molnar, Gyozo. II. Purdy, Laura.
  GV706.2.E75 2015
  306.4′83–dc23   2015004367

ISBN: 978-1-138-01528-9 (hbk)
ISBN: 978-1-138-70504-3 (pbk)

Typeset in Galliard
by HWA Text and Data Management, London

Contents

Notes on contributors

Michael Atkinson is Professor in the Faculty of Kinesiology Physical Education at the University of Toronto, Canada, where he teaches physical cultural studies, policy, bioethics and research methods. His central areas of teaching and research interests pertain to the experiences of human suffering in/as physical cultures, the cross-national study of bio-pedagogical practices, radical embodiment, issues in bioethics within global and local physical cultures, and ethnographic research methods. Michael's ethnographic research efforts have included the study of ticket scalpers, tattoo enthusiasts, fell runners, cosmetic surgery patients, greyhound and fox-hunting cultures, Ashtanga yoga practitioners, Straightedge and Parkour youth cultures, and triathletes. He is author/co-author of eight books including *Deconstructing Men and Masculinities, Battleground: Sports,* and *Key Concepts in Sport and Exercise Research Methods,* and is Editor of the *Sociology of Sport Journal.*

Alan Bairner is Professor of Sport and Social Theory at Loughborough University's School of Sport and Exercise Sciences, UK. He studied Politics at the University of Edinburgh, UK, gained a PGCE from Moray House College of Education, UK, and was awarded his PhD at the University of Hull, UK, for a thesis on the social and political theory of Antonio Gramsci. Prior to his arrival in Loughborough in 2003, he was Professor in Sport Studies at the University of Ulster, UK, where he had worked for 25 years. He is the author of *Sport, Nationalism, and Globalization: Europe and North American perspectives* (2001) and co-author (with John Sugden) of *Sport, Sectarianism and Society in a Divided Ireland* (1993). He edited *Sport and the Irish: Histories, Identities, Issues* (2005) and is joint editor of *Sport in Divided Societies* (1999), *The Bountiful Game? Football Identities and Finances* (2005) and *The Politics of the Olympics: A survey* (2010).

Adam Benkwitz is a Senior Lecturer in the Sociology of Physical Education and Sports Studies in the School of Human Sciences at Newman University, Birmingham, UK. He completed his doctoral thesis at the

University of Worcester, UK, based on an ethnographic study of football fans in Birmingham. His qualitative research interests centre on specific areas including fandom, rivalry and also physical activity interventions for mental health issues, and he is the founder and lead of Newman's Mental Health Research Group.

Tim Butcher is a Senior Lecturer at the RMIT School of Management, Australia. His research interests focus on identity, belonging and nostalgia at the intersections between community and organisation. As an organisational ethnographer, his published work covers a broad range of people in different organisational contexts including skilled machinists in aerospace manufacturing, European supply chain managers, coworking entrepreneurs, and remote Indigenous communities. Tim is a member of the Australia and New Zealand Academy of Management (ANZAM) and the European Group of Organisation Studies (EGOS), and he is a fellow of the Royal Academy of Engineering Panasonic Trust in recognition of his studies in sustainability. He is also the Program Manager of the Global Indigeneity and Reconciliation Program of the RMIT Global Cities Research Institute.

Carrie Dunn is a journalist and academic who has been combining research, teaching and professional practice since 2005. She teaches at Regent's College, UK, and the University of Surrey, UK, delivering modules on cultural studies, media and sociology. Her research interests include fandom, sport, feminism and the consumption of popular culture, and her PhD examined the experience of the female football supporter in the English professional game. As a journalist she divides her time between writing about sport and writing about popular culture, for publications including *The Times* and *The Guardian*.

Christian Edwards is a PhD student and Lecturer in Coaching Science at Cardiff Metropolitan University's School of Sport, UK. His research interests relate to sociological issues within sport, most notably that of coaches' power and social interaction in the coaching context. Christian's PhD work examines the social significance of humour and how it is used as a critical component in the negotiation of coaching relationships. He is a former international footballer and the Director of Cardiff Metropolitan University's Men's Football team.

Meridith Griffin's primary research interests are ageing, health and wellbeing, disability, gender and embodiment. Particularly, she is interested in exploring why, how, and when individuals tend to make health choices and/or change health behaviours, and the ways in which people experience different forms of embodiment over time in a variety of contexts. Her recent work has focused on active ageing, embodiment, and health consciousness within a non-elite women's-only running group, as well as an interest in the power of stories to create and direct action. These empirical and theoretical interests are framed by a methodological interest in interpretive forms of understanding including life history, ethnography, visual and narrative approaches.

Chris Hallinan has an extensive research background in Indigenous Studies and sports as well as the politics of ethnic, racial and national identities in sports and sports organisations. The principal area of specialisation critically examines major common assumptions concerning the politics of racial and cultural diversity within sport communities. He has published several books, and over 50 research articles and book chapters. Many of these publications have incorporated field work methods and design. With John Hughson he was the co-editor of a book that was one of the pioneer publications of ethnographic fieldwork experiences in sports studies. More recently he has conducted ethnographic based research studies with colleague Barry Judd about the experiential reality of sports participation for Indigenous Australians. He has also been employed at several universities in Australia and the United States and is currently with Monash Indigenous Centre at Monash University in Australia and the Department of Sociology and Anthropology at University of Toledo, USA.

John Harris is Reader in International Sport & Event Management at Glasgow Caledonian University, Scotland, UK. Harris is Leisure and Events Subject Editor for the *Journal of Hospitality, Leisure, Sport and Tourism Education* (JoHLSTE) and also serves on the editorial boards of the *Journal of Sport & Tourism* and the *International Journal of Sport Communication*. His published work includes the books *Rugby Union and Globalization* (Palgrave Macmillan) and *Football and Migration* (co-edited with R. Elliott, Routledge).

John Hughson is well known within the sociology and cultural studies of sport for his pioneering ethnographic research of young male football supporters in Australia in the early 1990s. He is currently Professor of Sport and Cultural Studies at the University of Central Lancashire, UK, and is involved internally and externally in the supervision of several PhD students, a number of whom are using ethnographic methods to research both sports participants and fans. His most recent field-based research focuses on football supporter culture in Serbia. John's most recent book is *The Making of Sporting Cultures* (Routledge). He is a senior member of the editorial team for the journal *Sport in Society* (Routledge) and is on the international editorial board of *Ethnography* (Sage).

Robyn L. Jones is a Professor of Sport and Social Theory at the Cardiff School of Sport, Cardiff Metropolitan University (UWIC), UK, and a Visiting Professor (II) at the Norwegian School of Sport Sciences, Oslo, Norway. He has published several books on sports coaching and pedagogy, the most recent being *A Sociology of Sports Coaching* (Routledge). He also serves as the General Editor of the newly launched Taylor & Francis journal *Sports Coaching Review*.

Barry Judd is a descendent of the Pitjantjatjara people of North West South Australia and British immigrants who settled on the Victorian goldfields in the 1850s. Barry has a growing research interest and expertise in explorations of Australian identity and the process of cultural interchange between Indigenous and non-Indigenous peoples in Australia since 1770. His PhD thesis, entitled 'Australian game, Australian Identity: (post)colonial identity in football', explored cross-cultural engagements between Aborigines and Anglo-Australians in the sport of Australian (Rules) Football. Barry engages with (post)colonial ideas of 'cultural hybridity' which claim colonial encounters between 'settler' and 'native' produce (post)colonial identity positions that rest somewhere 'in-between' those previously held by invader and invaded. Barry's research enables him to further develop his interest concerning constructions of Australian citizenship and Australian nationalism, Aboriginal affairs policy and administration. He is with the Centre for Global Studies at RMIT University in Melbourne, Australia.

Pirkko Markula is a Professor of Socio-Cultural Studies of Physical Activity at the University of Alberta, Canada. Her research interests include social analyses of dance, exercise, and sport in which she has employed several theoretical lenses ranging from critical, cultural studies research to Foucault and Deleuze. While her work is based on qualitative research methods (textual analysis, participant-observation, interviewing, ethnography), she is also interested in methodological experimentation including autoethnography and performance ethnography. Her work appears in *Qualitative Inquiry, International Review of Qualitative Inquiry, Sociology of Sport Journal, Journal of Sport & Social Issues, Journal of Sport Management,* and *Journal of Contemporary Ethnography.* She is co-author with Michael Silk of *Qualitative Research for Physical Culture* (Routledge, 2011), co-author with Richard Pringle of *Foucault, Sport and Exercise: Power, knowledge and transforming the self* (Routledge, 2006), editor of *Feminist Sport Studies: Sharing joy, sharing pain* (SUNY Press, 2005) and *Olympic Women and the Media: International perspectives* (Palgrave, 2009), co-editor with Eileen Kennedy of *Women and Exercise: Body, health and consumerism* (Routledge, 2011), co-editor with Sarah Riley, Maree Burns, Hannah Frith and Sally Wiggins of *Critical Bodies: Representations, identities and practices of weight and body management* (Palgrave, 2007) and co-editor with Jim Denison of *Moving Writing: Crafting movement in sport research* (Peter Lang, 2003).

Kerry R. McGannon is an Associate Professor in Sport and Exercise Psychology, Laurentian University, Ontario, Canada. Her work 'bridges' psychology and cultural studies to understand physical activity participation via interpretive qualitative methodologies to study marginalised identities and critical interpretations of sport and exercise. Her scholarship includes empirical and theoretically-driven contributions on over 66 national and international presentations and over 65 publications in refereed journals and scholarly books. She is co-editor of the books *The Psychology of Subculture in Sport and Physical Activity: Critical Perspectives and Community Based Research in Sport, Exercise and Health* and the forthcoming book *The Routledge International Handbook of Sport Psychology*. She is Associate Editor of the *Journal of Applied Sport Psychology* and serves on three journal editorial boards: *Psychology of Sport and Exercise, Journal of Applied Sport Psychology* and *Qualitative Research in Sport, Exercise and Health*.

Gyozo Molnar is Senior Lecturer in Sport Studies in the Institute of Sport and Exercise Science at the University of Worcester, UK. His current publications and research revolve around migration, globalisation, national identity, the Olympics and sport-related role exit. His most current research, with Dr Yoko Kanemasu, has focused on the migratory aspects of Fiji rugby. He is co-editor (with Prof. Alan Bairner) of *The Politics of the Olympics* (2010, Routledge) and co-writer (with Dr John Kelly) of *Sport, Exercise and Social Theory: An introduction* (2012, Routledge).

Cassandra Phoenix's research coheres around the concept of 'ageing well' and is framed by narrative approaches, visual methods, and ethnography. In particular, she is interested in exploring the embodiment of ageing across the life course; the impact of ageing on self, identity, and well-being; intergenerational relationships; disability; and the ageing body within the natural environment. This work currently spans three complementary themes: the role of physical activity in shaping expectations and experiences of ageing; the intersection of health, vulnerability and changing environment in the lives of older adults; and the advancement of qualitative methods and narrative theory through the combined use of, for example, mobile methods, visual methods, narrative analyses and creative analytical practices as a means of understanding the interplay between self, society, continuity and change.

Laura G. Purdy's research interests lie in delving deeper into high performance/elite sporting cultures, focusing on the everyday realities of coaches and athletes/players. In doing so, she has utilised ethnographic methodologies and methods to explore the lived experiences of coaches and athletes/players in relation to the concepts of identity, power and interaction. In addition to disseminating her work via *Sport, Education and Society* and the *Sociology of Sport Journal*, she has contributed to rugby and basketball coaches' CPD in a number of international settings. She is working in the Department of Sport and Physical Activity at Edge Hill University, UK.

Brett Smith is Professor of Qualitative Health Research at Loughborough University, UK, and leads the wellbeing team within the Peter Harrison Centre for Disability Sport. Working at the intersection of psychology and sociology, his research focuses on disability, physical activity, wellbeing, and the advancement of qualitative methods. This research has resulted in over 100 publications. He has also given over 100 invited research talks, including in the UK Houses of Parliament and for the Royal Society of Medicine. Brett is founding Editor of the award winning international journal, *Qualitative Research in Sport, Exercise, and Health*. He is also co-author of several books, including *Qualitative Research Methods in Sport, Exercise and Health: From process to product*.

Andrew C. Sparkes is Professor of Sport, Physical Activity and Leisure at Leeds Beckett University, UK. His research interests revolve around the ways that people experience different forms of embodiment over time in a variety of contexts. Recent work has focused on performing bodies and identity formation; spinal cord injury in sport and the narrative reconstruction of self; sporting autobiographies and body-self relationships, ageing bodies and shifting subjectivities; and the lives and careers of marginalised individuals and groups. These interests are framed by a desire to develop interpretative and critical forms of understanding via the use of life history, ethnography, and narrative approaches. He also seeks to represent lived experience to multiple audiences using a variety of genres. Andrew has published extensively on these research interests as well as on methodological issues across a range of disciplines in international peer reviewed journals and via numerous chapters in leading edited books. Andrew currently serves on the advisory or editorial board of 12 international journals. His latest co-authored book entitled *Qualitative Research in Sport, Exercise and Health: From process to product* was published by Routledge in 2014.

Alex Stewart is with the Department of PE & Sport Studies at the University of Bedfordshire, UK. Having conducted a five-year ethnographic study of amateur and professional boxers in England, his central research interests now lie in the examination of cultural and social aspects of the sporting experience. Reciprocally Alex's academic interests and teaching competences take in the following related areas: the socialisation process into and through sport; embodiment and identity formation; sport and issues regarding media representation and lifestyle; sporting subcultures; and sport development in relation to: culture and power, inclusion/exclusion, youth development, crime reduction and education. In a previous life Alex spent his time split between boxing competitively as an amateur and briefly as a professional boxer and backpacking and working his way around the globe.

Toni L. Williams joined the Peter Harrison Centre for Disability Sport at Loughborough University, UK, after being awarded a Glendonbrook Doctoral Fellowship. Her PhD explores the impact of activity-based rehabilitation on the health and well-being of people with spinal cord injury (SCI). Toni's research interests also include narrative inquiry, disability studies, psychology of injury and rehabilitation, and qualitative meta-synthesis. Her first meta-synthesis of qualitative research on SCI and physical activity has recently been published in *Health Psychology Review*. She was the co-chair of the 4th International Conference on Qualitative Research in Sport and Exercise and is currently editorial assistant for the journal *Qualitative Research in Sport, Exercise and Health*.

Chapter 1

Introduction

Gyozo Molnar and Laura G. Purdy

This is a brief introduction to what we believe is an intriguing, intellectually stimulating and inspirational collection of essays in the area of sport and exercise research. The extensive growth of the field of sport and exercise ethnography in the last decade is evidenced by the wide range of contributions and contributors to this anthology. Given ethnography's continuously mounting importance as a strategy and method of researching and interpreting the social world, we felt that there was an emerging need for a contemporary overview on the current state of ethnography and its application within sport and exercise. The majority of previous accounts considering the fields of sport and exercise ethnography either have focused on a specific topic – e.g., women, culture and exercise; ethnographies of injury and risk or evolutionary explanations of human performance – or have provided only a tokenistic account of the potential array of ethnographic approaches within sport and exercise. While these writings have merit in their own right, contemporary ethnography has diffused; has become richer in terms of data production, interpretation, representation and theoretical engagement. Although Robert Sand's (2002) seminal (though somewhat hagiographic) work may still serve as a good starting point to learning the basics about the trade, we now have access to the writings of scholars who have immersed themselves in many of the spheres of sport or exercise. However, as always seems to be the case, the field of sport and exercise studies is a late-bloomer in terms of letting itself be inspired by what we may refer to as the qualitative and ethnographic turn (Hughson & Hallinan, 2001). Whilst, by and large, we were still preoccupied with the actual nature and applicability of ethnography, in the mainstream social sciences, talks were already emerging around novel forms of this approach to research (see Goodall, 2000). In the spirit of embracing innovative forms of ethnography and creating a platform for raising and discussing recurring methodological as well as practical challenges, we aimed to focus on constructing a collection of essays which draws attention to considerably novel methodological implications, illustrative case studies and the inherent potential for a reality-congruent understanding of sport and exercise via ethnography.

The book has two main objectives, the first of which is to provide a current and accessible key source on the practical and methodological features of well-established and emerging ethnographic approaches in sport and exercise. Second, this book aims to serve to be a *tour d'horizon* of using ethnography in sport and exercise research, thereby filling a gap in the existing literature and providing a novel, analytical and contemporary collection of essays written by emerging as well as established researchers in this field. Our main goal is to provide clear accounts of ethnographic perspectives by explaining them in the contemporary world and showcasing their application through specific case studies. In doing so, the book will be a valuable companion to help students and academics in their quest for building a solid methodological foundation which, in turn, enable them to get better acquainted with qualitative research both at theoretical as well as practical levels.

Book content: increasing presence of ethnography in sport and exercise

The anthology begins with a historical overview of using ethnography in sport-focused research. Carrie Dunn and John Hughson pay heed to the significance of the Centre for Contemporary Cultural Studies in the emergence of football hooligan subculture research. They acknowledge the initial significance of the Leicester School in their covert participant observation of football fans and provide a critical insight into these early studies. One of the major critiques directed at the Leicester School was their lack of ethnographic self-immersion, which later studies aimed to address. Influenced by Paul Willis's seminal work, in-depth ethnographic studies were carried out in the 1990s centring on young male extreme fans' life world. Whilst football fan culture remained a central part of sport ethnography (e.g. Sugden, 2002), other areas of sport and exercise subcultural investigation began to emerge, including exercise (Spielvogel, 2003), skating (Rand, 2012), boxing (Wacquant, 2004), etc. Dunn and Hughson also direct our attention towards an on-going debate and tension between field research and ever-increasing institutional ethics scrutiny. The point raised, and, perhaps for the reader to ponder upon, is the potential danger of overly cautious ethics committees and procedures marginalising ethnographic-type field research. Dunn and Hughson note that "A prevailing 'medical model' approach to ethical evaluation within universities compounds the problem of over scrutiny for much of the research in social science and humanities areas." Ethnographic studies following a flexible and reflective approach to research are in a particularly vulnerable position because the possible risks to the researcher working in the field may not be as foreseeable as with more structured, linear forms of research. Consequently, it may be considered credible and significant to ponder upon the long-term contribution and sustainability of ethnography to research in sport and exercise.

As noted above, conducting field research is not without its challenges. In fact, it may be perceived as the most challenging aspect of conducting ethnographic work. Signalling the pertinence of the empirical phase of ethnography, multiple chapters in this volume discuss various aspects of collecting primary data and self-immersion in subcultural settings. Pirkko Markula's chapter provides an insightful, informative as well as theoretically robust account of fieldwork carried out in the fitness world. Specific focus is given to some of the dilemmas ethnographers encounter when choosing and entering the field. Firstly, with the help of Bourdieu, Markula defines the field as a culturally diverse terrain where the interactions of social agencies can be examined via a theory-informed ethnographic approach. Then she introduces different approaches that other ethnographers have successfully adopted to define and explore the field. One particularly interesting discussion is centred on 'field trouble' which points out that only a few ethnographers of fitness have acknowledged challenges when entering the field. While this process may appear trouble free given that "anyone can join a gym" – Markula notes – to do ethnography in fitness requires more than paying monthly membership dues. Here the relevance of ethical approval and gatekeepers re-emerges. Given that in most countries ethical clearance is a basic prerequisite of any primary data collection and, thus, formal approval from a gatekeeper is of the essence, it is of significance to acknowledge how their presence might have influenced the development of data collection strategies.

While gaining and negotiating access to the field is an unavoidable challenge in ethnographic research, so is self-immersion. For the sake of understanding the field and rich data collection, an ethnographer often has to make some tough, potentially life-altering choices to be able to carry out participant observation. In doing so, the researcher may have to put his/her body on the line to become an instrument of data collection. The next chapter, written by Andrew Sparkes, recognises the presence of an ocular-centric bias in contemporary ethnography and provides an in-depth discussion as to how researchers may use and have used other sensory perceptions to explore the complexities of selected social worlds. Since what has been described as 'sensory revolution' in social sciences, the hegemony of visual-centric research has been questioned and other sensory modalities have been brought to the fore. Sparkes observes that sensory engagement with the field goes beyond using the commonly acknowledged five senses and that others have argued for the presence of at least 13 sensory perceptions potentially utilised in research. Engaging the multiplicity of the senses in fieldwork manifest in 'sensory ethnography' involves the researcher's somatic faculties. Engaging the senses in research requires training and practice. To help us with our journey in sensory ethnography, Sparkes provides ideas to practise this craft and reawaken our 'sensory imagination', along with a range of useful examples of other researchers going beyond the boundary of ocular-centric description. For instance, we get a 'taste' of the auditory and olfactory aspects of running as well as haptic perceptions of both running and boxing. Subsequently, Sparkes focuses on representational challenges in sensory ethnography and outlines potential ways of managing them, for instance, via somatic layered and performative accounts.

Representing and communicating ethnographic research are areas of recurring debate, creating uncertainty in regard to the quality of work being produced. Ethnographers and qualitative researchers in general frequently ponder upon how to best represent their data and whether the quality of selected representation is sufficiently robust. Brett Smith, Kerry R. McGannon and Toni L. Williams note that the dominant way of displaying qualitative data is via realist tales and other similarly relevant approaches are currently under-utilised. Therefore, Smith et al. focus their attention on writing creative nonfiction in ethnographic research, which is "fictional in form yet factual in content". After introducing us to some of the key contributors to the sport and exercise field of creative nonfiction, Smith et al. provide an extensive critical analysis on why we may or may not choose this particular method of representation. They outline seven reasons for – e.g. protecting the identity of participants – and four reasons against – e.g. the potential danger of research losing credibility when associated with 'fictional' representation – employing creative nonfiction in research representation. Subsequently, they provide useful guidance as to how we might craft creative nonfiction. That is, how we may turn primary ethnographic data into a story. They prompt us to consider, among many other aspects, fundamental philosophical standpoints, theoretical engagement as well as writing a plot. Finally, Smith et al. outline helpful ways we might use to methodologically evaluate creative nonfictional representation in ethnographic research. Despite providing an extensive list of criteria, the authors acknowledge that the list may be modified in the future as ethnographers generate more experience with using creative nonfictional representation.

While methodological and theoretical discussions and considerations are the bedrock of all types of research, so is their practical application, around which the next section of the book is centred, consisting of seven ethnographic case studies. The first chapter in this section is written by Meridith Griffin and Cassandra Phoenix who offer an insight to ageing women's perception of their encounter with exercise – running. With the ever-increasing awareness of disease prevention there is more pressure on the general public to engage with exercise. However, the gender gap with regard to exercise participation is persisting and increasing when age is considered. Consequently, this chapter explores the outcomes of a 14-month-long fieldwork in a women-only running club. Griffin and Phoenix adopted a multi-method ethnographic approach and produced rich data via participant observation and informal as well as formal interviews. In doing so, they gained insight into the worries and anxieties that members of the running club had prior to joining up. For instance, participants often expressed their initial fears of 'not being sporty', being 'picked last for the team' or simple having an elitist, exclusivist perception of running which, for some time, held them back from participation. Essentially, participants displayed the presence of *narrative foreclosure* that prevented them from exercise participation. Eventually, the participants in the study overcame those fears and decided to try out running. One reason for joining the club was the all-inclusive promotional narrative released in the public domain, which was enriched by both visually and textually displayed success stories leading to *narrative hailing*. Women also decided to take up running because they wanted to stay/become healthy or they reached a certain significant age-related milestone (e.g., the big six zero). The issues identified and awareness generated by the data presented is pivotal in enhancing our understanding in respect to the barriers women have the tendency to face in exercise participation. Furthermore, Griffin and Phoenix recognised that while narrative hailing appears to work for some women to break through exercise participation-related barriers, there is a possibility that a high number of women's intention of taking up exercise is recurrently curbed by foreclosed narratives. Here the real danger is that "people can become the stories that they tell".

Whilst running was considered a health-centred option in Griffin and Phoenix's study, Michael Atkinson introduces us to an entire different type of running, specifically fell running. The key focus of the chapter is to make a contribution to the sociology of suffering by reflecting on 'the [suffering] limit' experiences Atkinson endured during a three-year period as a fell runner in the UK. Firstly, the chapter theoretically locates suffering in Physical Cultural Studies (PCS) and recommendation is made towards a 'forward-thinking sociology of sport and physical culture'. In doing so, Atkinson encourages the sociologists of sport "to break new ground, transgress disciplinary boundaries, pursue theoretically driven research with much vigour, and research beyond the comfortable subject so regularly studied". Then we gain an insight into the structure and nature of fell running, which predominantly consists of running up close-to-impossible inclines and coming back down whilst negotiating uneven, inhospitable terrain, wind, rain, shrubs, bogs and, sometimes, even herds of animals. In other words, "a good fell run assaults the runner's body". Given the constant suffering that is associated with the activity, fell runners form what Atkinson calls *pain communities*, in which withstanding pain is a key marker of collective identity. Atkinson then activates Roger Caillois' six social and personal features of play – free, separate, uncertain, unproductive, not entirely rule bound and fictive – to make sense of fell running (and runners) as a form of play where pain and suffering are part and parcel of the activity.

Pain and suffering are not alien to athletes, exercisers or leisure enthusiasts. It can even be argued that taking sport, exercise or leisure seriously always means the presence of some form of pain. In the next chapter, Alex Stewart, similarly to Atkinson, shows that perhaps enduring some form of physical agony can also form part of ethnographic fieldwork. Along with exposing the multitude of bodily injuries he endured as boxer, Stewart introduces us to his insider ethnographic research, which he carried out amongst amateur and professional boxers over a five-year period. His chapter focuses on some of the practical as well as theoretical issues around the ethnographer being the 'tool' of data collection and the interface through which the outside world learns about the subculture under investigation. The main challenge here is, Stewart observes, balancing between participant and ethnographer through developing a reflexive awareness that is often absent from methodological texts. He follows Paul Willis's comment that the ethnographer must engage in the temporal, symbolic and sensuous dimensions of the field. Consequently, after a viscerally engaging pro boxing scene, we get an in-depth and extensive insight into Stewart's personal, intricate and gradual journey – identity transformation – from being a pro boxer to going academic. In other words, he aims to articulate "the subtle and barely conscious subplot of...[his] identity transformation from 'boxing-insider' to 'researcher'". Reflecting on the epistemologically as well as methodologically challenging question of being an insider or an outsider when conducting ethnography, Stewart notes that the insider–outsider debate cannot be viewed through a static, essentialising cultural lens. Instead, the he argues that the "ethnographic-self is reflexively and dynamically crafted in response to the web of interactional and often contingent processes" the ethnographer experiences before, during and after, and within and beyond the fieldwork.

Becoming and being an insider – whether it be in the subculture under investigation or the academic establishment where the future of a budding ethnographer may lie – is a recurring practical as well as methodological challenge for ethnographers. Similar to Stewart, the author of the next chapter, Laura Purdy, grants us an insight into one of the empirical aspects of her completed PhD study. As a newcomer to ethnography, Purdy embarked on an in-depth, five-month-long exploration of a male, high-performance rowing subculture. Purdy provides a candid account of what encountering the field might mean to ethnographers and how challenging and frustrating it may be when research designs and expectations do not go according to plan due to events/people outside the control of the ethnographer. In Chapter 9, using her own journal entries, Purdy showcases the level and types of anxieties and worries she experienced as a consequence of difficulties with entering the field and raises questions which perhaps are a concern for all ethnographers during entrée. After successfully negotiating access to the field, further challenges arose revolving around personal uncertainties, (over)active participants and persisting feelings of being an outsider. To alleviate the feelings of uncertainty and vulnerability, Purdy engaged in the micro-politics of the field and developed strategies to 'earn her place' on the team and to 'write her into' the subcultural scene. These strategies involved a range of activities that the coaches and team members found productive and helpful, and, in turn, aimed to lessen the feeling of being an outsider, in tandem with strengthening the ethnographer's position in the field. On reflection, Purdy acknowledges that she may not have read all the micro-political aspects of the field correctly and, thus, may have neglected to appreciate other, simultaneously present micro-political forces. However, she notes that this fieldwork experience helped her prepare for "future projects by highlighting that the research process, particularly the data collection, involved appreciating and navigating various, sometimes conflicting, motivations, ideologies and goals".

The following chapter highlights another type of 'peril of ethnography' and provides further empirical transparency by shedding light on some of the major challenges the researcher encountered during fieldwork centring on football rivalry in Birmingham. Adam Benkwitz spent 15 months exploring the historically embedded Aston Villa–Birmingham City rivalry, during which period, as part of his participant observation, he attended football games, and became a frequent visitor to bars and restaurants associated with football fans. Whilst some of the dangers of self-immersion in a football fan subculture had been anticipated and specific measures had been taken to minimise risks, unforeseen courses of events affected data collection and sometimes the personal safety of the researcher. Benkwitz writes of being hit on the head by a coin presumably thrown by an opposing fan, being bombarded with advertisement boards and ketchup bottles, and poor stadium and crowd management by the police. He also acknowledges some of the ethical dilemmas he faced when witnessing violent and/or illegal acts. Though Benkwitz followed Sugden's (1996, p. 207) advice – "although I witnessed an illegal event, I did not take part in it and, as such, my presence in the field did not contribute to that act" – in the emerging fieldwork scenarios, he acknowledged the limitation of this standpoint and ponders upon potential grey areas ethnographers may need to consider during fieldwork. Then Benkwitz moves on to discussing some of the other key perils of his fieldwork such as going native, the time-consuming nature of data collection, the financial commitments and limitations, along with worries of a neophyte researcher. Arguably, the main message of the chapter is that while reading about and around ethnography is an important and essential part of the preparation for the fieldwork, nothing can fully prepare us for all the challenges producing primary data may entail in ethnographic research.

One of the recurring issues in regard to conducting fieldwork that the previous two chapters referred to was the uncertainty of the novice ethnographer in terms of collecting the 'right' data and recording everything potentially relevant. Christian Edwards and Robyn L. Jones give us a glimpse of an ongoing PhD research in relation to data collection, construction and interpretation. After a general introduction to ethnographic fieldwork, the authors critically examine the pros and cons of using ethnographic film in research. This is then followed by the reflections of the first author on his PhD research centring on "exploring the social significance of humour as a critical component in the negotiation of coaching relationships". As the research focuses on the use of humour in situ and the ethnographer continuously and simultaneously embodies different roles (i.e. researcher, participant and coach), the capturing of rich data through a traditional fieldnote technique was limited. Due to growing anxieties about recording rich data and seeing the 'right' data, Edwards decided to employ a video camera "to 'better' observe the inherent interaction in the context". The presence of the camera was soon forgotten and the recordings allowed the researcher to enrich his fieldnotes, providing a form of 'ethnographic training wheels'. Edwards notes: "the film had taken away (or lessened!) anxiety about missing things due to my multiple contextual roles. In turn, this confidence allowed me to work on, and better trust, my observational instincts."

The final case study in this section of the anthology is different from the previous chapters on two accounts: the study is in an early, pre-operational phase and it is located outside of the geographic realm of the UK. In this chapter, Tim Butcher, Chris Hallinan and Barry Judd explicate their aim to understand the ways in which Aboriginal men can actively engage with 'modern' sporting organisations – often perpetuating non-Indigenous hegemonies – whilst fulfilling 'customary' and 'traditional' family and community obligations. Specifically they intend to investigate how this can be done in a way that retains and nurtures 'customary/traditional' ontologies and spiritual connections. Their aims are to understand and explain the historical relations between the people of Papunya (a remote aboriginal community in Australia) and sporting organisations; and convey the organisational framework put in place to conduct an ethnographic investigation of the relationship that has developed between the Papunya community and the Central Australian Football League. They advocate that the exploration of such a remote area would be a perfect fit for an ethnographic approach. However, Butcher et al. also call for a decolonised ethnographic methodology that would be most appropriate in engaging a remote aboriginal community. This type of ethnography would need to "embrace cultural understanding, respect, the ability to build, maintain and nurture relationships, and a positive connectivity and legacy". In this spirit, the authors devise a clear and precise research plan to carry out research mindful of Indigenous cultural particulars. The relevance of the research plan is two-fold: firstly, it functions as a useful aid for novice ethnographers to develop their own research strategy and, secondly, it can be a helpful guide to those who might consider a similar type of participant population. In fact, given the paucity of ethnographic research around Indigenous populations, this original endeavour might serve as a potential future area of exploration for researchers interested in the unique cultural interchange of sport and exercise between different ontological dispositions.

The last section of the book revolves around future directions and considerations in relation to ethnographic research in sport and exercise. A potential technique of data collection and interpretation, which might grow in popularity, is introduced in the penultimate chapter. Alan Bairner discusses the intriguing concept and practice of *flânerie* and recognises the potential overlaps between flânerie and ethnography. The *flâneur*'s (we may refer to him/her as the idle wonderer) main activities include sauntering and looking and are almost exclusively associated with urban spaces. Bairner considers the early flâneur as an embryonic urban sociologist who reads the city as a text while keeping a relative distance from it. Therefore, it is important for the flâneur to have ample time available to 'cruse' the city and observe its complex social mechanisms. While observing and strolling the flâneur does not merely collect descriptive memories of the city but adds "a creative dimension to the ways in which we understand the social life of cities". In so doing, the flâneur witnesses the multitude of ways urban spaces may be used and interpreted by social actors. After discussing some of the key aspects of flânerie, Bairner provides three rich, flânerie-driven accounts of sport and the city. Firstly, there is an analysis of Belfast in terms of the juxtaposition of global and local sporting cultural features, which is followed by a snippet of bullfighting experience in Seville. The last city to be examined by the flâneur is Tokyo and its unique sumo wrestling subculture. All three city-descriptions offer a unique insight to specific aspects of the cities and highlight the complex connections between sport and urban space. The cultural depth of these accounts is, however, informed by more than just the idle wondering of the researcher. Bairner cautions us that "the social scientists who wish to use flânerie successfully must complement their wondering with wide reading of both fictional and nonfictional accounts of the particular urban setting".

While flânerie has only been marginally embraced by ethnographers, so has ethnography by some of the research areas focused on sport. One particular example is sport management where this approach still appears under-utilised. In the final chapter, as an area for future consideration, John Harris introduces sport management studies and explores the reasons why there is still a paucity of ethnographic research in this academic area. Harris attributes the dearth of ethnographic work in sport management to fascination with reliability, validity and hypothesis testing, the dominance of traditional methodological approaches and lack of engagement with emerging theories. Then he explores the potential of employing Sociological Imagination (Mills, 1959) to break through existing academic boundaries currently surrounding sport management and to help contemporary scholars involved in the field to overcome the traditionalist scientific establishment. It is also suggested that through continuous reflexivity it is pertinent to recognise that research itself is a socio-cultural product and as such is affected by the milieu in which it is carried out. When recognising that research is often "an expression of personal interests and values", Harris suggests that ethnography could offer "fantastic potential to uncover more about areas of sport management that have up until now remained under-explored and outside of the core focus of the field". Sport management, as an academic area, engages a wide range of interested parties. The understanding of the viewpoints of key stakeholders is essential in further developing sport, in general, and sport management, in particular. Ethnography certainly has the potential to tease out standpoints and opinions in an in-depth fashion, thereby significantly contributing to the academic exploration of sport management, in tandem with the broader area of sport and exercise.

One thing the captivating chapters in this book will certainly demonstrate is the wide-ranging potential and multiple use of ethnography in sport and exercise research. Ethnography is marked by diversity (Atkinson et al., 2007). The chapters that follow will demonstrate the numerous applications of and approaches to ethnography. They fulfil multiple functions: to inform, critique, discuss, caution and, last but not least, to inspire. It is our hope, as editors, that by engaging with this book and, in turn, with ethnographic approaches, our audience will make an ever growing and even richer contribution to the already burgeoning field of ethnographic research in sport and exercise.

References

Atkinson, P., Coffey, A., Delamont, S., Lofland, J. & Lofland, L. (Eds.) (2007). *Handbook of Ethnography*. Sage: London.

Goodall, H.L. (2000). *Writing the New Ethnography*. Rowman & Littlefield: Oxford.

Hughson, J., & Hallinan, C. (2001). The ethnographic turn in sport studies. In C. Hallinan & J. Hughson (Eds.), *Sporting Tales: Ethnographic fieldwork experiences* (pp. 3–6). Australian Society for Sports History: Kensington, NSW.

Mills, C.W. (1959). *Sociological Imagination*. Oxford University Press: New York.

Rand, E. (2012). *Red Nails, Black Skates: Gender, cash and pleasure on and off the ice.* Duke University Press: Durham.

Sand, R.R. (2002). *Sport Ethnography*. Human Kinetics: Champaign, IL.

Spielvogel, L. (2003). *Working Out in Japan: Shaping the female body in Tokyo fitness clubs*. Duke University Press: Durham.

Sugden, J. (1996). *Boxing and Society: An international analysis*. Manchester: Manchester University Press.

Sugden, J. (2002). *Scum Airways: Inside football's underground economy*. Mainstream Publishing: London.

Wacquant, L. (2004). *Body and Soul: Notebooks of an apprentice boxer*. Oxford University Press: Oxford.

Chapter 2

Ethnography in sport-related research
Influences, continuities, possibilities

Carrie Dunn and John Hughson

This chapter examines the emergence of ethnography in sport and human physicality studies and looks at how researchers initially began to engage with the method. It examines the problems researchers have encountered before moving on to consider more recent directions in research and newer challenges faced by academics and students for the continuing use of ethnography within the field. The chapter begins by assessing the history of the method, looking, *inter alia*, at the influence of ethnographic work from the Centre for Contemporary Cultural Studies (CCCS) – as its researchers interrogated the experience of working-class leisure time – and follows through to the development of ethnographic research in the 1980s, particularly in relation to the participant observation popularised in football research. Consideration is then given to subsequent directions in sport-related studies, including the introduction of autoethnographic research. In doing so, key developments in the parallel strands of sports participation and sports fandom are outlined, suggesting the necessity of exploring shifts in focus from the global to the local to the individual. The chapter also explores some of the gendered, classed and racial dimensions that have historically been present in the ethnographies of sport and exercise, while offering a critical engagement with the literature; it highlights how researchers may use their status as part of a privileged group to interrogate as yet under-researched facets of sports ethnography, and indicates potential future fields of investigation.

The use of ethnography in sports research

Some fifteen years ago one of the present authors commented, "It is perhaps fanciful to talk of an ethnographic turn in sports academe" (Hughson & Hallinan, 2001, p. 3). This may still not be the best terminology, but such talk would no longer be regarded as fanciful. And if by ethnography we mean social science-based studies using participant observation research, of both highly immersed and lesser engagement variants, then a good deal of work of this kind has been done and published within sports studies since the turn of the 21st century. This chapter will revisit the relevant background and

move along to consider how the 'ethnographic turn' within sport studies has progressed.

The promise of ethnography is the insight into social life it provides from a close-up look at what is going on within communal milieus and contexts. In the sociological academy this inspired the Chicago School-type tradition, associated primarily with W.F. Whyte (1955) and his classic book *Street Corner Society*. This book has influenced subsequent well-known ethnographic studies of participation in sport-related activities – involving men 'hanging-out' together for a particular purpose in public spaces they territorialise – for example of bodybuilders (Klein, 1993) and boxers (Wacquant, 2007). The practical difficulties of gaining research access to what are often rather insular, semi-formal, micro-cultures, has meant that the study of sporting teams has been slower to come. Studies of collective groupings have focused more on sports fans, with British scholarship, especially on association football supporters, being prominent. These studies on what have commonly and historically been referred to as 'football hooligans' have drawn upon social deviance aspects of the Chicago School ethnography and also the cultural identity theme as developed via the juncture of sociology and cultural studies.

The author of the touchstone ethnographic text in the history of British sociology, *Learning to Labour* (also published under the title Profane Culture), Paul Willis (1977, 1978) developed a comparative study of the 1970s biker and hippy subcultures located in and around the Birmingham area of England's West Midlands. Willis, a prominent member of the CCCS at the University of Birmingham (inaugurated in 1964), followed the advice of the Centre's first Director (and his PhD supervisor), the late Richard Hoggart – in a rephrasing of Joseph Conrad's words – to become "immersed in the destructive element".[1] Willis was the only researcher of his generation at the CCCS to undertake an ethnographic project involving a Chicago School degree of research engagement. However, other studies that did undertake observational work focused on youth subcultures, some with relevance to sport. For example, John Clarke (1976) examined the significance of football supporting to a skinhead subculture in London, wherein the young men within his study attempted a "magical recovery of community"; football following being a key means through which a reconnection with the working-class traditions of their parental generation could be made. Clarke's work has been cited by a subsequent growth industry in 'football hooligan' subculture studies, stemming from the figurational sociology based studies of the Leicester School to the 'social identity' based studies of Gary Armstrong and Richard Giulianotti (Hughson, 1998). Football hooligans provided a somewhat 'sexy' topic given the focus on football supporter related violence portrayed in the British media from the 1970s onwards. An overlap between academic work and the media occurred when members of the Leicester School research team, led by Eric Dunning, provided talking-head expertise in the Thames Television documentary *Hooligan* (1985), based on the notorious Inter City Firm followers of West Ham United Football Club.

Leicester's research ethos bore the influence of Norbert Elias, eminent professor of sociology and mentor to Dunning, himself a pioneering figure in the British sociology of sport. The Leicester School's position adhered closely to the figurational approach endorsed by Elias; whereby people are situated within networks of social interdependency, and power relations are dynamic and changing (cf. Giulianotti, 1999). Their concern was to investigate the subculture of football hooliganism, taking the figurational standpoint that the process of civilisation is ongoing, and currently a decivilising spurt was affecting the lower working-classes, resulting in uncivilised, i.e. violent, behaviour (see Elias & Dunning, 1986). The research claim to ethnography came by way of episodes of covert participant observation, undertaken by John Williams in conjunction with research team members Patrick Murphy and Dunning. The resultant findings acknowledged that no 'definitive answer' could be given to explain the causes of hooliganism, and admitted that the researchers "may stand accused by some commentators of asking entirely the wrong questions to begin with!" (Williams et al., 1984, p. xvii). Their trio of participant observational studies outlined the Leicester School's main research interests within the area: observing incidents of fan disorder inside and outside stadia, the build-up to events and the official reactions to them. Williams, the researcher tasked with carrying out this undercover work, also spoke to fans to elicit information on the ages, occupations and political leanings of fans, and the reasons they gave for following football and their memories of previous hooligan encounters, both in a domestic context and abroad (Williams et al., 1984).

Although the sociologists of sports at Leicester University had previously concentrated on hooliganism, the ground disasters and the lack of attention to their causes contributed to their new-found desire to study a broader sphere of football phenomena, and they and others working in the field began to move on to issues of history, identity and political economy. Murphy, Williams and Dunning (1990) made no gender distinctions in their explanation of a fan's attachment to their club and how these attachments first form and develop, and they began to engage more explicitly with the idea of subcultures at this point, though they went on to examine in detail only the subculture of hooligans. They introduced the idea of attachment, suggesting that people watch football because of a bond with the team, and they are introduced to the game via exposure to the 'subculture of football' from a 'significant other' such as a parent and will have been sustained through, for example, membership of a football-orientated peer group (Williams & Dunning, 1990). Various factors, such as geographical proximity, may lead an individual to feel a sense of kinship with a football club, but this kinship must be nurtured through a social network and a supporting network is important to strengthen each individual's ties to the club.

The work of the Leicester School researchers was trenchantly criticised in the early 1990s by Gary Armstrong, for whom it was not ethnographic enough (Armstrong & Harris, 1991). Along with Giulianotti (1996a), Armstrong (1996), citing Willis as a key influence, undertook the first highly immersed ethnographic studies of so-called football hooligan fan groups in the UK, based in Sheffield and Aberdeen respectively. A key aim of this work was to avoid an emphasis on violent behaviour as a 'social problem', in favour of a primary research concern with the collective lifeworld of the young men, presented from their own perspective. For example, Armstrong (1998) focused on how and why hooligans have chosen to participate in violence at football, arguing that 'hooliganism' at football is merely a performance of a ritual in a safe environment, signifying traditional working-class masculine strength, and placing football hooliganism in the tradition of 'masculine revelry'; the authorities condemn such activities because they fear the power of the mob. On a similar theme, Garry Robson (2000) took the standpoint that a club's fan culture is distinct and identifiable, but not generic. He took Millwall as his case study, again using participant observation to gain data, explaining that these supporters are a group about whom "so much is assumed and so little known", due to negative media representations linking them with violence and anti-social behaviour (Robson, 2000, p. ix). Robson's theories of football fandom are intrinsically bound up with (the performance of) masculinity; for example, he explained the fans' emotional investment in the game through "a need to sustain male contexts in which the core elements of pre-modern male subjectivities and cultures could survive and flourish" (2000, p. 2). He argued that Millwall fans are bound together through their shared understandings of class, masculinity and local history, and it is unimportant whether or not a supporter lives in the immediate vicinity. Following this theme through, he explained the ongoing rivalry between Millwall and West Ham by comparing it to the gangster rivalry between the South London Richardsons and the East London Krays, concluding that the families represent different sorts of masculinity championed in their particular areas of the city.

As epistemologically valuable as these studies have been, they suffer from researcher exuberance, and possibly masculine over-identification, a type of charge previously also levelled at Willis. Hence, the final aspect of Charlotte Brunsdon's caustic note that the subjects considered appropriate for study at the CCCS were "the public, the state and the male working class – the boyzone" (1996, p. 226). The studies by Armstrong, Giulianotti and Robson are open to similar criticism and have been regarded by Free and Hughson (2003) as failing – in their concentration on male identity – to specifically consider issues of gender relations and sexuality. The critical contention is that the performance or exaggeration of working-class masculinity is only possible when others (women and non-cohort males) are increasingly feminised, but the research of Armstrong and related colleagues remains rather silent on these matters and also assumes the studied male participants (as well as the researchers themselves) to be exclusively heterosexual.

Methodological reflection

In recent years, a number of socially reflective ethnographic studies have begun to appear. Social and political issues came to the forefront in sport – from the continuing hooligan problem, to the systemic neglect of grounds resulting ultimately in the deaths of 56 people in a fire at Bradford City's Valley Parade and 96 people in a crush at Sheffield Wednesday's Hillsborough (leading to a growing body of work with a very different view on the 'law and order' debate, cf. Scraton 2009, 2013; Taylor & Ward 1998); and from the sporting embargo on apartheid South Africa to the controversial 'rebel tour'.

The popular media and academic perception and treatment of sport has altered over time. The very real impact of sport on people's lives and its potential power has begun to be recognised more clearly as fans, players and administrators take a visible role in the debates within sport. Attention has shifted away from the concentration on disorder and on to experience, adopting ethnographic approaches more widely; rather than studying structures and large groups, there was an acknowledgement of the importance of the experience of the individual: postmodernist approaches – with their focus on the uniqueness, importance and significance of the individual subject and experience – began to take a firmer hold. The influence of Armstrong and Giulianotti must be acknowledged in this regard. Giulianotti (1995), meanwhile, looked back on his own work, and discussed the ambiguity of the researcher's position when conducting participant observation, and acknowledged that he had encountered problems with his early studies on football subcultures, such as finding an individual to introduce him to the Hibs 'casuals', and putting his personal safety at risk during the research.

Giulianotti, though, was overt in his research; the 'casuals' knew he was an academic who would be writing about them. Geoff Pearson's work for his PhD thesis used covert observation, requiring acceptance into the subculture being observed without being announced as an academic; and he later explored (2009) the ethical issue of whether a participant observation researcher could justify committing criminal offences if it was likely to retain their close link with the group they were observing. He reflected on his earlier work and admitted his methods could be 'difficult to defend' describing the criminal activity in which he had been involved despite avoiding arrest and not causing physical harm to anyone. This development in sport studies tied in with a broader trend for reflexivity in ethnography as researchers began to acknowledge more explicitly that their study of phenomena in societies were in themselves products of those societies, and that the 'reality' they were reporting was simply their single subjective perception of it (cf. Hammersley & Atkinson, 1983). Palmer and Thompson (2010), for example, made several significant points highlighting potential physical risks and ethical dilemmas facing the female researcher of male-dominated sports, particularly when employing participant observation, and regarding the consumption of alcohol affecting behaviour in sports settings (not just the participants, but the researcher as well). They argued that the researcher obviously has to be aware of potential risks to themselves, but also discussed the possible actions that a researcher might feel compelled to take due to their duty of care to participants.

As much as those of us imbued with a spirit of research integrity may welcome this reflexive honesty about the pitfalls in the field and how they might be overcome or avoided altogether, such declarations, especially when flagged ahead of the commencement of research projects, may well prevent many ethnographic-based studies from going ahead. The demands of 'ethical clearance' by universities for research projects – whether done by faculty members or (post)graduate students – is particularly encumbering upon observational and participant fieldwork. The real intent of the increasing scrutiny to which research academics and their students are subjected is debatable; i.e. are university administrations mainly concerned about the protection from harm of research subjects and researchers, or has the vigilance more to do with worries of being held financially liable should any legal problems arise as a result of the fieldwork? A prevailing 'medical model' approach to ethical evaluation within universities compounds the problem of over-scrutiny for much of the research in social science and humanities areas. In regard to sport-related ethnographic research, it is difficult to foresee how a number of the projects referred to in this chapter – most of which were conducted during doctoral candidature – could, in the present culture of fear, pass successfully through the unnecessarily arduous process of 'ethical clearance'. One can hardly imagine Richard Giulianotti fronting up to a member of the Aberdeen Casuals and asking him to sign a consent form.

Autoethnographic and autobiographical positioning

In popular literature, sports autobiographies boomed at the end of the 20th century, recording the lives of athletes as well as fans. In academic writing, autoethnography also began to develop (cf. Pringle, 2001, writing about his youth rugby participation).

The definition of 'autoethnography' has been contested; Anderson and Austin (2012) assess the developing understanding of the term, concluding that it meant an ethnographic study conducted by a researcher who is active and engaged in the field they are studying, and who reflects on their work and involvement. The 'narrative turn' within ethnography has resulted in researchers moving "away from assuming the stance of disinterested spectator toward assuming the posture of a feeling, embodied, and vulnerable observer" (Bochner, cited in Markula & Denison, 2005, pp. 166–7). In the best instances this approach adds a valuable humanistic dimension to ethnographic research, but in the worst it reduces the research offering to a confessional tale or an ego trip. Some researchers have preferred to avoid the term autoethnography. For example, Hoeber and Kerwin (2013) chose to refer to their study as a self-ethnography, arguing that their experience of sport was not 'intensely personal', which they saw as a required element of an autoethnography.

Carrington (2008) argued in favour of 'reflexive autobiography' when assessing the construction of race identities in sport, allowing for deconstruction of essentialised concepts of race. He suggested that the existing ethnographic data about race and sport was problematic because it had been collected by white researchers who had failed to consider their position in relation to the people and communities they were investigating. Equally, however, he warned of the danger of assuming an unproblematic research relationship based on a shared ethnic background. He also stressed the value that black researchers could have when interrogating white-dominated sporting communities, offering a more complex insight into the groups' intersections with race, class and gender (he used the phrase 'cultural passport' for this type of integration).

Woodward (2008) makes a significant observation when she reflects on her ethnographic studies of men's boxing, highlighting that she has never been a participant in the sport, and as a white middle-class researcher can be assumed to be an 'outsider' within the sphere. However, she argues that an 'insider' might produce a too-subjective set of data. Her research raises interesting questions in regard to the ethnographic study of both sport participants and supporters, implicitly challenging, for example, the unintentionally chauvinist view that only men from a similar background can undertake ethnographic investigation into male working-class subcultures.

We shall now turn to discuss some of the common themes of interrogation that have emerged in sports ethnography in recent years.

Patriotism, globalisation and identity

Work on English national identity increased after the ban on English football clubs competing in Europe was lifted (Giulianotti, 1999; Williams & Wagg, 1991); and this coincided with a thread of work looking at the supporters of national teams rather than domestic clubs, with ethnographies of England fans (Murphy et al., 1990; Williams et al., 1984); Scotland (Giulianotti, 1991); and the Republic of Ireland (Giulianotti, 1996b). Liston and Moreland (2009) also interrogated the creation of a sense of national identity through sport, looking at hockey's contribution to identity in Northern Ireland by interviewing ten female elite players and exploring their experiences of living and playing in an arena with intense nationalist tensions.

Many researchers (including Boyle, 1994; Williams, 1994; Williams & Giulianotti, 1994) examined sport's role in constructing late-20th-century male identity, coinciding with the rise of gender and male-specific studies. Williams (1994) addressed the topic of identity but still adhered closely to his previous work and the ethos of the Leicester School (and also Robson, 2000) in examining why football in particular is so important to so many people.

Giulianotti (2002) tracked the changes, or 'intensive hypercommod-ification', that have taken place in English football since the 1990 World Cup. He assessed the impact that the changing commercialised nature of the game has had on spectator identities, and drew up four categories of English football fans, all incorporating elements of consumption and financial investment. This work was not directly ethnographic but drew from the insights into football supporting that Giulianotti had gleaned from his previous ethnographic studies. Other researchers shared Giulianotti's interest in the role that money and consumerism has played and continues to play in sport, and highlighted the way it helps to constitute particular male identities. Redhead (1987, 1993, 1997), for example, positioned football as a strand of popular youth consumer culture, and tended to maintain that the consumer of football is a young male, and that football is a leisure choice, selected for its particular style- and identity-signifying properties. Redhead's work was not ethnographic as such but prompts further investigation, by way of ethnographic projects, into the ongoing connection between football and other domains of changing popular culture such as music.

Another area that would well benefit from ethnographic study is organi-sational research into sporting clubs (from grassroots to elite) and officiating bodies. However, a problem occurs here in regard to gaining research access to organisations, such as football clubs. The more focused such clubs become on financial return the less interested they will be in exposing themselves to any investigation that runs even a slight risk of damaging purely instrumental organisational goals. At the very best they are inclined to operate on a *quid pro quo* basis, and, in this light, it is understandable that a decision maker (gatekeeper) within such an organisation would not see the benefit in having an academic poking around the clubroom and having access to records and club personnel. One relevant study is Charles Korr's 'economic history' of West Ham United, conducted in the 1980s (Korr, 1986). Korr believes one of the reasons he was afforded privileged access to the inner workings of the club was because, at the time of the study, he was a young American scholar visiting England and, as such, enough of a cultural outsider to be deemed innocuous.[2] Korr's study did not engage an ethnographic dimension involving observation of or discussion with fans. He believed such an enquiry would be extraneous to his main concern with the day-to-day operations of the club, but such an opening of the research agenda today could give valuable insight into the relationship between clubs and fans in regard to themes such as the democratisation of club ownership and control.

Gendered dimensions of sports ethnography

The impact of class, as we have already discussed, was the subject of a great deal of interest from sports studies' inception; and even though gender has been generally neglected as a topic across sports studies, there have still been several key ethnographic interventions. For example, Imray and Middleton

(1983) highlighted the way in which club cricket was presented as a specifically gendered sphere, with women restricted to solely domestic/private-sphere functions. Over the past 30 years, women playing cricket has become more 'acceptable', with a burgeoning number of ethnographies on junior, senior, non-elite and elite women's cricket. For instance, Velija (2011) acknowledges that women in cricket have been perceived as 'outsiders', but her study into junior and adult female club cricketers shows that these dynamics are nuanced, with power variations between group members, largely along lines of sexuality and class.

Another sport which has historically excluded women from participation is boxing, which has only since 2012 included women's competition in the Olympics. Ethnography on female boxers, however, has been around for rather longer. Mennesson (2000) explored how women constructed and negotiated their identities within this 'masculine' domain by training in boxing gyms and building links with and interviewing female boxers and their (male) coaches. Sisjord (2009) highlighted the phenomenon of the 'babe' in her investigation of females' experience of snowboarding: female participants in snowboarding referred to a type of female snowboarder who does not dress appropriately, who does not participate appropriately, and encourages males to take females in snowboarding less seriously because of her behaviour.

As we have suggested, the bulk of writing on and research into sport specifically and working-class leisure time more generally has portrayed sport fans as male (cf. Clarke & Critcher, 1985). Specifically, the focus on how football reinforces 'ideals' of masculinity, particularly through the opportunities to engage in violence, recurs throughout this strand of literature, implying that the study of football fandom is only significant because of what is learnt about masculinity. King's work (1997) on 'the lads' and a particularly 'masculine', working-class identity consolidated through football fandom is a fine example of this.

More recent studies have indicated that a male-centric view of sports fandom is overlooking a sizeable minority of audience, with several ethnographies exploring the female experience of particular sport fandoms (cf. Crawford & Gosling, 2004, and their work on female fans of ice hockey; Farrell et al., 2011, and their exploration of female spectatorship of men's sports in the US; Pope and Williams, 2011, and their notes on female fans of rugby union). For example, Hoeber and Kerwin (2013) looked at female fans' experiences of sport more broadly, offering a critique of hegemonic masculinity in sport, particularly in North America, where, they report, nearly half of sport spectators and consumers are women.

It is appropriate to conclude this section by referring to Olive and Thorpe (2011), who, in their discussion of their work on action sports, argue in favour of a 'feminist ethnography' to interrogate issues in sport, prioritising reflexivity, and including a political dimension as well as a call to action – they are in favour of demonstrating the unfair operations of social power in sport, both in terms of participation, spectatorship and labour; they highlight the use, objectification and sexualisation of female bodies in sport, and suggest that there is a need to challenge sexism where it is seen rather than simply advising acceptance (or avoidance) of a toxic culture. Indeed, they discuss their work in the field with an impressive degree of honesty, including incidents of sexual harassment and assault as well as their own errors in their work (or 'feminist failings' as they term it). They argue that action sports – like most others – were devised by men for men's entertainment, creating a tension along gender lines for them as researchers as well as the problems of analysing a sport in which they are already participants.

Dimensions of race and religion

Similarly, race and religion remain under-investigated in sports ethnography, but there are some studies that highlight some important issues. For example, Carrington (1998) reported on the Caribbean Cricket Club in Leeds, presented as a discursively constructed black social space – a community institution and resource. Spracklen (1996, 2001, 2007) looked at 'race' and identity in a similar geographical area, but interrogating rugby league through participant observation; and later (Spracklen et al., 2010) reflected on the construction of working-class whiteness in the sport as well as the institutionalised racism preventing black players from career progression.

Burdsey (2010) also explored cricket, but examined the role of Islam in the lives of British Muslim players. He reported that all players said that Islam played a major role in their lives, but not necessarily in their cricketing career; and emphasised the heterogeneity of experience.

In a further study of cricket in the north of England, Thomas Fletcher (2012) has recently examined social identity at the intersection of ethnicity and place of regional inhabitancy. In doing so, he refers to 'Yorkshireness', a specific county identity. Unlike some other counties, the Yorkshire cricketing identity has tended to remain rigidly connected to its history as a white sport. This has created an obvious social division along racial lines as some areas of Yorkshire have dense Asian populations who follow and play the sport. In an ethnographic context, Fletcher played cricket with one 'predominantly white club' and with another club, 'predominantly Asian in membership'. He does not suggest that Yorkshireness provides a common social identity for members of both clubs, but that both cultural tension and the hope for its overcoming can be understood within a space allowing for a diversified but nevertheless shared regional identity.

Sports governance and labour issues

Roderick's autoethnographic contributions (2006) to sports studies provides an insight into life as a professional footballer, drawing on his own experience, and stressing the precarious nature of an elite sporting career; with his more recent work looking at job mobility (2013) and the impact of job losses (2013) on players. Roderick's background as an elite level football player is an example of how such a status can be successfully drawn upon by scholars within sport studies (those with such sporting backgrounds) to gain ethnographic access to sporting domains that might otherwise be difficult to enter and, also, challenging to interpret unless the researcher has played the sport him or herself at such a level.

The operation of sport governing bodies has had relatively little ethnographic attention, possibly because of issues around gaining access to these privileged spaces. However, Numerato and Baglioni (2012) have begun to explore this aspect of sport, looking at the role of social capital in the Czech and Italian governing bodies of football, handball and sailing, and how this impacts on policy-making. They note from the outset that their research and presence was 'not always welcomed', and admit that they were treated with 'distrust' which affected the way they interacted with some of the respondents.

Ethnographic study into the labour of sport can involve a focus on a number of related issues, including pain and injury. Although sports injury has been a topic studied more traditionally by bio scientists, sociologists, via ethnography, are now exploring how players and coaches respond to pain and injury, how in elite sport responses are conditioned by the financial costs of injury (cf. Killick et al., 2012), and how social pressures within a sports team affect responses to injury as well as the role that the placebo effect can play (cf. Howe, 2001).

Conclusion

In this chapter, we demonstrated that the breadth of sports ethnography has been increasing. Sports which have traditionally been on the margins of ethnography are now being studied. Previously neglected dimensions of sports and related activities, such as issues of gender, race, religion and social class, are also given academic attention. However, how ethnographic research continues under the ever-increasing scrutiny of university ethics committees is an issue to watch closely. The chapter has suggested that ethnographic studies of sports fans using immersed participant observation, sometimes covertly and in situations where the gaining of 'informed consent' is not possible in a traditional sense, will now, and in the foreseeable future, be difficult to launch. Against oppressive university governance, it is to be hoped that the richness of ethnography will not be lost to sport studies as increasing institutional nervousness promotes aversion against types of research that may be adjudged risky business.

Notes

1 Personal comment by Paul Willis to author (Hughson).
2 Personal comment by Charles Korr to author (Hughson).

References

Anderson, L. and Austin, M. (2012). Auto-ethnography in leisure studies. *Leisure Studies*, 31(2): 131–146.

Armstrong, G. (1996). *Fists and Style* (Unpublished PhD thesis). University College, London.

Armstrong, G. (1998). *Blade runners*. Sheffield: Hallamshire.

Armstrong, G., & Harris, R. (1991). Football hooligans: Theory and evidence. *Sociological Review*, 39(3), 427–458.

Boyle, R. (1994). 'We are Celtic Supporters...': Questions of football and identity in modern Scotland. In R. Giulianotti and J. Williams (Eds), *Game Without Frontiers* (pp. 73–102). Aldershot: Arena.

Brunsdon, C. (1996). A thief in the night: stories of feminism in the 1970s at Birmingham. In D. Morley and K.-H. Chen (Eds.), *Stuart Hall: Critical Dialogues in Cultural Studies* (pp. 276–86). London: Routledge.

Burdsey, D. (2010). British Muslim experiences in English first-class cricket. *International Review for the Sociology of Sport*, 45, 315–334.

Carrington, B. (1998). Sport, masculinity and black cultural resistance. *Journal of Sport and Social Issues*, 22(3): 275–298.

Carrington, B. (2008). What's that footballer doing here? Racialised performativity, reflexivity and identity. *Cultural Studies ↔ Critical Methodologies*, 8(4), 423–452.

Clarke, J. (1976). The skinheads and the magical recovery of community. In S. Hall & T. Jefferson (Eds.), *Resistance through Rituals: Youth subcultures in postwar Britain* (pp. 99–102). London: Hutchinson.

Clarke, J. & Critcher, C. (1985). *The devil Makes Work*. Basingstoke: Macmillan.

Crawford, G. and Gosling, V. (2004). The myth of the puck bunny: Female fans and men's ice hockey. *Sociology*, 38(3): 477–493.

Elias, N., & Dunning, E. (1986). *Quest for Excitement: Sport and leisure in the civilising process*. London: Blackwell.

Farrell, A., Fink, J. S. & Fields, S. (2011). Women's sport spectatorship: an exploration of men's influence. *Journal of Sport Management*, 25(3), 190–201.

Fletcher, T. (2012). Yorkshire, cricket and identity: An ethnographic analysis of Yorkshire cricket's imagined community. In J. Hughson, C. Palmer & F. Skillen (Eds.), *The Role of Sports in the Formation of Personal Identities*. Lewiston, NY: Edwin Mellen Press.

Free, M. & Hughson, J. (2003). Settling accounts with hooligans: gender blindness in football supporter subculture research. *Men and Masculinities*, 6(2): 136–155.

Giulianotti, R. (1991). The Tartan Army in Italy: the case of the carnivalesque. *Sociological Review*, 39(9): 503–527.

Giulianotti, R. (1995). Participant observation and research into football hooliganism: Reflections on the problems of entree and everyday risks. *Sociology of Sport*, 12, 1–20.

Giulianotti, R. (1996a). *A Sociology of Scottish Football Fan Culture* (Unpublished PhD thesis). University of Aberdeen.

Giulianotti, R. (1996b). Back to the future: An ethnography of Ireland's football fans at the 1994 World Cup Finals in the USA. *International Review for the Sociology of Sport*, 31, 323–344.

Giulianotti, R. (1999) *Football: A sociology of the global game*. Cambridge: Polity.

Giulianotti, R. (2002). Supporters, followers, fans, and flaneurs: A taxonomy of spectator identities in football. *Journal of Sport & Social Issues, 26*(1), 25–46.

Hammersley, M. & Atkinson, P. (1995). *Ethnography* (2nd ed.). London: Routledge.

Hoeber, L., & Kerwin, S. (2013). Exploring the experiences of female sports fans: a collaborative self-ethnography. *Sport Management Review, 16*(3), 326–336.

Howe, P.D. (2001). An ethnography of pain and injury in professional rugby union: the case of Pontypridd RFC. *International Review for the Sociology of Sport, 36,* 289–303.

Hughson, J. (1998). Among the thugs: The 'new ethnographies' of football supporting subcultures. *International Review for the Sociology of Sport, 33*(1), 43–57.

Hughson, J., & Hallinan, C. (2001). The ethnographic turn in sport studies. In C. Hallinan & J. Hughson (Eds.), *Sporting Tales: Ethnographic fieldwork experiences* (pp. 3–6). Kensington, NSW: Australian Society for Sports History.

Imray, L. & Middleton, A. (1983). Public and private: marking the boundaries. In E. Garmarnikow, D. Morgan, J. Purvis and D. Taylorson (Eds), *The Public and the Private* (pp. 12–27). London: Heinemann.

Killick, L., Davenport, T., & Baker, J. (2012). Pain and injury in sporting cultures of risk. In D. Hassan & J. Lusted (Eds.), *Managing Sport: Social and cultural perspectives* (pp. 129–142). Oxford: Routledge.

King, A. (1997). The lads: Masculinity and the new consumption of football. *Sociology, 31,* 329–346.

Klein, A. (1993). *Little Big Men: Bodybuilding, subculture and gender construction.* Albany, NY: SUNY Press.

Korr, C. (1986). *West Ham United: The making of a football club.* London: Duckworth.

Liston, K., & Moreland, E. (2009). Hockey and habitus: Sport and national identity in Northern Ireland. *New Hibernia Review, 13*(4), 127–140.

Markula, P., & Denison, J. (2005). Sport and the personal narrative. In D.L. Andrews, D.S. Mason & M.L. Silk (Eds.), *Qualitative Methods in Sport Studies* (pp. 165–184). Oxford: Berg.

Mennessen, C. (2000). Hard women and soft women: the social construction of identities among female boxers. *International Review for the Sociology of Sport, 35*(1), 21–33.

Murphy, P., Williams, J., & Dunning, E. (Eds.) (1990). *Football on Trial: Spectator violence and development in the football world.* London: Routledge.

Numerato, D., & Baglioni, S. (2012). The dark side of social capital: An ethnography of sport governance. *International Review for the Sociology of Sport, 47,* 594–611.

Olive, R., & Thorpe, H. (2011). Negotiating the 'f-word' in the field: Doing feminist ethnography in action sport cultures. *Sociology of Sport, 28,* 421–440.

Palmer, C., & Thompson, K. (2010). Everyday risks and professional dilemmas: Fieldwork with alcohol-based (sporting) subcultures. *Qualitative Research, 10,* 421–440.

Pearson, G. (2009). The researcher as hooligan: Where 'participant' observation means breaking the law. *International Journal of Social Research Methodology, 12*(3), 243–255.

Pope, S. and Williams, J. (2011). White shoes to a football match! Female experiences of football's golden age in England. *Transformative Works and Cultures* [online], 6.

Pringle, R. (2001). Competing discourses: Narratives of a fragmented self, manliness and rugby union. *International Review for the Sociology of Sport*, 36(4): 426–439.

Redhead, S. (1987). *Sing when you're Winning: The last football book*. London: Pluto Press.

Redhead, S. (1993). *The Passion and the Fashion: Football fandom in the new Europe*. Aldershot: Avebury.

Redhead, S. (1997). *Post-fandom and the Millennial Blues*. London: Routledge.

Robson, G. (2000). *No-one Likes Us, We Don't Care: The myth and reality of Millwall Fandom*. Oxford: Berg.

Roderick, M. J. (2006). *The Work of Professional Football: A labour of love?* London: Routledge.

Roderick, M. (2013). From identification to dis-identification: Case studies of job loss in professional football. *Qualitative Research in Sport, Exercise and Health*, 6(2): 143–160.

Scraton, P. (2009). *Hillsborough: The truth, 20th anniversary edition*. London: Mainstream.

Scraton, P. (2013). The legacy of Hillsborough: Liberating truth, challenging power. *Race and Class*, 55(2), 1–27.

Sisjord, M. K. (2009). Fast-girls, babes and the invisible girls: Gender relations in snowboarding. *Sport in Society*, 12(10): 1299–1316.

Spracklen, K. (1996). When you're putting yer body on t'line fer beer tokens you've go'a wonder why: Expressions of masculinity and identity in rugby communities. In G. Jarvie, L. Jackson, J. Lyle and K. Robinson (Eds), *Sport, Leisure and Society* (pp. 131–138). Edinburgh: Heriot-Watt University.

Spracklen, K. (2001) Black pearls, black diamonds: Exploring racial identities in rugby league. In B. Carrington and I. Mcdonald (Eds), *Race, Sport and British Society* (pp. 70–82). London: Routledge.

Spracklen, K. (2007). Negotiations of belonging: Habermasian stories of minority ethnic rugby league players in London and the South of England. *World Leisure Journal*, 49(4): 216–226.

Spracklen, K., Timmins, S., & Long, J. (2010). Ethnographies of the imagined, the imaginary and the critically real: Blackness, whiteness, the north of England and rugby league. *Leisure Studies*, 29(4), 397–414.

Taylor, R. & Ward, A. (1998). *Kicking and Screaming: An oral history of football in England*. London: Robson Press.

Velija, P. (2011). Nice girls don't play cricket: the theory of established and outsider relations and perceptions of sexuality and class amongst female cricketers. *Sport in Society: Cultures, Commerce, Media, Politics*, 14(1), 81–96.

Wacquant, L. (2007). *Body and Soul: Notebooks of an apprentice boxer*. New York: Oxford University Press.

Whyte, W.F. (1955). *Street Corner Society*. Chicago: University of Chicago Press.

Williams, J. (1994). Rangers is a black club – 'race', identity and local football in England. In R. Giulianott and J. Williams (Eds), *Game Without Frontiers* (pp. 153–183). Aldershot: Arena.

Williams, J. and Giulianotti, R. (1994). Introduction: Stillborn in the USA? In R. Giulianotti and J. Williams (Eds), *Game Without Frontiers* (pp. 1–20). Aldershot: Arena.

Williams, J. and Wagg, S. (Eds) (1991). *British Football and Social Change: Getting into Europe*. Leicester: University Press.

Williams, J., Dunning, E., & Murphy, P. (1984). *Hooligans Abroad: The behaviour and control of English fans in continental Europe*. London: Routledge.

Willis, P. (1977). *Learning to Labour: How working class kids get working class jobs*. Aldershot, Hampshire: Gower.

Willis, P. (1978). *Moving Culture*. London: Routledge and Kegan Paul.

Woodward, K. (2008). Hanging out and hanging about: Insider/outsider research in the sport of boxing. *Ethnography*, *9*, 536–560.

Part I

Ethnography

Methodological and theoretical considerations

Chapter 3

Finding the field

Ethnographic research in exercise settings

Pirkko Markula

As sport and fitness now permeate everyday lives worldwide, also ethnographic research on physical activity has become more visible. It is, therefore, important to discuss what type of field will reveal sufficient insights into these cultures. Although there are several perceptive ethnographies of sport (e.g., Bolin & Granskog, 2003; Howe, 2004; Newman & Giardina, 2011; Rinehart, 1998; Thorpe, 2011; Wheaton, 2004), I have, within the confines of this chapter, selected ethnographic research on fitness to illustrate ways of finding a field.

I first discuss the multiple meanings of culture and then, against this background, depict features commonly characterising a successful fieldwork operation. Because ethnographic fields can be diverse in composition, I highlight some of the dilemmas an ethnographer faces when choosing and then accessing the field. Throughout this discussion, I provide examples from existing ethnographic work on fitness to further illustrate the connections between the researchers' assumptions and their fieldwork.

What is an ethnographic field?

While some anthropologists claim that ethnography cannot be properly addressed without any reference to their scholarly discipline, others acknowledge (e.g., Clifford, 1986, 1988; Rabinow, 1986) that ethnography "is moving into areas long occupied by sociology, the novel, or avant-garde culture critique" to rediscover "otherness and difference within the cultural of the West" (Clifford, 1988, p. 23). Not limited to one scholarly discipline, ethnography refers to the cultural setting of the ethnographer's participant-observation. Ethnographers are, thus, to locate themselves within people's everyday lives, the field, to observe and describe their culture. The definition of culture, nevertheless, defines what is conceived as 'people', their 'everyday lives', and thus, ultimately the ethnographic field.

The ethnographers of fitness have approached their fields from two primary academic disciplinary orientations: sociology and anthropology. Therefore, while there are diverse conceptualisations of 'culture', my discussion in this chapter is informed by the main theoretical traditions guiding these ethnographies: French sociologist Pierre Bourdieu's reflexive sociology; combinations of several sociological theories; and interpretive, postmodern anthropology that emerged to challenge the dominance of structuralist anthropology primarily in the United States. The ethnographers approaching fitness from sociological perspectives appear to choose their theoretical approaches to negotiate the 'structure-agency' debate common within their mother discipline, sociology. I begin by introducing how Bourdieu's work addresses the impact of structure and agency in fieldwork.

'The field': Bourdieu's reflexive sociology

Bourdieu, who began his academic path as a philosopher, later transferred to sociology that according to him, allowed for more epistemological reflection and questioning of one's intellectual practice (Bourdieu & Wacquant, 1992). Through his "reflexive sociology" he explored society as a combination of "structures" and (a phenomenological analysis) of individuals' "cognitive forms" (Bourdieu & Wacquant, 1992, p. 14). He, thus, analysed the combined effects of structure and agency to the practice of everyday life. This approach required a sociological method that, rather than taking 'structures' of the social world (like structural-functionalist sociology or Marxism) or 'individual experiences' (like ethnomethodology or social phenomenology) as starting points, began by posing problems. To do this, Bourdieu replaced the notion of 'society' with his concepts of 'field' and 'space'. "Society", according to Bourdieu, is a collection of fields: sets of "objective, historical relations between positions anchored in certain forms of power (or capital)" (Bourdieu & Wacquant, 1992, p. 16). Each field prescribes its particular values and poses its own regulative principles that "delimit a socially structured space in which agents struggle, depending on the position they occupy in that space, either to change or to preserve its boundaries and form" (Bourdieu & Wacquant, 1992, p. 17). Therefore, the field is a space of play that individual agents enter and structure, but it is also comprised of "a patterned system of objective forces" (Bourdieu & Wacquant, 1992, p. 17) that present the structure of possibilities (rewards, gains, profits, sanctions) for its agents. The role of the sociologist is to observe the (often unwritten) rules framing individuals' actions. Accurate recording of the rules requires external, objective observation that needs to be combined with a theoretical understanding of social forces, forms of power ('capital') and individual 'habitus' (a type of individual embodied sedimentation of the social structures of the field). The role of the ethnographer interested in fitness is, consequently, to observe objectively the rules that regulate exercisers' 'habitus', as anchored in formations of capital, in their specific field. However, the precise definition of the 'field' of fitness, its values and regulative principles, is modified slightly by these ethnographers.

In her ethnography of personal training in the US, Jennifer Smith Maguire (2007) relied on Bourdieu's concept of field to define the cultural boundaries for her research. She distinguished between the fitness industry and fitness as a cultural field comprised of "a network of sites, texts, producers and consumers that generates practices for and meanings of the body" (p. 5). Following this theoretical framework, Smith Maguire identified several conditions for the emergence of a cultural field. Firstly, new social and cultural conditions simulate the production of new cultural goods and interest in them: "A field is made possible by new political pressures, economic models, technological possibilities and social movements" (p. 6). These same conditions continue to produce further interest in it. Secondly, there must be popular passions for the field. The field is divided, however, into hierarchically organised sets of positions that one obtains based on the investment in the field. This resembles Bourdieu's definition of habitus assumed by individuals in each field. For example, one can turn from inexperienced participant into devoted exerciser and further into instructor/personal trainer, club owner, or popular fitness expert based on one's investment in the field of fitness. Thirdly, fields tend to develop designated spaces, such as health clubs, to mark their activities. Fourthly, there is a definable network between the participants that is sustained either through immediate participation or participation in the textual realm of the field. In this schema, fitness is understood as a cultural field: "a set of relatively structured positions within which individuals and institutions, producers, and consumers struggle over the status and definitions of fitness and fit bodies" (p. 8). Furthermore, the cultural field of fitness contains several 'sites': the specified spaces designated to activities specific to the field. Therefore, Smith Maguire demarcated the 'health club' and information available from it as the 'site' for her research on fitness in general and the personal trainers in particular. From this Bourdieusian perspective, ethnographic research can take place in several sites (or focus on one or two) that illuminate the social forces, forms of capital, and habitus formation of the entire cultural field of fitness.

Parallel to Smith Maguire (2007), Matthew Frew and David McGillivray (2005) were informed by Bourdieu's theoretical framework in their ethnography of fitness culture in Scotland. They, nevertheless, provided a slightly differently interpretation of 'field'. Citing Bourdieu, they claimed 'the health and fitness club' to represent "a contested sub-cultural field (of sport and recreation) where the possession of physical capital is traded for distinction" (p. 163). What Smith Maguire defined as a 'site'—the health club—became a field within a larger field of recreational sport. In this sub-field, Frew and McGillivray observed the "consumption forces" that structured "durable dispositions of habitus", but also "the ability of agents to exercise strategies that could alter their cultural trajectories" (p. 162). While peppering their Bourdieusian approach with a Marxist flavour of consumption patterns of class groupings and the participants' socio-economic status, they, faithful to Bourdieu, accounted for both structural forces and the impact of individual agency in the subcultures of the three health clubs in Scotland.

In summary, Bourdieu defined 'the field,' such as *the fitness field*, as a relatively autonomous cultural entity with its own prescribed rules and values. This can be examined through theory-informed ethnography that accounts for the interactions between the structure and the individual agents inhabiting each field. The Bourdieusian fitness ethnographers have identified *the health club as a site* within the fitness field where the interplay between the multiple forces manifests. Consequently, the ethnographic field consists of multiple clearly identified sites for ethnographic observation. Other sociologically oriented fitness ethnographers have combined insights from different theorists to further highlight the structure-agency interaction.

'In the gym': combining various sociological approaches to find a field

Despite Bourdieu's intention of including both individual agency and structural forces, Nick Crossley (2006), in his ethnographic research, dismissed this theoretical approach among other 'grand sociological' theories such as Giddens' structuration theory or Foucault's theory of 'body-power' as too overgeneralised, unsuitable for accounting lived experiences in the 'gym', and "insensitive to the way in which the meaning of gym-going can change over the course" (p. 25). Drawing from the interpretive sociology of C. Wright Mills, Max Weber, and phenomenology, Crossley sought to draw more attention to the role of 'agency' in sociological research of 'gym' practices. Viewed from Bourdieu's perspective, this methodology appears to represent the social phenomenological (Bourdieu & Wacquant, 1992) approach to studying social life instead of an innovative sociological treatise. Nevertheless, to focus on individual motivations and meanings of participation, Crossley's field consisted of one 'gym' in which he was a participant for six years before engaging in ethnographic observations for two years. Although not denying social forces (such as strong norms of body weight and shape or the advantages of particular forms of 'physical capital'), Crossley's emphasis on the individual gym goers' meanings represents probably the clearest example of a sociological fitness ethnography focusing on individual agency instead of a broader emphasis on fitness (or his gym) in the intersection of social forces. Other ethnographers have combined an interpretive focus on individual agency with the impact of larger societal and cultural forces by employing a variety of theoretical perspectives.

In her ethnographic work, Roberta Sassatelli (2010), similarly to Smith Maguire (2007) earlier, distinguished between 'fitness culture' and the 'fitness gym': fitness gyms are at the core of the broader fitness culture (comprised of informal practices of jogging, keep-fit, exercising with videos or video games). She further classified the gyms into ones concentrating on a competitive activity (boxing, bodybuilding, martial arts) and fitness gyms: "non-competitive environments aimed at providing recreational exercise to boost physical form and well-being" (p. 6). According to Sassatelli (2010), such indicators as specific professionals, specific equipment, and specific fitness place the gym into the core of the fitness culture. The focus on fitness gyms allowed Sassatelli to concentrate on "gym practices as the more iconic, if not significant, aspect of the wider family of keep-fit exercise" (2010, p. 7). She employed the term "keep-fit exercise" to denote the broader fitness culture of recreational physical activities that the fitness industry might "exploit" (2010, p. 7) by introducing their modifications to fitness gyms. Her ethnography, nevertheless, exemplified the content and meaning of fitness in general, because "commercial fitness gyms are hegemonic formations within fitness culture" (2010, p. 7). She further located the fitness culture within the larger culture of consumerism where an individual experiences a dual process of passive and active self-construction. On the one hand, consumer culture dictates the norms of individual's body maintenance and culturally appropriate self-presentation, but also provides room for active self-orientation. Similar to Crossley (2006), she argued that "grand theories" do not "describe the world of the gym, their interaction mechanisms, the situated body practices of fitness training and the meanings that these practices have for those who decide to participate, drop out or continue to train assiduously" (p. 3). To capture the "dual process of subjectification", Sassatelli drew from the interpretive sociology of C. Wright Mills and Erving Goffman's "face-to-face interaction and the interaction order" (p. 8) as well as Harold Garfinkel's ethnomethodology combined with Bourdieu's notion of physical capital and Foucault's theory of disciplinary techniques to conduct a multi-site ethnography of several gyms in Italy and Britain. Combining ethnomethodology with Bourdieu's reading of capital is an interesting choice considering that Bourdieu was explicitly critical of ethnomethodology and had already developed his own methodology to count for 'dual subjectification'.

Focusing on the UK, Louise Mansfield (2011) also counted for both the structural forces of fitness culture and the individual exercisers' agency to challenge the dominant definitions of fit bodies in her ethnographic project. Like Sassatelli (2010), she located the 'fitness gyms' within the larger context of consumer culture explaining that individual exercisers' body consciousness and self-perceptions are "connected to long-term transformations in the economic, technological and political configurations in society that have contributed to the emergence of consumer culture" (p. 81). Similar to the previous fitness ethnographers, she assumed 'the fitness gym' as "a cultural space in which people manage the twin corporeal purposes of (internal) health and (external) appearance" (p. 81). Consequently, the fitness gym, as an ethnographic field, illuminated the construction and values of the broader fitness culture. Mansfield concentrated on examining the individual understandings of fatness through the interpretive sociology of Goffman and the societal construction of fatness through 'the socio-dynamics' of stigmatisation by Norbert Elias and John Scotson.

Shari Dworkin's (2003) ethnography in the US addressed the sociological structure-agency debate directly when she set out to "flesh out issues of agency and constraint" (p. 135) in women's weight training. Using multiple theoretical perspectives, but drawing heavily from Raewyn Connell's 'emphasised femininity', she discovered that most women preferred cardio-vascular workouts and feared 'bulking up' as a result of sustained weight lifting. In her US context, Dworkin identified feminine identity as the social constraint that exercising women actively negotiated. Her participant-observation took place in "one fitness site" (p. 132), a local gym, that Dworkin, nevertheless, divided into the weight room, the aerobics room, and CV room to further examine possibilities for women's empowerment and resistance through different exercise practices.[1]

In summary, ethnographers combining multiple theoretical approaches viewed fitness culture as structured by the general forces of *consumer culture*. Consequently, the *fitness culture* ultimately represents the consumerist society of which effects can be evidenced by observing the everyday life of the 'fitness gym'. Depending on the combination of theories, the ethnographic field varied from one (Crossley, 2006) to multiple gyms in several countries (Sassatelli, 2010). While most of these ethnographers, parallel to Bourdieu, considered both the structural forces and the gym goers' experiences, Crossley (2006) advocated most clearly for an interpretive approach to individual exercisers' understandings of the fit body.

From universal to culture in 'flux': the anthropological fields of fitness

Instead of focusing on the interplay between structure and agency in (the ethnographer's) society, anthropologists use 'culture' as the defining concept for their ethnographic work. The era of grand anthropological projects by Alfred Radcliffe-Brown, Bronislaw Malinowski, and Margaret Mead was characterised by modernist, structuralist or functionalist anthropology and their ethnographic fieldwork followed the theoretical principles of universal truths unearthed from authentic human culture. As Victor Turner (1974, p. 31) explained: "Functionalism...tried to present a unified theory of order and change based on a biological metaphor." From their field data, the functionalist ethnographers were able to develop generalisable theories that applied universally to developments of cultures. This goal assumed a certain homogeneity of cultures: all cultures are built based on a set of common, fundamental principles. Ethnographers were to remain objective, yet diligent observers, not critics, of cultural customs, practices, and beliefs to provide detailed cultural description of the general principles.

The universal truths about 'culture' were to be discovered in 'exotic' fields such as 'the tropics' or simple, small rural communities that had remained unchanged and that, unpolluted by the complexity of 'civilization', continued to display the 'authentic' social order characterising the beginnings of human culture (e.g., Clifford, 1988). While ethnographic work aiming to preserve 'authentic' culture endangered by globalisation has by no means disappeared, there are also strong critiques of the idea of culture as homogeneous, stagnate, and preserved for the ethnographer to record in detail (Clifford, 1988; Rabinow, 1986; Turner, 1974).

Instead of travelling to distant continents to examine the 'Others', many anthropologists now problematise the universal truths discovered in descriptions of authentic, exotic culture. Accordingly, the anthropological concept of culture itself is now understood as a cultural construction: what is considered exotic or authentic is based on very specific cultural definitions. James Clifford (1988), for example, accounted for globalisation and constant interaction between people as a necessary context for the formation of 'cultures'. In this 'inauthentic' and 'interconnected' world, everything is now 'strange';[2] anything around us can reveal significant information about a culture. Because "the exotic is now nearby" (Clifford, 1988, p. 10), the anthropologist's own everyday context is now included in the idea of culture. The ethnographers' 'westernised' cultures should be of equal interest in their strangeness to any other cultures and thus, "we need to anthropologise the West: know how exotic its constitution of reality has been" (Rabinow, 1986, p. 241). Because all cultures are constructed, their logics, their politics, their inventions and practices—"local tactics"—can be analysed "as a restrictive and expressive set of social codes and conventions" (Clifford, 1988, pp. 11–12). Consequently, anthropologists have now turned their observant eyes to their own conventions to question the 'truths' of their own cultures. Clifford's well-known definition can serve as a summary of the understanding of culture as constantly changing and socially constructed: "Culture is contested, temporal, and emergent. Representation and explanation— both by insiders and outsiders—is implicated in this emergence" (p. 19). Ethnography was opened to illuminate the contestations and emergencies of every day culture anywhere. For the anthropologists, ethnography now "is perpetually displaced, both regionally focused and broadly comparative, a form both of dwelling and of travel in a world where the two experiences are less and less distinct" (Clifford, 1988, p. 9).

As a graduate student in sport sociology, my own interest in ethnographic fieldwork was sparked through my coursework in anthropology. During the time, the field of anthropology in the US was being transformed by postmodern and poststructuralist ideas of culture in flux. Immersed in these theoretical debates, I come from the background of interpretive, symbolic, and postmodern anthropology by Victor Turner, Edward Bruner, James Clifford, George Marcus, and Paul Rabinow and feminist anthropology by Mary Louise Pratt, Marilyn Strathern, and Alma Gottlieb. Their work has supported my understanding of physical cultures and meaning(s) of ethnography. Instead of working in my native Finland, I travelled to the United States to conduct an ethnography on aerobics as a predominantly women's fitness practice (Markula, 1993, 1995, 2003). I have since pondered the oddities of fitness in New Zealand, the United Kingdom (Markula, 2004, 2008, 2011), and Canada to provide both regionally focused as well as broadly comparative accounts of the global fitness culture. Therefore, my ethnographic work has taken, as Clifford (1988, p. 9) suggested, "a form both of dwelling and of travel in a world where the two experiences are less and less distinct". In all the above countries, I have taken advantage of these locations to understand how the everyday fitness 'tactics' (Clifford, 1988) operate in fitness centres, health or sport clubs, but also enact the larger global fitness trends formed within the cultural forces of different westernised countries. The emphasis of my ethnographic work has often dovetailed the continual 'flux' of fitness culture that has, in its unique way, provided a cultural anchor in my otherwise continual cultural displacement. Although I recognise, similar to the sociologically oriented Bourdieusian fitness ethnographers, fitness as a cultural field, I do not regard its values and regulations as autonomous from the broader cultural orientations of its location. I draw from the poststructuralism of Foucault to examine how the discursive formation of fitness (including the knowledges informing fitness and health, the fit body, and exercise practices) operates within neoliberal power relations. Deleuze's rhizomatic philosophy[3] has guided my continual pursuit for developing more ethical fitness knowledges and practices. In this context, I—constantly displaced between cultures—enact, practise, observe, and write about fitness as it is incessantly moulded by various forces. Thus, my ethnographic field that encompasses diverse sites in different cultural settings, is no longer bound in 'a site' or in a clearly located 'field'. Laura Spielvogel (2003), whose ethnography mapped fitness culture in Japan, also located fitness within globalised, contemporary culture.

An American ethnographer, Spielvogel (2003) had resided in Japan previously and also had a Japanese university affiliation. Although primarily identifying as 'a foreigner' (*gaijin*), Spielvogel (while not explicitly discussing it) had the language skills to communicate with the participants and the local fitness club management. She limited her field to two popular health clubs in Japan: one in suburban and one in downtown Tokyo, but provided a lengthy justification for these locations assuming that many anthropologists "might view a project on body practices in Japanese fitness clubs as commonsensical and even trivial" (p. 5). Instead of defining the clubs as 'sites' of fitness field (Smith Maguire, 2007), Spielvogel argued that "the fitness club serves as the ideal location in which to explore the intersection of globalisation and consumption, of bodily discipline and display, and the constructions of health and illness in contemporary Japan" (p. 5). From her anthropological point of view, a fitness club presented "a unique window...to how everyday life is given meaning and relevance" (p. 5) in Japan. Spielvogel added that the specific history, space, and disciplinary techniques of the fitness club provided a window to general Japanese cultural assumptions regarding gender, beauty, and identity. She also analysed "the way the consumption of aerobics in Japan reflects the synthesis and, more often than not, the contradictions between Japanese and Western ideology" (p. 4). As an American ethnographer, she carefully explained her use of such a reductionist binary that she still detected in her ethnographic field where aerobics was defined predominantly based on the US fitness culture.

Spielvogel's work, similar to my fitness ethnographies, focused on group exercise. Consequently, while the health or fitness club acts as the location for the ethnography, the focus on group fitness narrows the space of participant-observations further into the fitness studios. In his ethnography of bodybuilding, Alan Klein (1993) offered a view into a different 'gym' space.

Klein's (1993) ethnography of professional bodybuilding illustrates an anthropological approach to studying fitness. Parallel to Spielvogel (2003), Klein examined how 'the body' is 'practised' and 'understood' through field research. To further justify his choice, Klein used a double tactic. He first established the bodybuilding gym as a locale of an, indeed, 'strange' culture occupied by curious 'Others' with rather extraordinary body shapes. He openly marvelled at the 'strangeness' of bodybuilding compared with his own East Coast academic culture within which he had never experienced anything resembling the sounds, smells, and sights of the gym. Secondly, he carefully established himself as 'a serious ethnographer' with a previous research interest in Native American culture but now transferring his ethnographic gaze to different types of 'Others' in his own culture. Klein's chosen field consisted of four gyms in California—considered the 'meccas' of bodybuilding among its serious practitioners—where he focused on the construction of gender, particularly hegemonic (hyper)masculinity.

In summary, the recent redefinition of culture has enabled anthropologists to view all cultures as 'strange', contested, temporal, and emergent. This has facilitated ethnographic examinations of fitness as a phenomenon that illustrates larger cultural issues such as globalisation, gender relations, consumerism, or the importance of body shape in cultural interactions. Despite these developments, the anthropologically oriented fitness ethnographers continually justify their topic choices and their *fields located within everyday life* as serious research. For example, Spielvogel (2003) travelled to Japan which, from the US perspective, can be viewed as a part of the 'exotic East' despite its status as a westernised, industrial country. Klein (1993) deliberately constructed bodybuilding as 'outlandish' activity practised in the rather curious location of the gym. As sport sociologists take pride in studying physical activity from a social science perspective, I have not faced a similar questioning of my choice of using ethnography to examine everyday fitness practices.

Although providing significant freedom to practise ethnography in diverse spaces and places, the notion of culture as temporal, contested, and emergent also obscures the conduct of ethnography. Staying for a sufficient length of time, yet perpetually displaced, to analyse how the local tactics operate in constantly moving cultures, can be challenging.

Field trouble?

If "'cultures' do not hold still for their portraits" (Clifford, 1988, p. 10), one can assume some trouble in identifying a suitable field. The contemporary fitness ethnographers, nevertheless, seldom report difficulties in finding or gaining access to their fields. This might be partly due to their understanding of a health or fitness club (or a 'gym') as a representative site of the fitness culture. These offer commercial services that welcome new members and thus, the ethnographers, who can effortlessly obtain a gym membership, readily access these spaces for casual participant-observation. However, the ease of conducting actual ethnographic research on fitness depends on the cultural assumptions of ethical research conduct. For example, both UK and North American research ethics boards/committees require official permission for conducting research with human participants including support from the management of the fitness clubs. However, only two fitness ethnographers, anthropologists Klein (1993) and Spielvogel (2003), report on the issues of access and the importance of gatekeepers for their work.

When first entering his 'gym', Klein (1993) felt great discomfort in an unfamiliar cultural surrounding. This was eased by his pre-arranged meeting with 'Swede', the manager of the gym. Klein was well prepared for the power of the 'gatekeeper' to limit or entirely block the ethnographer's research access, but Swede, after politely listening to Klein's carefully prepared research justification, openly welcomed the ethnographic observer to his gym and cheerfully provided introductions and connections to Klein. Although a success story, Klein did not detail how he gained access to Swede to schedule a meeting. Spielvogel's (2003) entrance to her field in Japan was not equally smooth.

There are cultural differences in accepted ways of entering a field and an awareness of such issues will help the ethnographer to develop appropriate strategies for negotiating access. Unlike Klein (1993) who conducted ethnographic research in his own country, Spielvogel (2003) had difficulty gaining access to the upper-level club managers who could secure her entry to fitness facilities in Japan, a foreign country for her. It required a preliminary six-week trip to Japan during which she, after a series of faxes and phone calls, was finally granted an interview with the managers of the fitness chain to which her two chosen clubs belonged. Similar to Klein (1993), she prepared to address her research rationale, methodology, and qualifications to convince the management of the quality of her project. Nevertheless, it was her identity as an American who was consequently considered an expert aerobics instructor that secured her access to the clubs. The upper-level management was far more interested in sponsoring Spielvogel as a foreign instructor—who, for free, could act as a living advertisement for the most fashionable trends in American aerobics choreography—than as an anthropologist conducting important ethnographic research. Although it was time-consuming to act as an employee (as well as an ethnographer), her status gained Spielvogel special access to the "backstage" spaces (2003, p. 18) reserved for hired personnel and the authority to interview club members.

Although preliminary access to the field often appeared unproblematic (anyone can join the gym), the support and assistance of 'gatekeepers' facilitate more in-depth fieldwork during which, in addition to participant-observation, the ethnographer can ensure connections for more formal interviews with participants, instructors, and the management. In countries where formal approval of research ethics is a requirement, officially endorsed access by the club management is vital. Several fitness ethnographers reflect upon their own engagement with fitness that, in turn, significantly influenced their access, their length of stay, and their rapport in the field.

Ethnographic self-reflexivity

The length of the fieldwork in fitness ethnography varied from 30 hours of observation (Waring, 2008) to several years. While Spielvogel (2003) stayed in her field for 13 months and Frew and McGillivray (2005) 18 months, Dworkin (2001) reported two years, Crossley (2006) eight years, Smith Maguire (2007) ten years, Mansfield (2011) more vaguely the past decade, and Sassatelli (2010, p. 11) "fragmented and complex engagement" for 15 years. I am still conducting research in the field of fitness although my foci have changed over the years. Such lengthy residences in the field are typical for ethnographers who are 'insiders' in the fitness field.

The field of fitness is, in many ways, gendered and the insider fitness ethnographers tend to examine activities aligned with their gender.[4] For example, Dworkin (2001, 2003), Mansfield (2011), Spielvogel (2003), and myself have focused on women's fitness. Crossley (2006), Smith Maguire (2007), and Sassatelli (2010) examined mixed gender activities where they blended easily in the relatively even mix of the other participants. The gender alignment might increase rapport with the participants, but has, in addition, provoked several self-reflections by the insider ethnographers.

As Spielvogel (2003) commented, participant-observation, the methodological bedrock for ethnographic work, embodies an inherent contradiction: participation requires insider knowledge, but observation necessitates some distance for an ethnographer to assume an analytic point of view to the culture. However, becoming too much of an insider, 'going native', has troubled anthropologists for decades.[5] Alongside the broadened conceptualisation of culture to include the ethnographer's own everyday setting, instead of being a problem, insider status is seen as valuable in terms of gaining access to the field and creating rapport with the participants as long as the ethnographers engage in continual critical self-reflection of their field observations and fitness practices. For example, Mansfield (2011) whose participation in the field included exercising together with her participants, explained:

> I was always mindful of the impact [of] my involvement…A feminist sense of critical self-reflection has been important in this regard to managing myself in the research setting, in balancing the tasks of sociologist as participant and inquirer and in bringing an appropriate balance of passion and reason to the analysis. (p. 83)

Spielvogel (2003, p. 17), an aerobics participant, instructor, and ethnographer, characterised herself as "an expert participant": a status which, as indicated earlier, gained her more exclusive access to her gyms. In this sense, her active involvement provided her opportunities with 'serious' conversations in the field. The only limitation she identified was "an almost celebrity-like charisma and mystique" (p. 18) surrounding an aerobics instructor that made some members intimidated or embarrassed by the presumed old-fashion ways of practising aerobics in Japan compared with the United States. As an instructor, I have been elevated to a similar expert position: some participants assumed that I was testing their fitness knowledge or asked my advice regarding various aspects of fitness and nutrition instead of providing their own understandings of exercise participation. In my later work with fitness instructors, instructor qualifications (and experiences) have, however, been advantageous: in these situations experts of equal voice can trust to share visions, problems, and solutions.

The 'outsider' ethnographers Klein (1993) and Sassatelli (2010) reflected upon the status as ethnographers rather than fitness participants. Klein devoted an entire chapter to his confessions from the field. In this chapter, he focused largely on how he, an outsider to the culture, overcame his preconceived notions of bodybuilding and bodybuilders to accept the field as the 'insiders' expressed it. He did not comment lengthily on his own involvement in actual bodybuilding, but it was clear that he did not have previous experience of the activity before entering the field. Sassatelli described herself as "a reluctant participant" who only "gradually developed something of a 'liking' for fitness training" (2010, p. 10). She acknowledged, like many of the fitness ethnographers, the importance of "a direct, sustained embodied participation" (2010, p. 11) without becoming "totally submerged in the activity" (2010, p. 10).

Bourdieusian ethnographers Smith Maguire (2007) and Frew and McGillivray (2005) did not offer details about their own involvement in fitness. Citing Bourdieu, Frew and McGillivray (2005) further explained that grounding one's ethnographic work on false theoretical binaries (e.g., theory/empiricism, quantitative/qualitative, structure/agency) increases the ethnographer's intellectual bias and thus, needs to be avoided. This call for ethnographer's impartiality appears somewhat curious considering Bourdieu's emphasis on reflexivity. However, while Bourdieu titled his theoretical approach as reflexive sociology, his understanding of reflexivity did not refer to the sociologists' personal confessions of their troubles during the fieldwork, but a larger reflection and critique of "the social and intellectual unconscious embedded in analytic tools and operations" (Bourdieu & Wacquant, 1992, p. 36) such as a critique of taken-for-granted binaries embedded in social theory. Reflection aims to secure objective and thus, sound sociology by engaging the researchers in continual critique of their theoretical views. Reflexivity is to reveal any blurring in sociological gaze that is a result of the ethnographers' social origin (class, gender, ethnicity), their positions in the academic field, or any 'intellectualist bias' that prevents the researcher construing the world as a set of concrete problems to be solved practically (Bourdieu & Wacquant, 1992, p. 37). For Bourdieu, "reflexivity calls less for intellectual introspection than for the permanent sociological analysis and control of sociological practice" (Bourdieu & Wacquant, 1992, p. 40). He was a merciless critic of postmodern anthropology, its insistence on situating the observer within the act of observation, including personal reflections of the fieldwork, and using the first person in the final write-up of the research. Bourdieu saw no need to include his own private revelations in his work, arguing that reflexivity is "achieved by subjecting the position of the observer to the same critical analysis as that of the constructed object at hand" (Bourdieu & Wacquant, 1992, p. 41). In Bourdieu's reflexive sociology, accordingly, personal confessions from fieldwork limit the ethnographer's objectivity.

Conclusion

Characterising ethnography as a study of culture, I reflected the definitions of 'the field' against the fitness ethnographers' theoretical conceptualisations of culture. Three main theoretical 'strands' underlined their field selections: Bourdieu's reflexive sociology, combination of several (sociological) theories, and symbolic, postmodern anthropology. The sociologically oriented fitness ethnographers emphasised choosing a field that illustrated an interplay between the larger societal structures and the individual exercise agents. The sizes of their fields and the focal points of their field observations were then guided by the preferred theoretical perspectives. The anthropologically oriented fitness ethnographers indicated that a field should illuminate aspects of the culture in general (e.g., gender relations, the meaning of bodily practices). Ethnographers, before embarking on the time-consuming labour of field research, should, nevertheless, clearly stipulate their theoretical assumptions to ensure meaningful research conduct. The ethnographers' theoretical choices resulted in fields of diverse sizes and compositions, but a typical site was a health or fitness club (or 'the gym') where the ethnographers often spent several years.

While access to the field did not emerge as a problem for the fitness ethnographers, many contemplated their roles as 'insiders' in fitness culture. Familiarity with the field was considered positive because of increased access to participants and deeper embodied knowledge of the actual practice. Even the 'outsider' ethnographers, such as Sassatelli (2010), emphasised the importance of the physical experience of fitness during the fieldwork. It must be noted that the majority of the ethnographers featured in this chapter can be considered 'insider' ethnographers, including some of the Bourdieusian ethnographers who provided no or scarce detail about their own involvement in fitness. Therefore, the fitness culture appears to be of most interest to its practitioners.

In conclusion, a coherent connection between one's theoretical assumptions and the choice of one's field is imperative. This connection determines the other successful elements of fieldwork such as the length of stay, access to and rapport with the participants, and the choice of (multiple) methods. Finally, it shapes the write up including the choice of using personal reflections as critical elements of insightful ethnography. While concerns regarding finding the field differed slightly depending on one's disciplinary orientation (sociology, anthropology) and one's insider or outsider status, acknowledgement of one's research assumptions is central for successful ethnographic work in physical culture.

Notes

1 In another ethnographic project, Dworkin (2001) explored how women in "several local gyms" (p. 336) in Los Angeles, practised weight lifting. During her fieldwork in one elite and one mid-range gym, Dworkin found that women either did not lift weights or moderated their weight training in fear of becoming too muscular. Similar to her later ethnography, Dworkin focused on social constraints of emphasised femininity and women's agency to negotiate it through fitness practices.

2 The functionalist anthropologists generally looked for something 'strange' and thus, excluded any problematisation of their own culture (that was familiar). Thus, in 1988 it was important to argue that everything was strange to expose all types of cultures to anthropological examinations.

3 As a poststructuralist philosopher Deleuze, like Michel Foucault, was a critic of neo-liberal capitalism that, he believed, was the foundation for contemporary inequality (e.g., Deleuze & Guattari, 1987). Deleuze considered that capitalist power relations were effectively maintained by deeply rooted knowledge formations (or strata) locked into pre-determined logic of the world as unified

totality. These needed to be replaced by rhizomatic thinking, knowledge, and practices that account for life's multiplicity.

4 Although certain fitness activities are preferred by women, fitness culture includes both men and women. This is not the case with other fields of physical activity. For example, feminist sport ethnographers Rebecca Olive and Holly Thorpe (2011) struggled to operate within their predominantly masculine fields of surfing and snowboarding, respectively.

5 In his examination of the historical connection between anthropology and ethnography, Clifford (1988) observed a traditional division between 'a man on the spot,' an amateur local who could make some observation of the 'natives' and the sociologists or anthropologist of the city, who, as a scientist, provided the educated accounts of the culture. These were later replaced by a 'fieldworker-theorist', the university trained scholar (such as Malinowski, Radcliffe-Brown, and Mead) who tested and derived theory from first-hand research. Like 'the man on the spot' earlier, the fieldworker was, indeed, to stay in the field and even learn to understand some of the native language without losing the objectivity necessary for a scholarly endeavour. The objective observation required a predominantly 'outsider' status that was threatened by the mastery of 'native' values and practices. The field-worker theorist evolved into an ethnographer whose fieldwork could now be shortened by a theoretical focus on selected aspects of the culture such as structure, individual life cycle, or ritual complex.

References

Bolin, A., & Granskog, J. (2003). *Athletic intruders: Ethnographic research on women, culture, and exercise.* Albany, NY: SUNY Press.

Bourdieu, P., & Wacquant, J.D. (1992). *An invitation to reflexive sociology.* Cambridge, UK: Polity.

Clifford, J. (1986). Introduction: Partial truths. In J. Clifford & G.E. Marcus (Eds.), *Writing culture: The poetics and politics of ethnography.* Los Angeles: University of California Press.

Clifford, J. (1988). *The predicament of culture: Twentieth-century ethnography, literature, and art.* Cambridge, MA: Harvard University Press.

Crossley, N. (2006). In the gym: Motives, meanings and moral careers. *Body & Society, 12,* 23–50.

Deleuze, G., & Guattari, F. (1987). *A thousand plateaus: Capitalism & schizophrenia.* New York: Aethlone.

Dworkin, S. (2001). "Holding Back": Negotiating a glass ceiling on women's muscular strength. *Sociological Perspectives, 44,* 333–350.

Dworkin, S. (2003). A woman's place in the…cardiovascular room?? Gender relations, the body, and the gym. In A. Bolin & J. Granskog (Eds.), *Athletic intruders: Ethnographic research on women, culture, and exercise* (pp. 131–158). Newbury Park, CA: Sage.

Frew, M., & McGillivray, D. (2005). Health clubs and body politics: Aesthetics and the quest for physical capital. *Leisure Studies, 2,* 161–175.

Howe, P.D. (2004). *Sport, professionalism, and pain: Ethnographies of the injury and Risk.* London: Routledge.

Klein, A. (1993). *Little, big men: Bodybuilding culture and gender construction.* Albany, NY: SUNY Press.

Mansfield, L. (2011). Fit, fat, and feminine? The stigmatization of fat women in fitness gyms. In E. Kennedy & P. Markula (Eds.), *Women and exercise: The body, health, and consumerism* (pp. 81–110). New York: Routledge.

Markula, P. (1993). *Total-body-tone-up: Paradox and women's realities in aerobics* (Unpublished PhD dissertation). University of Illinois at Urbana-Champaign. Urbana, IL.

Markula, P. (1995). Firm but shapely, fit but sexy, strong but thin: The postmodern aerobicizing female bodies. *Sociology of Sport Journal, 12,* 424–453.

Markula, P. (2003). Postmodern aerobics: Contradictions and resistance. In A. Bolin & J. Granskog (Eds.), *Athletic intruders: Ethnographic research on women, culture, and exercise.* Newbury Park, CA: Sage.

Markula, P. (2004). 'Tuning into one's self:' Foucault's technologies of the self and mindful fitness. *Sociology of Sport Journal, 21,* 190–210.

Markula, P. (2008). Affecting bodies: Political pedagogy of Pilates. *International Review of Qualitative Research, 1,* 381–408.

Markula, P. (2011). 'Folding': A feminist intervention in mindful fitness. In E. Kennedy & P. Markula (Eds.), *Women and exercise: The body, health and consumerism* (pp. 60–79). New York: Routledge.

Newman, J.I. & Giardina, M.D. (2011). *Sport, spectacle and NASCAR nation: Consumption and the cultural politics of neoliberalism.* Basingstoke, UK: Palgrave Macmillan.

Olive, R. & Thorpe, H. (2011). Negotiating the 'F-word' in the field: Doing feminist ethnography in action sport cultures. *Sociology of Sport Journal, 28,* 421–440.

Rabinow, P. (1986). Representations are social facts: Modernity and post-modernity in anthropology. In J. Clifford & G.E. Marcus (eds) *Writing culture: The poetics and politics of ethnography* (pp. 234–261). Los Angeles: University of California Press.

Rinehart, R. (1998). *Players all: Performances in contemporary sport.* Bloomington, IN: Indiana University Press.

Sassatelli, R. (2010). *Fitness culture: Gyms and the commercialization of discipline and fun.* Basingstoke: Palgrave.

Smith Maguire, J. (2007). *Fit for consumption: Sociology and the business of fitness.* London: Routledge.

Spielvogel, L. (2003). *Working out in Japan: Shaping the female body in Tokyo fitness clubs.* Durham, NC: Duke University Press.

Thorpe, H. (2011). *Snowboarding bodies in theory and practice.* Basingstoke, UK: Palgrave Macmillan.

Turner, V. (1974). *Dramas, fields, and metaphors: Symbolic action in human society.* Ithaca, NY: Cornell University Press.

Waring, A. (2008). Health club use and 'lifestyle:' Exploring the boundaries between leisure and work. *Leisure Studies, 27,* 295–309.

Wheaton, B. (2004). *Understanding lifestyle sport: Consumption, identity, difference.* London: Routledge.

Chapter 4

Ethnography as a sensual way of being

Methodological and representational challenges

Andrew C. Sparkes

As part of their quest to understand the life worlds of other people, many ethnographers share a commitment to gaining first-hand experience of a selected social or cultural setting on the basis of (though not exclusively by) *participant observation*. Atkinson (2012) describes his three-year ethnographic study of Ashtanga yoga, as a "process of knowing a subject by *doing and becoming through immersed observation*" (p. 35). This, he points out, requires time, patience, energy, and the willingness to immerse physically, socially, cognitively and emotionally in the cultures of others. Such 'full-scale' ethnographies can totally encompass and connect one's professional and personal lives. Atkinson states, "When one chooses to study sport and physical culture worlds ethnographically one's entire modality of living shifts" (p. 35). Likewise, Spencer (2012), in his four-year ethnographic study of Mixed Martial Arts (MMA) notes that this is a way of life, a way of being-in-the-world, not just in terms of the amount of time required training in the gym, but also in the way it comes to dominate thought processes and relationships with one's body on a daily basis. Speaking of his commitment to experiencing his subject matter with his body as an instrument of data collection, Spencer notes the following.

> During this ethnography I pulled my groin twice, my kneecap popped out on two occasions (residue of a past injury), I fractured my fifth metacarpal in my right hand, I suffered the pain associated with having cauliflower ear, and I received stitches under my left eye. I limp on days when I have had a hard training session and aside from when I am wearing a hat, my ear shows the wear and tear of my participation in MMA. I am marked by this ethnography. My body tells my story for all to see.
>
> (Spencer, 2012, p. 1)

The process of participant observation, involving as it does a willingness to immerse oneself in the cultures of others in ways that can lead to shifts in personal modalities of living, signals the centrality of the researcher's fleshy body in the ethnographic enterprise as both a way of knowing and a way of being in the field. Ethnographically 'being there' as a participant observer in the action, calls upon a 'way of being' that involves a form of intentional, reflexive, and embodied engagement with a chosen phenomenon over time. This, by definition, is multisensorial in nature. Ethnography as an embodied practice can, therefore, involve intensely sensuous ways of knowing about the mundane and the strange.

This is not to infer that participant observation is the only form of inquiry that involves the senses of the researcher or that other 'methods', such as, interviews and photo-elicitation, cannot access the senses. As Sparkes and Smith (2012, 2014) emphasise, they can, and do. Equally, it needs to be recognised that ethnographers themselves will call upon multiple methods of data collection in the field alongside and connected to their participant observation. As Spencer (2012) states, "Ethnography is, in its best version, a method assemblage that deploys manifold methodological techniques to uncover fractals of a given object of study" (p. 164). He further reminds us that the ethnographer's body, as the pivot in the world, is intimately linked with the research process from start to finish. Given the centrality of the researcher's body as the main 'instrument' of sensual data collection, it is this aspect of the ethnographic process that will be the focus in this chapter.

In the past, ethnographers have acknowledged that the experiences gained via participant observation rely on all the senses. As Sparkes (2009) pointed out, however, not all of the senses have been represented with equal care and attention. The culture of the eye has dominated and informed an ocular-centric bias that relegates the senses of sound, touch, taste and smell (among others) below that of the visual. This relegation ignores the complexities of our *carnal* ways of knowing about the world that, according to Mellor and Shilling (1997) is "thoroughly embodied and connected to people's senses and sensualities" (p. 56).

In recent years, this ocular-centric bias and hegemony of sight has been challenged by what Howes (2005) describes as the 'sensorial revolution' in the social sciences. Paterson (2008) points out that not only have attempts been made to reassert the validity of nonvisual experiences but also questions have been raised about Graeco-Roman notions of a sensory hierarchy based on Aristotle's fivefold classification of the senses. For Macpherson (2011a), the commitment to the existence of only a relatively small, specifiable and discrete number of types of senses forms part of what she calls the 'sparse view' of the counting question. Macpherson argues that this view is difficult to sustain because there is evidence that more than five senses *actually* exist, and from these cases we can go on to extrapolate, and thus come to believe, that the number of *possible* sensory modalities is large.

Vannini, Waskul and Gottschalk (2102) note that the taken-for-granted five senses belong to those sensory modes that provide information about the world *external* to us. These are the exteroceptive senses: sight, hearing, taste, smell, and touch. Vannini and his colleagues then identify at least three more senses that provide information about the *internal* world of the human body. These interoceptive senses are, the sense of pain (nocioception), thirst, and hunger. For them, these eight, however, are not enough. They go on to ask:

> What about our sense of our own internal muscles and organs (proprioception)? What about the sensations that mediate between the external world and the internal body, such as our sense of balance (equilibrioception), movement (kinesthesia), temperature (thermoception), or even our sense of time (at least in terms of polychronicity and monocronicity, if not more)? Now our list has grown from five senses to thirteen, and still we experience senses that are clearly not accounted for in these categories.
>
> (Vannini, Waskul, & Gottschalk, 2012, p. 6)

Given the plethora of actual and possible senses, Vannini et al. (2012) argue that to think of the senses as only confined to the five exteroceptive sensory modes "is grossly to oversimplify human sensual experience, both within and across cultures" (p. 7). Adding a further complication, Macpherson (2011b) questions the common assumption that sensory modalities are perceptual systems isolated from one another and unaffected by the others. For her, "in the face of recent incontrovertible empirical evidence, the idea that the sensory systems do not interact has been discredited" (p. 2). Speaking of the sentient body, Blackman (2008) notes that although the senses are often discussed as separate processes, "it is now agreed that they work in combination and communication with each other rather than as isolated forms of bodily awareness. The term that is used to describe these networked connections and processes is synaesthesia" (p. 84). In view of this intersensoriality, researchers are now concerned with the connections and interactions between the sensory modalities in terms of how they generate cross-modal experiences.

Seeking the senses and methodological challenges

Various scholars have advocated different ways of conceptualising the ethnographic enterprise that foregrounds the senses in the process. For example, Pink (2009) speaks of 'sensory ethnography' that takes as its starting point the multisensoriality of experience, perception, knowing and practice that is integral to the "lives of people who participate in our research *and* to how we as researchers practice our craft" (p. 1). Likewise, Vannini et al. (2012) in seeking to develop a 'sociology of the senses', posit an approach to senses and sensations that is thoroughly *social* and *interactive*. Central to this approach is their notion of *somatic work*. This refers to the "range of linguistic and alinguistic reflexive experiences and activities by which individuals interpret, create, extinguish, maintain, interrupt, and/ or communicate somatic sensations that are congruent with personal, interpersonal, and/or cultural notions of moral, aesthetic, and/or logical desirability" (p. 19). They point out that people manage carnal sensations by performing somatic work according to negotiated 'somatic' rules that vary by personal, interpersonal, contextual, social, cultural, material, geographic, and historical circumstances. Sensing, therefore, is a social practice, and not just a chemical or physiological effect.

At a basic level, given the embodied nature of participant observation it could be argued that, at the level of method, all researchers who adopt this role are necessarily involved in somatic work and a sensual ethnography of some kind. This is not the case. Participant observation is not just a technique or method of data collection. Wolcott (1995) emphasises this when he makes the important distinction between doing fieldwork *versus* (just) being in the field. For him, the essence of fieldwork is revealed in the *intention* behind it, rather than by the label itself, inferring as it does that *merely being present* can constitute this activity. Of course, being there is a necessary condition for participant observation to take place. But, just being there is not enough. Vannini et al. (2012) support this view and point out that, "*Any* research activity has the potential to work insofar as we perform a bit of somatic work. So, it does not really matter *what* a researcher does; what is important is *how* he/she does it" (p. 68).

Vannini et al. (2012) point out that we can walk from 'point A' to 'point B' in a habitual manner, on auto-pilot, in an effortless, 'mindless', and *insensitive* way that involves little sensory reflexivity. In contrast, we can walk the same route in a more 'mindful', reflexively conscious, and sensitive manner that opens up the body to the experiential dynamics of this corporeal movement through time, space, and place. Vannini and his colleagues, therefore, stress the need for ethnographers to develop what they call 'sensory intelligence' which involves the ability to understand one's and others' sensations.

> It is the skilled use of sensibility to approach life situations. It is the ability to utilize one's senses as skills to manipulate and adapt to one's environment. It is the combined emotional, visceral, and cognitive ability to engage in somatic work. Without sensory intelligence there can be no sensuous scholarship. Indeed, we will go further and suggest that all sensuous scholarship is a form of sensory intelligence.
>
> (Vannini et al., 2012, p. 67)

The need to develop the reflexive ability to sensually engage via direct participation in the environment, and practices of others, in order to produce multisensorial and emplaced ways of knowing, is further commented on by Pink (2009). For her, "Learning to sense and make meanings as others do thus involves us not simply observing what they do, but learning how to use all our senses and to participate in *their* worlds, on the terms of their embodied understandings" (p. 72). Accordingly, she talks of developing the 'sensory imagination' and 're-sensing' the process of participant observation. In part, this involves moving from a sensory bias to a sensory subjectivity that entails a reflexive appreciation of one's own sensorium. That is, in order to cultivate a cross-sensory awareness that other cultures and groups do not necessarily work with the same sensorium or experience as the researcher, in the first instance, the researcher must develop an awareness of her or his sensory biases in the field. Pink suggests that this process should be initiated before ethnographic fieldwork begins and could involve exercises that encourage researchers to break down an experience into its sensory categories.

Sparkes (2009) argues that students undertaking research methods courses should be encouraged to develop their sensory intelligence and reflexive appreciation of their own sensorium. One way of doing this, he suggests, is to assist students to get to know the same location over time in different ways using different senses. For example, task one might be to visit a gym and describe it in terms of what is seen via the use of photographs and fieldnotes. Task two, on another day, might be to go in and describe the soundscape of the same gym in terms of the role that sound plays. On another occasion, the focus will be on the haptic, the skinscape, and how touch and textures work in the gym to create and sustain meaning. Likewise, the senses of smell (the panaroma) and taste would be the focus of attention on different days.

The purpose of these tasks is to reawaken the senses in the budding ethnographic researcher and to help them realise that all the senses are involved in understanding the life of the gym, or any other place, as a sensescape. As part of this reawakening, crucial questions can be raised about how, as people engage in somatic work in various settings, the senses interact in various combinations and hierarchies to shape the experiences and meanings of those involved in terms of various categories, such as gender, ethnicity, (dis)ability, age, social class, sexual orientation, and religion.

The process of re-sensing, and developing a sensory imagination and intelligence, as described by Pink (2009) and Vannini et al. (2012), is no easy task and should not be undertaken lightly. It is important to recognise, however, that as part of the sensorial revolution and the somatic turn in the social sciences, a growing number of scholars in sport and exercise have engaged with, and illuminated, the senses in action via their ethnographic studies. This work provides a rich resource for those wishing to do likewise. Due to limitations of space I can only touch lightly on a few of these.

Drawing inspiration from the work of Wacquant (2004) and his call for a 'carnal sociology', Spencer (2012) embarks on a sensual apprenticeship in Mixed Martial Arts (MMA) to explore how the pugilistic habitus is fabricated and deployed within this activity. Keeping with the mandates of sensory ethnography as described by Pink (2009), Spencer depicts the carnal dimensions of MMA at the level of his own multisensory, embodied, and emplaced experience to introduce us to bodies that touch, see, smell, taste, and hear combat.

Spencer (2012) begins by illustrating the temporal and spatial dimensions of his MMA club and the role that sight and sound play in how fighters come to know and act within it. He also focuses on the haptic dimensions of this process that are most evident when fighters are in the clinch standing or on the floor grappling with each other. In such moments, the fighters are in constant contact with their opponent and touch becomes the paramount experience. As he describes it, "Combatants must feel when to move, a touch sensitivity that is built up over time and practice. Not only must fighters have a heightened sense of their own bodies, but they must also feel their way through the body of their opponents" (p. 43).

Grappling on the floor and holding each other in clinches get fighters close enough to smell each other. Regarding the olfactory dimension of combat, Spencer (2012) notes that the smelling of a person's body odour is the most intimate perception of them, and that "our sense of them, their significance to us, and our histories of them are formed in and through smell" (p. 47). In his MMA club, particular odours came to be attached to particular individuals, and the olfactory sense of them had the potential to dominate memories of significant events. The smell of individual bodies, including one's own, mix together in the spaces of the club. Spencer notes how on entering, a collage of the thick salty odour of sweat and the sweet pungent smell of mat-cleaning products fills the nostrils, and how the changing rooms are almost entirely drenched with the smell of muscle liniment and sweat.

> The smells of these spaces intensifies according to the accumulation of bodies. In terms of the temporality, intensification of odor corresponds to the time of the classes and the forms of dueling that dominate the experience of MMA. Whereas the mats have the faint smell of cleaning products prior to night classes, odors reach their highest intensity after three hours of grappling or stand-up sparring as bodies shed heat and sweat.
>
> (Spencer, 2012, p. 48)

Mingling with the other senses in the MMA club is the taste of the rudiments and products of combat. Spencer (2012) notes how after and during a long training session, "water is transformed into a divine liquid. The mundane taste of water becomes extraordinary" (p. 50). The dominant taste for the fighter, however, is that of the plastic mouth guard which can range from sweet fluoride, to neutral, to bitter. Another experience that marks the experience of MMA is that of blood that is often accompanied by the sensation of pain from being struck. According to Spencer, the taste of blood both signals the event of battle and characterises the sensory experience of fighting. Here, "the breakdown of bodies is reflected in the taste of blood. Its salty-iron flavor reflects the bodies' fissure" (p. 51). To taste one's blood and to bleed in the gym alongside fellow fighters provides a sense of belonging and signifies one's membership amongst the wider MMA community.

The MMA gym, as described by Spencer (2012) through the corporeal realities of his lived fighting body, is self-evidently multisensorial in nature. Even though for convenience, he deals with each sense separately, it is clear that MMA fighters rarely experience training in club or combat though a singular sensory modality, but rather in multisensory ways, with two or more senses working together in concert. This is consistent with the views of Hockey and Allen-Collinson (2007) who, in seeking to better understand the phenomenology of the sensual sporting body, depict a range of sensory activities involved in doing sport that include movement and rhythm, the aural and respiration, the visual, the olfactory, and the haptic.

Allen-Collinson and Hockey (2013) and Hockey (2006) explore the visual experiences of distance runners as they negotiate their training routes. In addition to the visual, Hockey examines the auditory and olfactory dynamics of sensing the route. Regarding the latter, he notes that, like the fighters in Spencer's (2012) MMA club, when runners train they produce and engage with immediate smellscapes particular to themselves and their routes. This consists of an amalgam of odours or aromas that change according to activity, space, place and atmospheric/seasonal conditions. For Hockey, those odours relevant to distance runners help individuals substantiate their athletic identity in a number of ways: in an embodied sense; in a biographical sense; and in a space-time sense.

Reflecting on how smell operates in an embodied sense, Hockey (2006) notes how odour becomes a symbol of the running self as both a physical and moral being in which the "pungency that permeates distance running bodies and equipment is symbolic of training and racing effort, and is recognised as so by runners" (p. 192). This is made evident in the extract he provides from his individual running log.

> The weather has been bad for weeks and I have been wearing a Gore-Tex jacket and a thermal top underneath it – and the sweat pours out of me during every session. My crotch, back and armpits give off a kind of gross ripe smell and my kit is saturated with it. It's a stink I am used to, that is me when I am out there working hard, putting the miles in.
>
> (Hockey, 2006, p. 193)

The haptic dimensions of temperature and pressure are contrasted by Allen-Collinson and Hockey (2010) in distance running and scuba diving. For both divers and runners, the heat of the elements through which they move are central to their embodied experiences. In diving the touch, 'texture', movement and temperature of the water are intertwined in the experience, influencing the choice of clothing (e.g., don a wet or dry suit), which in turn affects the sensations experienced in the underwater environment. Analogously for runners, the touch and temperature of the air are important elements of the outdoor (and indoor) running experience. The touch of the elements can be experienced as pleasure or displeasure. For example, the touch of warm air caressing bare skin can be pleasurable. In contrast, windy, cold air with its lack of heat touching the body can generate intense displeasure that can involve discomfort and pain.

Regarding the tactile aspects of diving, Allen-Collinson and Hockey (2011) note that felt pressure is a key structure of experience because as one descends into deeper water, the pressure mounts. If remedial action is not taken, these feelings of pressure can be followed by discomfort and then pain. Experienced divers, therefore, become skilled at gauging very small gradations in pressure and making improvised, continual compensatory adjustments to their air pressure as they become attuned to their pressured aquatic environment. For runners too, such corporeal awareness and attunement is important, particularly in relation to the terrain which is more than mere neutral ground, as it also holds connotations of fitness for running purpose. The intentionality of runners is strongly focused on the terrain they cover, together with the feel of the running shoes or their bare feet. Accordingly, as they move over different kinds of terrain, there is an interplay in felt experience, of ground and sensory receptors, mechanoreceptors (pressure detecting), thermoreceptors (temperature detecting) and nociceptors (pain-detecting experienced as pleasure or dis-pleasure). The resulting experience can be either pleasurable or painful.

More recently, Allen-Collinson and Owton (2014) further explore the role of the haptic senses in running and boxing, and particularly the 'touch' of heat, in producing periods of intense embodiment in which the senses work together to generate a kind of bodily 'high'. They focus on the sense of heat as a core experience in two interrelated areas that are relevant to all sports; warming up, and thermoregulation.

Warming up can take many forms, but however it is undertaken, as Allen-Collinson and Owton point out, "it requires of the practitioner a heightened awareness of somatic sensations in muscles, tendons and joints, to gauge when the body is sufficiently prepared" (p. 12). Besides this, they illustrate how warming up can incorporate an energising element (often involving listening to music) in which a sense of heat can be experienced as feelings of internal energy and bodily readiness. In this form, "it is experienced as less a form of touch and more as a distinct 'sense'…this corporeal readiness incorporates a *psychological warm-up*" (p. 12).

Following the warm-up, one of the challenges faced by runners and boxers alike is heat regulation, the maintenance of an optimum (or at least comfortable) balance between keeping warm and overheating. Allen-Collinson and Owton reveal how both activities involve experiencing tactile forms of heat where the body is literally touched by the elements to produce feelings of intense pleasure or pain. With regard to thermoregulatory efforts, they note how practitioners, besides seeking to control the inner heat of the body to maximise their performance, also attribute meaning to its corporeal indicators, such as profuse sweating. In running and boxing subcultures, sweat has strong connotations of corporeal immersion in the hard physical labour of the activity, displaying to self and others a willingness and preparedness to work hard and suffer discomforts.

This brief review of a selection of the work on the senses indicates that this topic is now being taken seriously by researchers in sport and exercise. It also reveals that the scholars involved are adopting a much more nuanced stance towards just what constitutes the senses, how they operate together, and how these might be accessed by the ethnographer in various ways. Of course, accessing the senses in sport and exercise is one challenge. Representing the senses as felt, and experienced, is quite another. According to Spencer (2012), "Quotidian and academic descriptions, while hinting at the various ways the senses are registered in sport, fail to adequately engage with the full spectrum of the senses and how sensory dimensions are experienced in concert" (p. 33). Or, as Wacquant (2013) puts it, "there is no point in carrying out a carnal sociology backed by practical initiation if what is revealed about the sensorial magnetism of the universe in question ends up disappearing later in the writing" (p. 31).

Representational challenges

In his book *Body and Soul*, Wacquant (2004) grappled with the challenges of how best to ethnographically describe to readers the sensuous intoxification of apprentice boxers, and the interplay of the senses in their conversion to the world of prize fighting, via expressive forms suitable to communicating it without, in the process, annihilating its most distinctive properties. Reflecting back on this challenge, Wacquant (2013) poses it as the simple question: "How to go from the guts to the intellect, from the comprehension of the flesh to the knowledge of the text?" In answer to his own question, he states the following.

> To restitute the carnal dimension of ordinary existence and the bodily anchoring of the practical knowledge constitutive of pugilism – but also of every practise, even the least 'bodily' in appearance, including sociological analysis – requires indeed a complete overhaul of our way of writing social science. In the case at hand, I had to find a style breaking with the monological, monochromatic, linear writing of the classic research account from which the ethnographer has withdrawn and instead elaborate a multifaceted writing mixing styles and genres, so as to capture and convey 'the taste and ache of action' to the reader.
>
> (Wacquant, 2013, p. 30)

Wacquant (2004) mixes three types of writing, intertwined with each other, but each given priority in one of its three parts, in an attempt to allow the reader to slide smoothly from concept to precept, from analysis to experience.

Wacquant (2013) states that the first part of *Body and Soul* operates in a classic sociological style and an analytical mould to provide the reader with the necessary tools for explaining and understanding what is going on. The second part of the book is set by ethnographic writing in the strict sense in that it provides a "dense depiction of the ways of being, thinking and feeling and acting proper to the milieu under consideration" (p. 30). In the third part comes the experiential moment in the form of what he calls a sociological novella that seeks to "deliver felt action, the lived experience of the subject who also happens to be the analyst" (p. 31).

Others grappling with the challenges of representing the sensuous body in textual form have drawn directly on the seminal work of Stoller (1997) and his calls for *sensual scholarship* in which "writers tack between the analytical and the sensible, in which embodied form as well as disembodied logic constitute scholarly argument" (p. xv). Developing this notion, Vannini et al. (2012) speak of writing sensuously as a way of inviting our audiences to a double layer of reflection.

> The first layer is descriptive, not in order to claim that we are portraying reality objectively (writing cannot accomplish this), but in order to evoke and create in our audience sensations that evoke research settings, people, and the phenomena that interest us. The other layer links the ideographic with the nomothetic, private sensations with public discourses, somatic experience with sensory order, somatic careers with sensory histories, private recollections with collective memories.
>
> (Vannini et al., 2012, p. 74)

Such writing, Vannini et al. (2010) argue, can take the form of a *somatic layered account* that is proportionately prosaic and poetic, drawing as it does upon multiple forms of consciousness or ways of knowing, such as the embodied, the somatic, the affective, the imaginative, the linguistic and the non-symbolic, and the intellectual and analytical. Having suggested a number of strategies that authors can use to write somatically, Vannini et al. (2012) emphasise that producing such accounts and writing sensuously is not an easy or automatic task. For them, it "requires deploying representation technics and techniques; it demands skill, and constitutes a creative act, a form of poiesis" (p. 80).

For Pink (2009), scholarly writing remains a central, and she believes crucial, medium for the transcription, evocation, argument and theoretical debating of ethnographic research that attend to the senses. Various forms of writing *can* connect sensory experience and theoretical discussion in instructive ways. This said, she notes the following.

> Yet, conventional scholarly practice is limited in its capacity to communicate about the directness of the sensory and affective elements

of emplaced experience. Alternative routes to representing sensory knowing have been developed in arts practice and there are opportunities for these practices to both inform and be developed collaboratively with sensory approaches to ethnographic representation.

(Pink, 2009, p. 132)

As part of a growing interest in arts-based and performative methodologies across the social sciences, these alternative routes for representing the senses, include autoethnography, poetic representations, ethnographic fiction and nonfiction, ethnodrama, and ethnotheatre, dance, musical performance, and installations, to name but a few (Sparkes, 2002; Sparkes & Smith, 2014). According to Bagley and Castro-Salazar (2012), such arts-based research has the potential to "engage with the emotional, sensual, and kinaesthetic complexity of everyday lived experiences; to challenge dominant cultural norms, beliefs and values; and to uncover, recover and portray research to audiences in new ways" (p. 257).

Douglas and Carless (2013), suggest that performative methodologies can provide a different way of 'coming to know', more inclusive forms of representation, a vicarious re-experiencing of the world, a blurring of the self–other divide, and an alternative vision of what might be. In contrast to more traditional forms of academic writing, they argue that "good performative research does not force upon an audience a single finalized perspective, but instead offers a provocative 'picture' which preserves complexity and multiplicity, retaining some degree of openness and ambiguity that characterises many aspects of the social world" (p. 4). Despite these offerings, they acknowledge that many challenges face the researcher with a serious interest in developing their own performative practice.

Moving into the realm of performance, as a way of representing the senses, will take many researchers into unfamiliar territory and call for the development of new skills and sensibilities. Recognising this, Sparkes and Smith (2014) suggest that researchers in sport and exercise seek guidance and support, as part of a process of developing mutually beneficial and respectful collaborations, with those who have specific expertise in the performing arts. They emphasise that one does not have to be, for example, a trained theatre artist in order to write an ethnodrama and produce ethnotheatre. For them, however, collaborative ventures between social scientists and arts-based researchers are more likely to produce high quality performances that work 'on stage'. That this is the case is evidenced in a number of successful collaborations that include the following: Bagley and Cancienne (2001, 2002), with one an educational researcher the other a dancer and choreographer; and Llewellyn, Gilbourne and Triggs (2011), with one being a theatre and drama specialist and the other two being sport psychology researchers.

Besides the specific performance genres named above, Dicks, Soyinka and Coffey (2006) point out that ethnographers currently have a broad range of media at their disposal for conducting fieldwork, for aiding analysis and, "most challengingly, for representing their completed work" (p. 27). These include digital media such as photographs, video film, audio-recordings, graphics and others besides. They note how through the computer 'writing space', these media can be integrated together, alongside more conventional written interpretation, into hypermedia environments. While this development offers exciting opportunities, Dicks and her colleagues outline a number of potential problems that such integration poses. In particular, they argue that different media can be seen to 'afford' different kinds of meaning. They believe that ethnographers thinking about using multimodal representations need to give careful consideration to the kinds of meaning afforded by different media, and pay attention to the overlaps among, and distinctiveness of different modes as this alerts us to the ways in which different media can be used for representing multimodality. Importantly, they emphasise, ethnographers should not assume that "multimedia automatically gives us multimeaning, satisfactorily reflecting the multimodality of the field" (p. 94).

Pink (2009) also reflects on the inevitable falsity of separating out the senses in ethnographic representation and then focusing on one modality as a time as many studies do. She notes that most scholars who practise or write about sensory representation are well aware that no sense can be totally isolated from others, and that in their focus on one sensory modality they often seek to evoke a fuller embodied, multisensory experience for the audience. Rather than offering simple solutions, Pink provides challenges and possible ways of addressing these based on innovative practices in the social sciences along with the work of contemporary artists. This mingling, she suggests, of more established and emergent ethnographic genres and styles along with sensory arts practice offers ethnographers a series of inspiring models. Despite such inspirations and possibilities, the fact remains, however, as Pink states, that "ethnographic representation is a complex task" (p. 153).

The methodological and representational challenges described above need to be addressed if the notion of ethnography as a sensual way of being is to be developed in the future. At the most basic level this requires that we acknowledge the centrality of the researcher's fleshy, messy, material (biological), and sentient body throughout the ethnographic process, and be willing to cultivate carnal ways of knowing about sport and exercise. Given that, most of the time, our bodies are experienced as an absent-presence in our daily lives, strategies need to be developed that stimulate the sensory imagination of ethnographers and assist them to develop their sensory intelligence in the field. The pedagogical implications of this task suggest that a reconceptualising of how ethnography is taught to students on 'research methods' courses may be necessary. For example, such courses often introduce students to the concept of 'mixed methods' research in an unproblematic manner as part of their curriculum (Sparkes, 2015). We might, therefore, reflect on how the concept of a 'mixed' and multisensory researcher might be introduced and developed in practice on such courses, in ways that challenge the hegemony of sight, and encourage an intense engagement with *all* the available senses operating in any social setting. As part of this process, we might also reflect on how best to encourage and support students to cultivate sensuous forms of scholarship that involve new ways of knowing about and representing themselves and others as part of the ethnographic enterprise. None of this, of course, will be easy. Such challenges will, however, need to be met if a more sensory research agenda in sport and exercise is to flourish in the coming years.

References

Allen-Collinson, J., & Hockey, J. (2011). Feeling the way: Notes towards a haptic phenomenology of distance running and scuba diving. *International Review for the Sociology of Sport, 46*, 330–345.

Allen-Collinson, J., & Hockey, J. (2013). From a certain point of view: Sensory phenomenological envisionings of running space and place. *Journal of Contemporary Ethnography*. DOI: 10.1 177/0891241613505866.

Allen-Collinson, J., & Owton, H. (2014). Intense embodiment: Senses of heat in women's running and boxing. *Body & Society*. DOI: 10.1177/1357034X14538849.

Atkinson, M. (2012). The empirical strikes back: Doing realist ethnography. In K. Young & M. Atkinson (Eds.), *Qualitative research on sport and physical culture* (pp. 23–49). Bingley: Emerald.

Bagley, C., & Cancienne, M. (2001). Educational research and intertextual forms of (Re)presentation: The case of dancing the data. *Qualitative Inquiry, 7*, 221–237.

Bagley, C., & Cancienne, M. (2002). *Dancing the data*. New York: Peter Lang.

Bagley, C. & Castro-Salazar, R. (2012). Critical arts-based research in education: Performing undocumented historias. *British Educational Research Journal, 38*(2): 239–260.

Blackman, L. (2008). *The body*. Oxford: Berg.

Dicks, B., Soyinka, B., & Coffey, A. (2006). Multimodal ethnography. *Qualitative Research, 6*, 77–96.

Douglas, K., & Carless, D. (2013). An invitation to performative research. *Methodological Innovations Online, 8*, 1–12.

Hockey, J. (2006). Sensing the run: The senses and distance running. *Senses and Society, 1*, 183–202.

Hockey, J., & Allen-Collinson, J. (2007). Grasping the phenomenology of sporting bodies. *International Review for the Sociology of Sport, 42*, 115–131.

Howes, D. (2005). Introduction: Empire of the senses. In D. Howes (Ed.), *Empire of the senses: A sensual culture reader* (pp. 1–17). Oxford: Berg.

Llewellyn, D., Gilbourne, D., & Triggs, C. (2011). Representing applied research experiences through performance; extending beyond text. In D. Gilbourne & M. Andersen (Eds.), *Critical essays in applied sport psychology* (pp. 23–38). Champaign, IL: Human Kinetics.

Macpherson, F. (2011a). Taxonomising the senses. *Philosophical Studies, 153*, 123–142.

Macpherson, F. (2011b). Cross-modal experiences. *Proceedings of the Aristotelian Society, CXI, 3*, 429–468.

Mellor, P., & Shilling, C. (1997). *Re-forming the body.* London: Sage.

Paterson, M. (2008). Review essay: Charting the return of the senses. *Environment and Planning, 26,* 563–569.

Pink, S. (2009). *Doing sensory ethnography.* London: Sage.

Sparkes, A. (2002). *Telling tales in sport and physical activity: A qualitative journey.* Champaign, IL: Human Kinetics.

Sparkes, A. (2009). Ethnography and the senses: Challenges and possibilities. *Qualitative Research in Sport, Exercise & Health, 1,* 21–35.

Sparkes, A. (2015). Developing mixed methods research in sport and exercise psychology: Critical reflections on five points of controversy. *Psychology of Sport & Exercise, 16,* 49–59.

Sparkes, A., & Smith, B. (2012). Embodied research methodologies and seeking the senses in sport and physical culture: A fleshing out of problems and possibilities. In K. Young & M. Atkinson (Eds.), *Qualitative research on sport and physical culture* (pp. 167–190). Bingley: Emerald.

Sparkes, A., & Smith, B. (2014). *Qualitative research methods in sport, exercise and health: From process to product.* London: Routledge.

Spencer, D. (2012). *Ultimate fighting and embodiment: Violence, gender, and mixed martial arts.* London: Routledge.

Stoller, P. (1997). *Sensuous scholarship.* Philadelphia: University of Pennsylvania Press.

Vannini, P., Ahluwalia-Lopez, G., Waskul, D., & Gottschalk, S. (2010). Performing taste at wine festivals: A somatic layered account of material culture. *Qualitative Inquiry, 16,* 378–396.

Vannini, P., Waskul, D., & Gottschalk, S. (2012). *The senses in self, society, and culture.* London: Routledge.

Wacquant, L. (2004). *Body and soul: Notebooks of an apprentice boxer.* Oxford: Oxford University Press.

Wacquant, L. (2013). Habitus as topic and tool: Reflections on becoming a prizefighter. In R. Garcia & D. Spencer (Eds.), *Fighting scholars: Habitus and ethnographies of martial arts and combat sports* (pp. 19–31). London: Anthem Press.

Wolcott, H. (1995). *The art of fieldwork.* Walnut Creek, CA: AltaMira Press

Chapter 5

Ethnographic creative nonfiction

Exploring the whats, whys and hows

*Brett Smith, Kerry R. McGannon
and Toni L. Williams*

The traditional or most common way to communicate qualitative research, including ethnographic work, is through a realist tale. In a realist tale the researcher is almost completely absent from the finished text, an extensive set of closely edited data (e.g. interview quotes) is presented, and a tight theoretical account of the data is given (see Sparkes, 2002; Sparkes & Smith, 2014). Despite the dominance of the realist tale, there are many other legitimate options for communicating the results of ethnographic research (Griffin & Phoenix, 2014). In this chapter, we consider the use of creative nonfiction as one relatively novel way for representing work done in this qualitative tradition. To understand *what* creative nonfiction is and might look like when produced, a description and example of this genre is first offered. Next, *why* creative nonfiction might be used is considered. The chapter then gives attention to *how* a creative nonfiction might be crafted and *how* we might judge this format in terms of its quality.

What is creative nonfiction?

Creative nonfiction is a type of creative analytic practice (CAP) that tells a story which is grounded in research data and draws on literary conventions. Thus, when researchers speak of producing a creative nonfictional representation of ethnographic data, they are making it clear to the reader that their stories are not made up or wholly imagined but are based on empirical data systematically collected. Each story is fictional in form yet factual in content. It is grounded in real events and people's lived experiences that a researcher observed in some fashion (e.g. interviews, participant observation, internet blogs) whilst 'being there' in the field. As Clayton (2010) stressed, in a creative nonfiction "empirical evidence is represented within a fictional form of writing" (p. 272). Or, as Cheney (2001) put it, "Creative nonfiction tells a story using facts, but uses many of the techniques of fiction for its compelling qualities and emotional vibrancy. Creative nonfiction doesn't just report facts, it delivers facts in ways that move the reader toward a deeper understanding of a topic" (p. 1).

Within the field of sport and exercise research, a number of scholars have opted to use creative nonfiction as a way of representing their qualitative findings. Recent examples include the study by Gearity and Mills (2012) on strength and conditioning coaching; Smith's (2013) research on experiences of sustaining a spinal cord injury through sport; Smith, Papathomas, Martin Ginis, and Latimer-Cheung's (2013) efforts to translate knowledge on physical activity and spinal cord injury; McGannon and Cameron's (2013) stories of female exercisers' experiences of body anxiety and fear of fat; Carless, Sparkes, Douglas and Cooke's (2014) investigation of an adapted sport course for disabled military personnel; Curran, Bingham, Richardson and Parnell's (2014) work on football and community-based physical activity; Krane et al.'s (2014) exploration of what it means to be a girl athlete; and McMahon and Penney's (2014) examination of athletes' perceptions about their parents in relation to performance and perfection in sport.

Another example can be found in the research by Clayton (2010) on masculinities and the classroom exploits of a cohort of male collegiate football players reading for a module concerned with gender at a UK university. Grounded in "the fruits of ethnographic fieldwork, interviews and focus groups" (Clayton, 2010, p. 372), the following extract gives a taste of what an ethnographic creative nonfiction *might* look like. We stress 'might' because, as Smith (2010) warned, if research is to flourish it is important not to adopt a facsimile approach, whereby more of the same is repeated in content and form. Past research can provide very good exemplars. But we should avoid thinking of these as prescriptive formats to simply follow lest we risk producing a lot of formulaic, safe, straightforward, predictable, and sterile research. In the case of a creative nonfiction the creative element would likely be washed out as well. With these points in mind, here is a flavour of this genre of representation from Clayton's (2010) study of male footballers studying for a degree in sport.

'We should probably do something', Daniel announced with an air of antipathy, leaning forward in his chair to peruse the thoroughly academic task.

A blissful moment of scholarly silence filled the room as the other Boys followed Daniel's lead. The Lecturer sat back in his chair, extending his legs out under the desk.

The silence was soon broken.

'Are you gonna do anything?', Sean gaped at Alex before turning to the Lecturer, holding his arms slightly aloft.

A faint noise somewhere between a groan and a laugh disseminated around the room.

Alex remained focused on the same semi-naked celebrity, barely recoiling from Sean's belligerent intrusion. The Lecturer momentarily pondered how long it can take to read a tabloid tit-bit about a semi-naked celebrity.

'Fascinating as I'm sure that is, Alex, any chance we could stick to the task at hand?', he posed a deliberately oratorical request.

'Keep it real', Steve mocked in retaliation.

The Boys laughed, the Girls rolled their eyes, the Lecturer summoned another wry smile and Alex, finally, looked up from his newspaper.

'Christina Aguilera', he announced in a bizarre state of contemplation.

The Lad's exclusive laughter was quickly replaced with a more encompassing silence born of both perplexity and irritation. The Girls looked at Alex, then at the Lecturer. The Lecturer looked at Alex, then at the Girls.

Alex continued, 'It's relevant, isn't it, because she is to do with gender and that'.

The Lecturer closed his hands together in a prayer-like motif. 'Yes', he probed further with a slight sense of trepidation.

'Well, she's feminine, isn't she?', Alex elaborated. 'Stereotypically, like'.

'She wants bending over and giving a right seeing to', Steve interrupted in a manner as abrupt and inappropriate as an interruption can be.

'Shit, yeah', Brad stepped in. 'Does she get 'em out, does she?'

Alex had a quick glance down at the semi-naked celebrity. 'Oh, man, I'm telling ya', he exclaimed. 'She don't show it all. She's kind of got her hair coming down and covering up the nips'.

The Lecturer slammed his mug to the desk-top bringing the furore to an end, picked up a marker pen and walked to the board. 'Okay', he calmly exhaled. 'Brad, you seem to know something of the female body, and Alex seems to feel strongly about the relevance of Christina Aguilera's breasts to the task, so relate your comments to the task for me'.

The Girls folded their arms and leant forward on the desk with something resembling a smirk. The Boys fell silent for moment, Brad and Alex exchanged a look, both prompting the other to speak.

'Well', Brad cleared his throat. 'She's like the top woman that men are supposed to go for, like that exaggerated femininity thing, that ideology, 'cus she represents hegemony... male hegemony'.

The Lecturer nodded, having to concede that Brad's response had some merit.

'Jesus!', Alex exclaimed. 'Why don't you just bend him over the desk and make sure of the first?'

The Boys laughed. The Lecturer didn't....

(Clayton, 2010, pp. 375–6)

Clearly then, ethnographic creative nonfictions are very different from how research is traditionally represented. These differences, neither good nor bad, invite us to think reflexively and critically about the ways we choose to represent, that is written about, the results of our research. This is important for several overlapping reasons. The term ethnography derives from not just the Greek *ethnos* (meaning 'people') but also *graph* (meaning 'writing'). Given that writing is central to what ethnographers do, and that there are differing ways a qualitative researcher can write, how an ethnographer represents their research cannot be ignored. Researchers need to command an awareness of the different ways in which they might represent their research. They also need to make informed, principled, and disciplined choices about just which kind of genre they might use to represent their research (Sparkes, 2002; Sparkes & Smith, 2014). Vital in this process of making a choice is the consideration of why a certain genre of writing might be used (Blodgett, Schinke, Smith, Peltier, & Pheasant, 2011).

Why do a creative nonfiction? – Some benefits and weaknesses

While creative nonfiction might seem easier to do than other ways of representing research, similar to other kinds of research writing, this genre of representation is challenging to do well. There may also be the belief within certain quarters of the qualitative community that a creative nonfiction is superior to realist tales; it is not. No genre of representation is perfect. Other available genres of representation often serve different purposes and, therefore, are chosen in light of these. Choosing any form of representation because it is fashionable also will not suffice. Moreover, a talent for more arts-based approaches or a genuine love for these are not in themselves adequate reasons for doing a creative nonfiction, even if they are useful attributes of a researcher wanting to do this kind of work well. With these caveats in mind, the following are some reasons for why a researcher may choose a creative nonfiction to represent their research data.

First, because analysis takes place in the process of writing, a creative nonfiction can provide a valuable analytical dimension to a project. As Richardson (2000: 923) argued:

> I consider writing as a *method of inquiry*, a way of finding out about yourself and your topic. Although we usually think about writing as a mode of 'telling' about the social world, writing is not just a mopping-up activity at the end of the research project. Writing is also a way of 'knowing' – a method of discovery and analysis. By writing in different ways, we discover new aspects of our topic and our relationship to it. Form and content are inseparable.

Second, a good creative nonfiction has theoretical benefits. According to Ellis (2004), because a story is theoretical in its own right and can do the work of communicating theory, a creative nonfiction story can show theory. As part of showing theory in and through a story, other theoretical possibilities also emerge. A creative nonfiction allows a researcher to show an array of research findings along with multiple theoretical points in one paper. This can be done because a story can uniquely contain complex information. Another possibility is that a creative nonfiction can display interpretive openness when it comes to theory. It can encourage additional theoretical insights beyond what the researcher considered or purposively aimed to show within the story. As Frank (2010) argued, rather than closing down interpretive insights, stories have the capacity to open up multiple understandings. In so doing, rather than remaining firmly anchored to one way of seeing the world, readers may be spurred to revisit the world from a different direction and transported into understanding human life in other possible ways. Thus, instead of theoretically finalising human lives, that is offering the last or final theoretical word on them, a creative nonfiction can generate a rich smorgasbord of understandings and possible ways of being.

Third, a creative nonfiction can have an ethical benefit. It can help protect the identity of research participants without stripping away the rawness of real happenings.

Fourth, according to Clayton (2010), a creative nonfiction allows the reader to viscerally and emotionally inhabit the lifeworld of participants and/or researchers. It also "condenses the action in a tale that spans and adjusts time and place, revealing actual (witnessed) occurrences from within the period of data collection, but decontextualising each occurrence and reorganising in a way that reveals the lived experience in a less fragmented form" (Clayton, 2010, p. 372). Likewise, for Carless et al. (2014), creative nonfictions have the benefit of providing insights into the complex, ambiguous, and contingent of human life.

Fifth, this genre of representation can be a useful medium for bearing witness in that a story can not only offer testimony to a truth but also implicate others by calling on the reader to become a witness of others, that is, to share the story with others.

Sixth, creative nonfiction offers a deeply embodied, sensorial and relational account of human lives. This is vital. Bodies are lived, social, and biological entities that shape human conduct. Human lives are not experienced in a sensorial vacuum but are sometimes guided by a combination of smells, tastes, textures, sounds, touch, and what we see or do not see (Sparkes & Smith, 2012). Our actions, behaviours, and emotions emerge from social relationships, not from individual minds.

Seventh, according to Smith et al. (2013), an ethnographic creative nonfiction has the benefit of being able to reach multiple audiences instead of only academics. The traditional ways to represent qualitative research (i.e. a realist tale) and quantitative research (i.e. the scientific tale) deliver important knowledge when done well. However, due to the highly specialised academic terminology used, scientific and realist tales are comprehensible largely to academic audiences only. As such, the reach of findings is often limited to a small group of people. A creative nonfiction has, however, the strength of being highly accessible to many people beyond academia. It is more accessible because, as suggested in Smith, Thomsone, Latimer-Cheung, and Martin Ginis (2015), good creative nonfictions are stories that use everyday language, are emotionally engaging, contextualise experiences, have credible characters, promote meaning-making, stimulate imagination, resonate with people, show theory and humanise the mind, behaviour and action. One implication of highly accessible research is that, as evidenced in Smith et al. (2015), it can enhance the process of knowledge translation and dissemination. Another implication highlighted by Smith et al. is that with more accessible research larger numbers of people may be affected. Practical impact can be wide and significant. This impact could include teaching, reminding, reinvigorating, and reassuring people as well as encouraging dialogue amongst individuals.

Of course, in highlighting various benefits of creative nonfiction as a scholarly process and production, some weaknesses and risks must also be acknowledged. These include the following key points. First, as Frank (2010) makes clear, stories are always out of control. When one offers a story in the form of an ethnographic nonfiction there is no guarantee that the purpose behind the story, analytical insights, theoretical points, attempts to translate knowledge, or desire to generate impact, will be realised. Thus, when the story is circulated, researchers need to learn to live with uncertainty in terms of what they seek to communicate and what they hope the story might do. This can be tough or unsettling for some researchers who are historically located in a certain view of science that privileges a quest for absolute certainty in human matters.

Second, despite creative nonfictions being grounded in data collected systematically, when the word fiction is linked in any way to the word 'research' the work in some quarters may struggle for legitimacy (Sparkes & Smith, 2014), particularly when interpreted against taken-for-granted notions of validity, reliability and truth that often permeate the research process. In this regard, there may further be concern from colleagues who work with more traditional forms of research criteria that the research 'is all made up!' or not grounded in scientific rigour (Sparkes, 2002). As a result, such work could be disregarded.

Third, and related to this second point, is that although there are many excellent journals that accept creative nonfictions, some journal editors will not accept this kind of representation. Equally, some university project supervisors and PhD committees may greet creative nonfictional work with suspicion, even hostility, and questions are raised as to whether it constitutes 'proper' research and/or relegate such work to the 'appendix' section of the document. None of these issues are helped, we should stress, when poor creative fictions are produced whereby researchers do not reflexively attend to issues of epistemology and theory and how these impact and co-construct the researcher, researched and the 'tale' that is ultimately produced.

In many respects, all of the foregoing points bring us to the question of how might we judge creative nonfiction. That is, how can we distinguish the 'good' from the 'bad' so that quality is kept high and the fire of any critics is not fuelled further. We address the issue of how we might judge this work shortly. But now, we turn to how we might write a creative nonfiction.

Writing a creative nonfiction: how might this be done?

Drawing from Barone and Eisner (2012), Cheney (2001), Ellis (2004) and Ellingson (2009), the following are some tips for how to craft a creative nonfiction. For reasons noted when we spoke about what creative nonfiction *might* look like, these tips should not be seen as a set of prescriptive techniques or a recipe. Rather, we hope that some of the tips are useful for thinking about how to transform data into a story.

- *Epistemological and ontological awareness*: Throughout writing, be attentive to how, as a researcher, one's epistemology and ontology informs the story. Also consider the world views of the people in the story and how these are inseparable from culture and the social world. For example, because the interests, history, and so on of a researcher influence the knowledge they develop in and as a story, it is important to be critically reflexive about what content is privileged in a creative nonfiction, how it is composed, and with what possible effects on people's worlds.
- *A purpose*: A creative nonfiction needs to have and communicate an important point. This helps enable stories to succeed not only as artful literary pieces, but as human science research, too. Make sure the purpose is clear to readers. For instance, some stories gathered from the field might be interesting to the researcher, but this alone is not a good enough reason for one to write an academic creative nonfiction. A researcher needs to consider what the empirical, theoretical, moral, ethical, practical, and so forth point of the story is. They need to have a good response to the 'so what' question – what does the story add to knowledge, how does it extend or challenge theory, and/or, for example, how might this story change our social and personal worlds?
- *Analysis and theory*: For instance, some researchers might first choose to operate as a storyanalyst (see Smith & Sparkes, 2009). When operating as storyanalyst the researcher places narratives *under* analysis and communicates results in the form of a *realist tale* to produce an analytical account *of* narratives. When narratives are placed under analysis, the researcher uses one or more specific types of analysis, such as a thematic analysis or narrative dialogical analysis, to scrutinise, think about, and theoretically interpret certain elements of a story. Following this, and

with results from operating as a *storyanalyst* at hand, a researcher may then make a move to what is known as a *storyteller*. When operating as a storyteller the researcher recasts data and results to produce a story and the story (e.g. in the form of a creative nonfiction) *is* a theory. Accordingly, as in the work of Smith et al. (2015), a researcher might use the results and theoretical interpretations generated when operating as a storyanalyst to help assemble a story. Researchers may also add findings from other research to their story. This can help create a more complex picture and show tensions, contradictions, and connections between research. Collating all analytic results and theories in a table can sometimes be useful; it condenses points to be made, is easily accessible, and can help jog the memory about ideas to be included when crafting the story.

- *Show rather than tell*: Showing is about delivering a rich, vivid description that aims to create images and conjure up emotions within a reader. Telling concisely catalogues actions and emotional life. Here is an example of telling, provided by Gearity (2014): "It was hot outside and my coach yelled at us" (p. 212). In contrast, here is showing: "Sand kicked up as the gruff coach, hoarse from a long afternoon of berating me and twenty-five of my teammates to sprint again and again, stomped his worn cowboy boots across the heat scorn Mississippi field. Beads of sweat poured steadily..." (p. 212).

- *Verisimilitude*: Seek truthfulness, not the Truth. The story needs to demonstrate how true to an experience a narrative can be and with that, the evocation of emotion and feeling from the reader(s). For instance, as in the work of Carless et al. (2014), this might include creating an account that feels close to the participant's own telling, attempting to be faithful to the experiences and emotions described, the meanings they inscribed, and their own styles of speech.

- *Select and develop characters*: How many characters are needed to tell the story, who the characters will be and become, how they will drive the story along, what stories each will tell, and how they will interact with each other, are some issues to consider to help select and develop characters. Make characters complex too. For example, simply depicting someone as a good or bad coach or another character as always happy following a traumatic sporting injury or always sad would often be too simplistic and not do justice to the complexity of human lives across time.

- *Use dialogue*: Show what has happened, the point of the story, emotions, and so on through conversations where appropriate. Using dialogue is important because humans often engage with each other through this medium of talk. It can bring a sense of 'real life' to the story as well as vibrancy. It allows also readers to hear differences across and within people. Here is an example of dialogue from a study on spinal cord injury, physical activity and sport.

'That might be,' interrupts Martin. 'But disabled sport isn't for everyone. It's not for me. It bores me. No adrenalin rush. And these guys that I see play in the gym, they're full of bravado. They're all talk.'

'I don't know, they seem to be having fun, and getting fit,' Greg says, casually throwing thoughts into the air.

'Maybe. But, I tell you,' says Martin. 'I bet they were crap at sports before they ended up in here. They were the kids at school who got picked last to play. No, disabled sport isn't for me. It's not me. Where's the skill in it? Where's the rush, the enjoyment? And anyhow, I won't be in this chair forever, so why bother playing?'

'I really hope that's the case man,' replies Greg. 'But maybe you shouldn't put all your hope on walking again soon...'

(Smith et al., 2013, p. 2052)

- *Embodiment*: Evoke a sense of the characters' body in motion and being still. Show bodies being emotionally expressive (or not) and enacting on, within and against stories. Let the characters act out the story in relation to other people and reveal things about themselves to others through these actions. Here is an example from Sparkes' (2007) study of academic culture.

On entering the office, Paul collapses into a chair. To Jim he looks smaller than when he last saw him two weeks ago weight-training in the university gym. Now his body wilts, it sags, as if the sap has been drained out of him. His skin is pale, the cheeks of his face hollow and pinched. The eyes are tired and red. They do not look at Jim but down at the table.

'So what brings you to this neck of the woods. Haven't you got any work to do?' Jim jokes to hide his unease at Paul's physical appearance. Paul's eyes remain fixed on the table in front of him. When he speaks, the usual vibrancy of his voice is absent. The words come out in a quiet whisper.

'They've told me I'm going to lose my job. They're going to sack me.'

Jim watches his friend's shoulders sink inside his jacket. Almost inaudibly, Paul sighs.
'I don't know what to do. I just don't know. ...'

Jim sees the tears glisten in Paul's eyes and feels his own begin to swell, clouding his vision as he watches his friend's muscular frame crumple in front of him. As the tears begin their slow descent to his cheeks, Jim stands and moves quietly over to Paul.

'Do me a favour Big Fellah. Stand up and let me give you a hug.'

(Sparkes 2007: 529–30)

- *Write evocatively*: As shown in the examples above, evocativeness involves using words to evoke and vividly reveal lived meanings. For instance, it can also be useful to use flashback, metaphor, and dramatic evocation. Writing evocatively can also include showing lived meanings through dialogue as well as using words to evoke different senses (e.g. smell, sound, taste) to vividly illuminate emotions, create suspension, and engage the readers viscerally as well as cognitively. An example of the use of senses can be found in Sparkes (2009).
- *Develop a plot*: A plot cannot always contain tension, as everyday life is not like that. But a story needs to have some dramatic tension. It needs to connect points across time, be cohesive, and have a consequence(s). A story needs a beginning, middle, and 'end' (not the final word), but not always told in that order. As shown in the work of Sparkes (2007), and Clayton (2010) earlier, to help drive the plot along also consider the characters, what obstacles along the story they will face, what they care about, and how they might change, even if only very subtly.
- *Scene setting*: Think about where (e.g. places) and when (e.g. morning breakfast) to locate people and their conversations (including internal dialogues with phantom others). Ask yourself about the backstages and front stages people behave in as well as how many scenes readers are willing to move in and out of.
- *Selectivity*: No one can tell the 'whole' story of a research topic. Select what needs to be told in that paper, to meet a certain purpose (e.g. to answer your research question), and to communicate an important point to a particular audience. Don't try to pack all you know and found in!
- *Think with your body*: When reading drafts of the story, draw on your felt experiences and listen to the many voices you have heard in and through your body. Does the story 'feel' right? What niggles within you about the story?
- *Edit*: Revise your work numerous times – editing, revising, editing more, and revising again – over a period of time (often this is over many months). Make every word count. Don't make the story too long.

How might we judge creative nonfictions?

Similar to any piece of qualitative or quantitative research, it is challenging to write high quality nonfictional representations of ethnographic research. And when or "if one chooses to use fictional techniques in the writing of ethnography, how are those ethnographies evaluated? How might one judge them? What might be the criteria?" (Richardson and Lockridge, 1998, p. 328). This is important because, as Richardson and St. Pierre (2005) rightly state, creative analytical practices like a creative nonfiction need to be "held to high and difficult standards: mere novelty does not suffice" (p. 960).

Clearly, therefore, not 'anything goes' when it comes to using different representational forms and judgements about quality are routinely made. How then, might the process of judgement operate? For creative nonfiction to be judged appropriately, and thus given a fair chance, there needs to be a shift from a *criteriologist* approach to a *relativist* approach (Schinke, Smith & McGannon, 2013; Sparkes & Smith, 2009, 2014). A criteriologist approach is informed by a set of assumptions that might loosely be described as post-positivist, neorealist, or foundational in nature (Smith & Deemer, 2000; Smith & Hodkinson, 2005, 2009). It assumes that the criteria for judging qualitative research needs to be, and can be, *pre-established, static, permanent* and *universal.* That is, there is a fixed recipe or standardised template for judging *all* qualitative research on *all* occasions.

There are various problems that go with a criteriologist approach. One of these is that in a world of multiple, mind-dependent realities there can be no pre-established, static, permanent and universal criteria to apply on all occasions in order to sort out trustworthy interpretations from untrustworthy ones (Smith & Deemer, 2000; Smith & Hodkinson, 2009). Another problem with a criteriological approach is that if our research community wants innovative, interesting, and useful research that continues to push the boundaries and add to the knowledge base, then it is neither possible nor desirable to mandate pre-established, static, permanent and universal criteria to judge all qualitative research. This is because when specific predetermined criteria are called upon to judge all qualitative research there is, as Sparkes and Smith (2009, 2014) point out, the problem of producing a closed system of judgement that can only operate within a very narrow range of what constitutes legitimate research. When this happens, Sparkes and Smith (2009, 2014) note, criteria are wittingly or unwittingly used in exclusionary manner. Such an exclusionary practice means that new fields and forms of inquiry are, by definition, excluded or policed from the very start. There is also the danger that innovation is stifled, difference is suppressed, imagination is dampened, and potentially useful research is rejected before it has even been engaged with (Sparkes & Smith, 2009).

Given such issues, it would be sensible to adopt a relativist approach. A relativist approach adheres to the view proposed by Smith (1993) where criteria are seen as *characterising traits* that have, at best, mild implications as a prescription for inquirer behaviour and do not necessarily refer to something that is held to be foundational or fixed in stone. Here, researchers might discuss the characterising traits of a particular qualitative approach to inquiry and simply note that these criteria are the way(s) researchers seem to be conducting their particular kind of inquiries at the moment. The difference with this characterising trait approach from the criteriological approach is that, as Sparkes and Smith (2009, 2014) point out, those holding a relativistic position are willing to describe what one *might* do, but are not prepared to mandate what one *must* do across all contexts and on all occasions prior to any piece of research being conducted.

For Smith (1993), and Smith and Deemer (2000), once criteria come to be seen as characterising traits or values that influence our judgements, then any particular traits or values will always be subject to constant reinterpretation as times and conditions change. Criteria from this perspective have a *list* like quality. In saying this, we do not wish to imply that the more criteria met on any given list the better the quality of the study. Matching ten criteria from a list does not necessarily make the study twice as good as a study that 'only' matches five criteria (Sparkes & Smith, 2009). Smith and Deemer (2000, p. 888) explain:

> The use of the term *list* should not be taken to mean that we are referring to something like an enclosed and precisely specified or specifiable shopping or laundry list. Put differently, to talk of a list in this sense is not at all to talk about, for example, an accumulation of 20 items, scaled 1–5, where everyone's presentation proposal is then numerically scored with a cut off point for acceptance. Obviously, to think of a list in these terms is to miss the entire point.

Smith and Deemer (2000), and Smith and Hodkinson (2005) see any list of characteristics as always open-ended, and ever-subject to constant reinterpretation so that items can be added to the list or taken away. They emphasise that the items on the list cannot be derived from a distillation of some abstract epistemology but rather derive from practical experience and the standpoint we adopt on any given issue. Therefore, the criteria used to judge a piece of research can change depending upon experiences, the context, and the purposes. This is because a characteristic of research we thought important at one time and in one place may take on diminished and further importance at another time and place.

Against this backdrop, how might supervisors, researchers, reviewers, and editors go about passing judgement on a creative nonfiction? As part of an ongoing list, here are some possible starting points. These are partly developed from Richardson (2000) and Barone and Eisner (2012).

- *Substantive contribution and worthiness*: Does the research contribute empirically, methodologically, theoretically, and/or practically to our understanding of social life, and how? Is the topic of the research relevant, timely, significant, and interesting? Has the work provided new knowledge, fresh insights, or a deeper understanding? Did the work provide me with things I didn't know before?
- *Focus*: Is there a purpose or point to the research? Is there a sense of focus throughout or does the story go too far off track?
- *Aesthetic merit*: Does this research succeed aesthetically? Do the stories open up the text, and invite interpretive responses? Is the text artistically shaped, satisfying, complex, and not boring? Do they 'work'?

- *Expression of a reality*: Does this text embody a fleshed out, embodied sense of lived experience? Does it seem 'true' – a credible account of a psychological, cultural, social, individual, or communal sense of the 'real'?
- *Evocation and illumination*: Does the work emotionally and/or intellectually illuminate a terrain, a process, individual, group, and/or theory? Does the researcher begin to feel meanings within the story being told?
- *Engagement*: Does the research keep me emotionally and intellectually interested? Do I want to carry on reading half way through?
- *Incitement to action*: Does the research move me, intellectually and emotionally? Does it generate new questions? Does it move people to act? How well does the work create a plausible and visceral lifeworld and charged emotional atmosphere as an incitement to act within and outside the context of the work? What might I do with this research?
- *Meaningful coherence*: Does the study achieve what it purports to be about? Does it use methods and procedures that fit its stated goals? Does it meaningfully interconnect literature, research questions/foci, findings, and interpretations with each other?

In offering this list of criteria, we should reiterate that it is ongoing. The list can be added to, modified, and subtracted from depending on purpose and context. We encourage the development of other criteria that may emerge from others' engagement with creative nonfictions in the future.

Conclusion

With a view to giving a relatively novel form of writing about ethnography within sport and exercise deeper exposure, in this chapter we have considered the genre of creative nonfiction through four questions: what is it, why might it be useful, how might we write one, and how may we judge this genre of representation? Creative nonfiction is not however bounded to ethnography. Researchers operating in other qualitative traditions, like narrative inquiry or phenomenology, can also utilise creative nonfictions to represent their findings. Moreover, it needs to be recognised that we do not encourage the use of this genre if one wishes to experiment with writing simply for the sake of experimenting. Nor do we advocate choosing this genre because it is quite novel or because the more traditional way of representing qualitative work (i.e. realist tales) is not to one's taste. Choices about how to represent research need to be made in informed, principled and disciplined ways. It is hoped this chapter has helped in the process. Borrowing from and adapting what Griffin and Phoenix (2014) termed narrative literacy, we hope too that it has helped enhance some people's *representational literacy*, that is, it has helped people become aware of the types of representational genres they have been caught up in. We hope the chapter further plays a small part in expanding the ways in which we might represent data, and judging fairly and appropriately work others have written or performed.

References

Barone, T., & Eisner, E.W. (2012). *Arts based research.* London: Sage.
Blodgett, A., Schinke, R., Smith, B., Peltier, D., & Pheasant, C. (2011). Exploring vignettes as a narrative strategy for co-producing the research voices of Aboriginal community. *Qualitative Inquiry, 17,* 522–533.
Carless, D., Sparkes, A.C., Douglas, K., & Cooke, C. (2014). Disability, inclusive adventurous training and adapted sport: Two soldiers' stories of involvement. *Psychology of Sport and Exercise, 15,* 124–131.
Cheney, T.A.R. (2001). *Writing creative nonfiction: Fiction techniques for crafting great nonfiction.* Berkeley, CA: Ten Speed Press.
Clayton, B. (2010). Ten minutes with the boys, the thoroughly academic task and the semi-naked celebrity: Football masculinities in the classroom or pursuing security in a 'liquid' world. *Qualitative Research in Sport and Exercise, 2,* 371–384.
Curran, K., Bingham, D., Richardson, D., & Parnell, D. (2014). Ethnographic engagement from within a Football in the Community programme at an English Premier League football club. *Soccer and Society, 15*(6), 934–950.
Ellingson, L. (2009). Engaging crystallisation in qualitative research. London: Sage.
Ellis, C. (2004). *The ethnographic I.* Walnut Creek, CA: Altamira Press.
Frank, A.W. (2010). *Letting stories breathe.* Chicago: University of Chicago Press.
Gearity, B.T. (2014). Autoethnography. In. L. Nelson, R. Groom, & P. Potrac (Eds.). *Research methods in sport coaching* (pp. 205–216). London: Routledge.
Gearity, B.T., & Mills, J. (2012). Discipline and punish in the weight room: A Foucauldian inspired narrative. *Sport Coaching Review, 1,* 124–134.
Griffin, M., & Phoenix, C. (2014). Learning to run from narrative foreclosure: One woman's story of aging and physical activity. *Journal of Aging and Physical Activity, 22,* 393–404.
Krane, V., Ross, S., Barak, K.S., Lucas-Carr, C., & Robinson, C. (2014). Being a girl. *Qualitative Research in Sport, Exercise and Health, 6,* 77–97.
McGannon, K.R., & Cameron, K.A. (2013). Exercising fat control, resistance and self-compassion: Two ethnographic stories from the field. In R.J. Schinke & R. Lidor (Eds.), *Case studies in sport development: Contemporary stories promoting health, peace, and social justice* (pp. 75–89). Morgantown, WV: Fitness Information Technology.
McMahon, J., & Penney, D. (2014). Sporting parents on the pool deck: Living out a sporting culture? *Qualitative Research in Sport, Exercise and Health.* DOI:10.108 0/2159676X.2014.901985.
Richardson, L. (2000). Writing; A method of inquiry. In N. Denzin & Y. Lincoln, (Eds.), *Handbook of qualitative research* (2nd edition) (pp. 923–948). London: Sage.
Richardson, L., & Lockridge, E. (1998). Fiction and ethnography: A conversation. *Qualitative Inquiry, 4*(3): 328–336.
Richardson, L., & St. Pierre, E. (2005). Writing: A method of inquiry. In N. Denzin & Y. Lincoln. (Eds.), *Handbook of qualitative research* (3rd edition) (pp. 959–978). London: Sage.

Schinke, R., Smith, B., & McGannon, K. (2013). Pathways for community research in sport and physical activity: Criteria for consideration. *Qualitative Research in Sport, Exercise and Health, 5*, 460–468.

Smith, B. (2010). Narrative inquiry: Ongoing conversations and questions for sport psychology research. *International Review of Sport Psychology, 3*, 87–107.

Smith, B. (2013). Sporting spinal cord injuries, social relations, and rehabilitation narratives: An ethnographic creative nonfiction of becoming disabled through sport. *Sociology of Sport Journal, 30*, 132–152.

Smith, B., & Sparkes, A.C. (2009). Narrative analysis and sport and exercise psychology: Understanding lives in diverse ways. *Psychology of Sport and Exercise, 10*, 279–288.

Smith, B., Papathomas, A., Martin Ginis, K.A., & Latimer-Cheung, A.E. (2013). Understanding physical activity in spinal cord injury rehabilitation: Translating and communicating research through stories. *Disability & Rehabilitation, 35*, 2044–2055.

Smith, B., Tomasone, J., Latimer-Cheung, A., & Martin Ginis, K. (2015). Narrative as a knowledge translation tool for facilitating impact: Translating physical activity knowledge to disabled people and health professionals. *Health Psychology, 34*(4): 303–313.

Smith, J. (1993). *After the demise of empiricism: The problem of judging social and educational inquiry.* Norwood, NJ: Ablex Publishing Corporation.

Smith, J., & Deemer, D. (2000). The problem of criteria in the age of relativism. In N. Denzin & Y. Lincoln (Eds.), *Handbook of qualitative research* (2nd edition) (pp. 877–896). London: Sage.

Smith, J., & Hodkinson, P. (2005). Relativism, criteria and politics. In N. Denzin & Y. Lincoln. (Eds.), *Handbook of qualitative research* (3rd edition) (pp. 915–932). London: Sage.

Smith, J., & Hodkinson, P. (2009). Challenging neorealism: A response to Hammersley. *Qualitative Inquiry, 15*, 30–39.

Sparkes, A. (2002). *Telling tales in sport and physical activity: A qualitative journey.* Champaign, IL: Human Kinetics.

Sparkes, A.C. (2007). Embodiment, academics, and the audit culture: A story seeking consideration. *Qualitative Research, 7*, 521–550.

Sparkes, A.C. (2009). Ethnography and the senses: Challenges and possibilities. *Qualitative Research in Sport, Exercise and Health, 1*, 21–35.

Sparkes, A.C., & Smith, B. (2009). Judging the quality of qualitative inquiry: Criteriology and relativism in action. *Psychology of Sport and Exercise, 10*, 491–497.

Sparkes, A.C., & Smith, B. (2012). Embodied research methodologies and seeking senses in sport in sport and physical culture: A fleshing out of problems and possibilities. In K. Young & M. Atkinson (Eds.), *Qualitative research on sport and physical culture* (pp. 169–192). Emerald Press.

Sparkes, A.C., & Smith, B. (2014). *Qualitative research methods in sport, exercise and health: From process to product.* London: Routledge.

Part II

Case studies

Chapter 6

Women's lived experiences of health and ageing in physical activity

Meridith Griffin and Cassandra Phoenix

What it means to grow older today differs from what it meant even a generation ago. Improvements in health and life expectancy affect people of all ages and genders, and have concomitant implications for their relationship with their bodies and their identities across the life course (Higgs & Jones, 2009; Jones & Higgs, 2010). As ageing is continually re-defined, our understandings of 'natural' and 'normative' ageing are undermined (Jones & Higgs, 2010; Kirkwood, 2001), and the "new reality of ageing intersects with the somatic aspects of a consumer society based on difference and choice" (Jones & Higgs, 2010, p. 1514). Paired with the individualised imperatives of postmodern culture, there is a decided shift from earlier metanarratives of ageing that emphasised decline and dependency to a different – yet related – narrative of normative ageing which is organised around the reflexively constituted culture of fitness (Bauman, 2005).

Simply stated, it is increasingly difficult to ignore the proliferation of health advice. Indeed, most people can competently cite what they (and others) should be doing to lessen their risks of future ill-health (Blaxter, 2010). Yet while most age and social groups are well-acquainted with the messages of disease prevention, few people, in practice, enact 'healthy' lifestyles either entirely or in part. For example, although knowledge about the specific health benefits of physical activity tends to be comprehensive and widespread, the majority of older adults do not actually achieve sufficient levels of activity to result in health gains (Blaxter, 2010, Crombie et al., 2004).

Further, statistics on sports participation reflect the gendered nature of leisure activity (Wiley, Shaw, & Havitz, 2000). For example, in the UK, men are considerably more likely than women to participate – and to participate frequently – in organised and informal sports activities (Evans, 2006; WSFF, 2007). The literature is replete with social and psychological research regarding various identifiable barriers to physical activity specific to women, such as a lack of (or constrained) time, low confidence, lack of social support, and so on (see Bond & Batey, 2005; Green, 1998; Haughton-McNeill, Kreuter & Subramanian 2006; Henderson, 2003; Im et al., 2008; Little, 2002; Segar et al., 2002; Shaw, 1994). The gendered participation disparity increases even more with a consideration of age. Indeed, older women number among the groups with the most sedentary lifestyles, with participation rates falling significantly after the age of 45 (Dumas & Laberge, 2005; WSFF, 2007). Historically, sedentary behaviour was further entrenched by many older people's perceptions of what the older body should and should not do, which was fuelled by their understanding of the biological processes of ageing as well as pervasive ageist social and cultural attitudes, expectations, and prejudices (Blaikie, 1999; Grant, 2001). This disproportionately affects women, who continue to live longer on average and who readily report sociocultural barriers including the perception that much sport and physical activity is 'unfeminine', and a lack of physical confidence to take part (WSFF, 2007).

Recent interdisciplinary work in the field of health studies has highlighted that analyses of health must consider the way that health discourses have come to make sense of women's bodies: the way 'scientific' knowledge, popular conceptions, and the various media have impacted on gender, racial and class identities (Rail & Beausoleil, 2003). These are the relational contexts within which health identities, ideas of health, and health practices emerge:

> Health identities are features of the clustering of relations around specific aspects of embodiment, such as sport and exercise, body modification, disability or growing old... Health identities are neither prior, nor are they determined. Rather they emerge from concrete embodiment practices in relation to material, cultural, technological and emotional contexts.
>
> (Fox & Ward, 2006, p. 475)

Within this view, health constitutes a social text, something at least partially created by the densely interwoven network of experiences and interpretations we bring to it (Rail & Beausoleil, 2003). Thus, to understand people's health practices and behaviours, it is important to be aware of the symbolic meanings and emotions which inextricably cling to each lifestyle 'option' (Lupton, 1994). For example, why and how do people choose certain behaviours and activities over others? When do they make decisions to pursue behaviours and/or seek out activities? What do these choices mean for individuals in terms of personal and social identity? In this chapter, we explore these questions by delving into women's lived experiences of health and ageing (and the intersection of these) within a particular physical context: a non-elite, women-only running group. This was accomplished through an ethnographic investigation of embodiment, opening up opportunities to explore issues of if, why, how, and when women engaged with health and 'active ageing' messages across the life course.

We will first present details on the social and cultural context under scrutiny – the women-only running group – alongside a description of the ethnographic approach undertaken therein. We will briefly describe the analytical and theoretical approaches employed within this work, followed by a presentation of a selection of data demonstrating key findings, processes, and experiences. Specifically, we explore what influenced women to move from health consciousness (or awareness of the health benefits of physical activity/ running) to actually lacing up a pair of trainers, attending a session, and taking those first hesitant steps. We will conclude by outlining the implications of this work for health promotion and policy, and reflect on the power of ethnography in capturing these women's perspectives and experiences.

Methods and methodology

Data for this chapter are taken from an ethnography of a nationally successful women-only running organisation in the United Kingdom. Following the established tenets of ethnography, the research design was emergent and involved multiple methods and data sources (Hammersley & Atkinson, 2007; O'Reilly, 2005 – see Table 6.1 for details). Specific methods included 14 months of participant observation, during which the first author ran with several different groups associated with the organisation in the South West of England. Participant observation was undertaken in several different associated contexts, including weekly running sessions with varying leaders, numerous events and races, and in the office of the organisation. Following the multi-method ethnographic approach, participant observation was augmented by innumerable informal (in 'the field') and 20 formal, in-depth qualitative interviews with women who ranged in age from 29 to 66. In-depth case studies were also conducted, allowing greater insight into three women's personal experiences of running, health, ageing, and their bodies. Further, a variety of visual methods were employed, including collection and analysis of material artefacts, media and promotional material, and using techniques of photo elicitation and autophotography with a selection of the sample (see Noland, 2006; Robinson, 2002).

Upon gaining access and receiving ethical approval, the first author made contact with individual leaders and began attending running group sessions. Her role as researcher was overt, in that at each group she introduced herself and identified her purpose for attendance. That said, the role evolved into that of semi-overt over time (O'Reilly, 2005) – because attendance was on a drop-in basis and different women were present each week. Traditionally, ethnographic interviews are conducted on site, or in situ, during long-term field studies (Heyl, 2001). Certainly, this was the case during attendance at weekly running sessions with the running group, wherein every opportunity was taken to ask questions, listen, and engage in conversations (or informal interviews) with numerous members of the group before, after, and during running sessions. At the beginning, this was primarily comprised of established and highly involved members 'teaching', or telling us how the group operated,

Table 6.1 Data sources

Data source	Type	Number	Detail
Participant observation	'Regular'/weekday session	22	All abilities/levels
	Speed/track session	9	For those aiming to increase speed or achieve a PB in an upcoming race
	Beginner's group	8	'Learn-to-run' programme
	Half marathon training group	11	More 'experienced' women, though still all abilities
	Events	5	Summer Race Series, Race for Life, Great West Run
Misc. fieldwork	Volunteering at the office	2 days	Helping to prepare grant application for funding from Sport England
Questionnaire	Conducted by the running group	342 responses	Consisted of 5 open-ended questions
Visual resources	Website Media clippings/ coverage Promotional material Visual elicitation Auto-photography task		Any available images Pamphlets, posters, brochures, beginner's logbook, etc. 15 images per case study
Interviews	Staff	5	To gain a greater understanding of the organisation as well as their personal experiences of the group
Case studies	Members	15	To gain an understanding of individual embodied experiences within the social context of the group
	3 interviews each	3	To gain a more in-depth understanding of three women's experiences: one drop-out, one beginner, and one long-term member/participant

including discussion of processes, techniques, and the sharing of information. As time went on and we became more familiar with the women present at the sessions (and vice versa), this evolved to their sharing of personal stories and experiences, having informal 'chats' on just about every possible topic, combined with continual (though more relaxed) interest and questioning.

Another style of ethnographic interviewing employed in this context centred on a set of semi-structured, in-depth interviews with key informants:

people from a variety of settings and backgrounds who had certain kinds of experiences (Heyl, 2001). Specifically, we interviewed five members of staff to gain a greater understanding of the organisation as well as their personal experiences of the running group. In addition, 15 members of the running group were also interviewed, to gain an understanding of individual embodied experiences within the social context of the group. The sample was opportunistic in nature – an open invitation was made by email to all members, and we interviewed all those who came forward as volunteers. Snowball sampling was also employed to reach newer members and those less heavily involved in the group. Overall, a concerted effort was made to include women of varying ages, running levels and abilities, and degrees of involvement within the group.

Case studies were employed to gain a more in-depth understanding of three women's experiences: a drop-out, a beginner, and a long-term member/participant. These case studies were instrumental in nature, with the aim of understanding something other (or beyond) the particular person (Stake, 1995). As Stake (1995) explains, a case study is expected to capture the particularity and complexity of a single case, coming to understand its activity within important circumstances. These three individuals were of interest for both their uniqueness and their commonality (Stake, 1995). As such, they were selected and invited to participate because we felt that they were typical of prevalent 'types' of members within the running group. The visual methods referred to above (photo elicitation, autophotography) were primarily employed within these case study settings. Alongside all of these methods and throughout the entire process, reflexive fieldnotes were recorded by the first author.

Following Frank (2006), narrative provided a sensitive lens through which to explore conceptions of health. For him, health depends on "which stories are heard, which are taken seriously, and what sense is made of those stories" (Frank, 2006, p. 422). Frank (2006) further argues that what individuals notice about their bodies, what they attend to or disregard, how they act on what they notice, what they worry about and what they take satisfaction in – all of these are continuously informed by the flow of stories that affect an embodied sense of health. As such, a multi-level narrative approach was taken in the analyses of the collected data: categorical-content analysis to examine the thematic similarities and differences between the narratives collected (Lieblich et al., 1998); attention to setting and context using the narrative framework of big and small stories (Bamberg, 2006; Georgakopoulou, 2006; Phoenix & Sparkes, 2009); holistic-form analysis to focus on the plots and structures of collected stories (Lieblich et al., 1998); holistic-content analysis to explore the content of individual complete stories (or case studies – Lieblich et al., 1998; Stake, 1995; 2003); and visual narrative analysis (Riessman, 2008) to consider the visual material collected and created within the ethnographic project.

Why now?

Health consciousness within a foreclosed narrative

Women involved in the project were keen to speak about health, what it meant to them, and how the activity of running matched their personal conceptions of health. References to health in general occurred in both formal interview settings as well as during informal conversation within the setting of the running group itself. Definitions, understandings, and explanations of health and health practices emphasised both the physical *and* biological basis of health. Across the board, however, these women expressed an understanding of participation in running as beneficial to bodily health. Common reasons for taking part in running included: to lose excess or maintain current weight, to return to a former weight (e.g., pre-childbirth), to gain or re-gain fitness, and to prevent osteoporosis via weight-bearing activity. One participant described a level of awareness of health and exercise that was, at least partially, in response to messages about healthy living portrayed in the media:

> I realised recently that I wasn't getting enough exercise. I read an article in the local newspaper about the importance of weight-bearing exercise – especially for women – to prevent osteoporosis. I want to enjoy my retirement, and not have any physical limitations. I want to be able to play with my grandchildren… So health is very important to me.

Participants often made references to *control* and *health* in the same breath; specifically in relation to weight control and in particular, weight loss. Running as a form of cardiovascular physical activity was understood to be a means of addressing weight-related aims. However, control was also referred to when women spoke of age-related health changes. As in the quotation above, for many women, menopause acted as an indicator of age, which in turn served as an impetus to seek out health information and make attempts to change behaviour. The example above articulates women's common acknowledgement of the medicalisation of the ageing body (Tulle-Winton, 2000), in that ageing was seemingly automatically linked to osteoporosis, particularly for the midlife (pre/peri/post-menopausal) woman.

Despite widespread 'health consciousness', or awareness of the benefits of physical activity to health, the majority of participants described a previous and longstanding antipathy towards participation. In asking women how, when, and why they got involved in the running group, they tended to begin by explaining why they had not participated in running in the past. These reasons spanned the typical 'barriers' to physical activity participation: lack of time, lack of confidence, lack of knowledge, and so on. But first and foremost, they recounted poor past experiences with physical activity, often going as far back as physical education in school. For example:

I was always picked last for the team.

I had very bad school experience which convinced me I simply wasn't built for, or able to run; and that idea became more engrained the older I got.

It was a fear of failure, I guess. I was never a sporty girl, and had pigeon-holed myself as such.

Statements such as these within participants' stories revealed the influential and longstanding impact of poor physical activity experiences in their formative years. Identities were thus forged on the basis of a lack of athletic ability, and fears and insecurities about the athletic realm were pervasive and long-standing. Oftentimes this was linked into concerns about excess weight, and the capacity of the overweight body to engage in an activity such as running. Quotations from two women provided examples of this experience:

I have always been overweight, and never sporty. Running was something I was 'made to do' at school, and it didn't occur to me that I could run and enjoy it!

I am overweight and didn't like going out running alone, and I have always had a major fear of running since cross country at school!! I was embarrassed to run out on my own, but I knew I had to face my fears after turning 30 last year.

As such, an extremely common response when women were asked why they had not participated in running in the past was, "I didn't know I could do it," or even more strongly, "I didn't think I could."

Another reason that participants cited for non-participation was that previously, they considered themselves too old to begin running. Statements expressing this sentiment included: "I never thought I could, being the wrong side of 50", or "I can't run – I'm too old…" Others described having thought that running was actually harmful to older bodies. A 46-year-old participant explained: "I was worried before, about injury and the advisability of strenuous exercise at my age." Similarly, another stated that she had been "…unsure whether it might be damaging for my joints". Also echoing metanarratives around the medicalisation of ageing, these stories link to ideas around the perceived frailty and thus incapacities of the female, ageing body (Tulle-Winton, 2000; Vertinsky, 1991; 1998; 2000; 2002). One woman retrospectively summarised this in a humorous way, saying "Me, run?!? Never!! Too old, too fat, too self-conscious. I'm not a runner!!" These stories revealed a very real, identity-based disconnect between what these women felt was their physical reality, and the mere possibility of running. Following

Freeman (2000; 2011), we conceptualised this as a form of narrative foreclosure, in which women were 'caught' in a story that was both limiting and lacked imagination. The longer that these women had told a particular story about themselves over time (i.e., 'I'm not the running type'), the more entrenched it became.

Participants also described previously having a very clear sense about what a runner's body looked like, and by comparison, discounting themselves from ever fitting into that category. On her first session at the group, one participant expressed that she had always been interested in running, but just did not see herself reflected within popular running culture:

> I kept picking up things like Runners' World magazine, or watching elite athletics on telly. Then I'd look down and catch a glimpse of my rather more substantial belly or thighs, and the idea would just be shelved again.

As such, women expressed that representations of running – and of the running body, specifically – were not often inclusive of their body concepts and experiences. Running culture and the aesthetics therein were also perceived as exclusive social and cultural domains. For example, one 29-year-old participant expressed that she "…thought all running groups were for 'proper' runners". Similarly, women frequently expressed reservations at wearing running-specific clothing, as it was too tight and "shows up all the lumps and bumps!"

All ages, all sizes, all abilities: narrative hailing

These women all became members of the running group, so at some point their perceptions, and/or barriers and constraints shifted, changed or evolved. In exploring why and when this shift occurred, we first considered the unique social and physical context represented by the running group under scrutiny, and the stories circulating therein. The target audience for this running group was middle-aged to older, previously inactive women. Knowing this, the advertising, marketing, and media coverage of the group tended to identify and attempt to downplay what they knew were the insecurities and barriers to participation often cited by these women. Both images and text included within their promotional material supported the ubiquitous and oft-repeated ethos of the organisation: 'All ages, all sizes, all abilities'. For example, one pamphlet depicted three women (of varying ages and sizes) holding hands and crossing a finish line, with superimposed text reading:

> It can be daunting to get started – if you haven't done anything athletic in years, were never that sporty at school or gave up exercise when you had children… Fit or unhealthy, young or old, experienced or a newcomer, we promise everyone a warm welcome.

These stories were re-told within both local and national media. 'Success' stories were highlighted, 'average' women were celebrated, and the ethos was repeated at every juncture. Exploring this, we focused on both visual and textual narratives within the running group media, and noted the prevalence of *narrative hailing* – a particular type/style of storytelling that acts as a 'call' for individuals to take a specific story on board (see Griffin, 2010). For example, within the stories circulated and re-told about and for the running group, competition was actively downplayed – a deliberate distancing from 'other', more 'typical' running groups (their language). Instead, notions of 'safety', 'support', 'fun', empowerment, weight loss, and charitable motivations were highlighted. Echoing neoliberal health imperatives, there was an emphasis on taking personal responsibility for health, body image, and the ageing body. Moral and gendered language was employed, alongside personal stories of 'successful' and 'inspirational' members as encouragement. This running group, it claimed, was made up of 'people just like you' who had overcome obstacles, big and small, by means of their participation.

Of course, many women who had been exposed to these same stories and images were not hailed (i.e., did not join the group) for a wide variety of reasons. Our sample consisted of women who responded to this narrative hailing by joining and running with the group. We investigated how and what they responded to within these organisational storylines. The vast majority of women reported learning of the running group via some form of print media (newspaper article, brochure, pamphlet, website, etc.). For many women engaging with this media was no more complex than a transfer of information, for example, they read a short news article in the local paper which advertised a new or existing group in their area. Either they had been looking for an opportunity of this sort, had heard of the group previously but had not lived near enough to participate, or they were hailed by the language in the article itself: "I saw that it said 'Beginners welcome!' so decided to give it a try", said one participant when asked how she learned of the group. Another replied, "Well, it said it was for beginners – and that's certainly me – and that it was all ages, sizes, and abilities. And non-competitive – that was key. I probably wouldn't even have read further if it hadn't said that!" One more participant described being hailed not just by the language within the description of the group, but by the image that ran alongside the article: "I saw this article in the local paper about the [group] with just a brilliant picture – lots of ordinary, normal women, all looking a bit nervous and uncomfortable in their lycra – just like me!" Many others reported seeing posters in local shop windows, composed of just an image and the contact information for the local leader.

However, other acts of engagement with the narratives within print media were more complex than described above: going beyond just a transfer of information, and one step removed from women being able to imagine themselves as directly and currently embodied within the represented subject positions. Participants described being called by stories that depicted subject positions that they did not see themselves in, per se, but desired to embody in the future. Alternatively, many women also identified that they were inspired by admirable or inspirational stories of other women who had overcome stereotypes, hardships, or other barriers in order to participate. Somehow, seeing that these 'feats' were indeed achievable made it more possible for women to imagine their own participation, and to identify with the subject position in question. For example, one 63-year-old participant put this quite simply when she said, "I was inspired by women in their 60s running marathons. You see it and you think, well, if she can do that, why can't I?"

Critical moments

Lastly within this question of 'Why now?', we considered the specific timing of the health choice/decision to join the running group, and explored the stories that women told surrounding their decision to actually attend their first running group session. For some, it was word of mouth – positive experiences of friends and acquaintances passed onward and trusted. For others, it was exposure to the promotional material of the group – at the right time and place in their lives, they were hailed by images and language used and persuaded to sign up (Griffin, 2010). For many others however, it was being hailed at a *specific* and *significant* point in time in their lives that was noteworthy. Indeed, many participants reported the consequential character of particular events within their lives – as being why they chose to 'take action'. We have characterised these events, which took a multitude of forms, as critical moments (Denzin, 1989; Giddens, 1991; Thomson et al., 2002). Milestone birthdays served as an impetus for many participants:

I reached 50 and needed something else in my life…

I didn't want to hit the big 6–0 and just slip into a gradual decline!

For these women, a chronological marker of age was enough to make them think about where they were and what they wanted from life. These numbers, or markers of age, coincide with socially constructed life-stage categories and associated age identities (Gullette, 2004). Within these, women had very clear conceptions of what they wanted to be doing – or what they *should* be doing – and who they wanted to be, having reached a certain age.

Other critical moments took the form of health scares (personal, or someone in their family/social circle), bereavement, divorce and/or relationship break-up, geographical relocations, children moving out, and so on. For example, a 62-year-old participant revealed why she had joined the group by saying:

I thought it would help me to stay strong and healthy. I had been quite ill after my husband died unexpectedly, and I wanted to somehow acknowledge that I was still alive – but within a safe setting... Running has given me such a feeling of confidence, which spills over into other areas of my life. It has empowered me, has enabled me to come to terms with personal tragedies, and above all has kept me feeling healthy and strong.

Each of these critical moments represented a turning point in the participants' story, wherein the risks of inaction became 'real' and somehow tangible. Running – or participation in the running group – was perceived as one avenue through which to either directly address these risks, or to make emotional connections to those who were perhaps experiencing similar struggles or transitions.

Staying involved

Embodied learning

Important for the majority of participants was not just getting involved in physical activity, but staying involved as they encountered familiar and unfamiliar barriers, setbacks, or constraints. Many participants described how they had tried (a variety of activities) in the past, and then given up their participation – because they either felt unsuccessful in the activity, or as though they were not progressing as desired:

I tried running on my own before, and I just couldn't do it properly. So I thought, well, maybe I *can't* do it. I didn't think it was something you could learn – I thought running was something you could either do or you can't. What didn't register was that there's actually a right way of doing it, of progressing slowly and so on.

Within a structured and supportive environment, participants learned to run by building up slowly and safely, through advice on nutrition, stretching, and recommendations for shoes and clothing. They were exposed to this information in formal, coach-led sessions, as well as by informal contact and conversation with existing running group members. This learning took place on numerous levels – going beyond mere informational knowledge transfer (i.e., "this style of socks won't give you blisters"). Within the running group, women described learning how to be in their bodies in a new way: a way in which they were unfamiliar with, unaccustomed to, and – in many cases – initially resistant to. The body thus became part of, if not the technique for learning about the physical and social context of the running group (Yarnal, Hutchinson, & Chow, 2006). One participant articulated this, in saying:

I've never really pushed myself, physically... At the beginning, I was afraid I was going to have a heart attack or something. You know, collapse on the side of the road. I thought that being out of breath meant that you'd pushed yourself too far. So in the beginner's group I learned how to push myself, when to push myself – when I was 'injured' versus when I was just sore, like, in my muscles. And I learned how to celebrate small accomplishments rather than talk myself out of them. Really, I learned an awful lot about myself.

For beginners, new bodily sensations and experiences involved both formulating and telling a new story to oneself and to others. Learning to tell this new story (via learning how to run) increased the embodied agency of participants – the capacity to tell new stories about themselves, their bodies, and their capabilities (Frank, 1995; Shapiro, 1999; Sparkes & Smith, 2011).

As an example of this phenomenon and to demonstrate the use of visual methods within this ethnography, one of the case study participants provided a series of photographs from her recent vacation (Figure 6.1). Explaining her choice for sharing these photos, she said:

And I'm scared of heights...!! Last year, I said I'd love to try it, but I don't think I could do that. But this year, I went for it. Looking at these pictures now and seeing myself up there again, that's confidence. And I've got no doubt that's running that's done that. Because now I can run, I can do that, it's almost like – well, if I can do that, I can do this. Yes, my stomach turned over a few times. I did feel a little bit queasy. But I got up there. And I look at those now and I just think, 'I'm so proud of myself'. Because I feel like I've actually achieved something. Because if I can do something I couldn't do before, like running, then what's to say I can't do parasailing?

This participant enthused at great length about how her running group experience had affected all aspects of her life: improving her health, completely reframing her body image, making her more comfortable with

Figure 6.1 Case study participant parasailing on vacation

herself and her appearance. Perhaps the greatest effect was a psychological one, as she referred repeatedly to how participation had boosted her confidence and expanded her comfort zone – both within and outside of running itself. She called this "a 180 degree transformation", and attributed all of these changes to running and, specifically, to her experience with the beginner's group.

Social identity

Once within the social setting of the running group – and over time within this social and physical culture – many participants experienced a shift in identity: a process of constructing a new sense of self in that particular context. From a narrative perspective, immersion within the setting allowed the beginner access to locally specific narrative resources that they could then begin to integrate into their own self constructions, or self-stories (McAdams, 2006; Taylor, 2006). Working from this view, although all individuals are unique and have unique responses to local storied culture, their identities are still always constructed in and through embodied interactions with others. As such, immersion in a running group context tended to create and propagate a collective identity, built on similarity. This was evident in two separate (though overlapping) senses. Firstly, women described the process of coming to identify as a 'runner':

> 'Check this out.' [*participant leans over and pulls down her sock to reveal her heel*]
> 'Oooh – Ouch!'
> 'No, no, it doesn't hurt anymore. My first blister! My leader said to me, "Oh, you're a proper runner now! You've had a blister!" [*laughs*]. So I went and got proper running socks. See how they have this cushioning here? So I'm gradually learning about all of the little things like that…'

Immersion within the running group community, comparing and sharing experiences, and learning about the culture and world of running fostered a shift in – and an adoption of a – running identity. This is even more remarkable given that such a shift was previously considered to be impossible by many participants.

Secondly, participants referred to the process of identifying as a member of this specific running group. Group membership represented a desirable social identity (Haslam et al., 2009; Tafjel, 2010), wherein participants expressed feeling a sense of support, community, camaraderie, and cohesion in the group setting:

> I was struggling up the hill near the end of the race. Honestly, I nearly stopped. But about halfway up, another member came up alongside me

and encouraged me all the way to the finish. Nearing the line, there was a sea of sky blue [*the running group kit*] and I kept hearing my name and everyone was cheering. I really felt like I was a part of something.

For many participants, this was the first time they had experienced the feeling of inclusion in a physical activity setting, and it was this social and emotional support that strongly encouraged their sustained participation. Indeed, one of the unique aspects of this running group was very often the social role that it played in participants' lives. Remarking on this, one member explained:

It was the first time I felt a part of something… It was lucky, because you don't always feel that comfortable when you join a new group… It's a really nice feeling of well-being and being part of something. And people now know me. And I think that's been really, really nice. Really nice. And so supportive… And so kind. And I feel very much a part of it.

Reflections and conclusions

Findings from this work have implications for health promotion, and specifically for exercise and physical activity programme planning, design, and interventions for older, previously inactive, adults. It is crucial that the complexity and interaction of barriers to physical activity participation are acknowledged. Barriers and constraints to participation are often linked to life stage and are highly gendered, but these rarely occur – and thus can rarely be addressed – in isolation. This ethnographic examination of a women-only running group demonstrated the importance of recognising the impact and influence of early experiences with physical activity. There are a lot of older adults who are not interested in physical activity, and the reasons for this are varied and innumerable. However, from a narrative perspective, this ethnography revealed that there is a real possibility that a good number of women are living with a foreclosed narrative in relation to physical activity involvement in later life (Freeman, 2000; 2011). Despite health consciousness and a desire to make healthy choices, including physical activity participation, they are accustomed to telling a particular story about themselves, who they are, and who they can be.

Frank (2010) warns that there is a danger that people can become the stories that they tell – for better, or for worse. According to Freeman (2000), narrative foreclosure relates to the degree to which the culture in which one lives fails to provide adequate narrative resources for living one's life meaningfully and productively. Narrative foreclosure is an eminently social phenomenon that connects to the reification of cultural storylines and the tendency, on the part of many, "to internalize storylines in such a way as to severely constrict their own field of narrative expression: the story goes this way, not that" (Freeman, 2000, p. 83). Therefore, Freeman argues, by accepting the prevailing endings to cultural stories one accepts a certain kind of narrative fate and this potentially reduces the possibility of self-renewal as one grows older. Going forward, the question becomes how to unsettle more of these stories, and empower increasing numbers of older adults to make the move from health consciousness to action.

As part of this, pathways into physical activity participation require further investigation, regarding individuals in later life. The public storyline that this running group offered acted as a counterstory: one that fit into the gaps between what the prescriptive master narrative demanded of these women, and what they actually (can) do or are (Nelson, 2001). A lesson from this ethnography is that it is necessary to circulate more – and diverse – stories about who can do what with respect to physical activity and ageing. Options for older adult participation need to be created and publicised that encompass a continuum of activities, intensities, and interests. Further, it is crucial that stereotypes and assumptions about ageing and the ageing body continue to be unsettled and destabilised. To do so, it is essential that stories which celebrate diversity and difference are shamelessly circulated (e.g., Hinchliff & Gott, 2008; Phoenix & Smith, 2011). This has the potential to increase the opportunity for older adults to be 'hailed' (Griffin, 2010), or to connect therein. Many more stories are needed about what active ageing looks like and who has the capacity to 'achieve' it – both within and outside the realm of physical activity.

Lastly, it is critical that we remember that older adults do not hit 60+, and suddenly develop a new attitude to, or perception of, physical activity. Those who are new to an activity have to *learn how* to be active in their changing, ageing bodies over time (i.e., embodied learning leads to embodied agency). Active ageing, for many, has to be learned – and without consideration of this, metanarratives of health consciousness and active ageing will not resonate. The embodied learning and resulting embodied agency discernible amongst these running group participants is not to be confounded with athletic competence (although it takes that form among these social actors, in this social context). Instead, for these women, embodied agency can be additionally understood as the ability to control and broaden their ontological position without feeling culturally obligated to deny their corporeal existence (Tulle, 2008). Here, we are therefore arguing for a reconstruction of ontology as social, and open to renegotiation, growth and flux at any age.

Certainly, the ethnographic data also revealed the salience of neoliberal cultural trends of late modernity, namely the engagement with body projects to attain socially valued norms of physical appearance and the rationalisation of the body required to attain those norms. In addition, however, we have drawn attention to the other side of the ageing story: the progressive, growth-focused thicker narratives that may be more representative of the third age and what now constitutes normal ageing (Gilleard & Higgs, 2005; Jones &

Higgs, 2010). In amplifying stories that would not otherwise be heard, this ethnography has generated awareness of alternative stories of ageing – and, in doing so, has provided more meaningful ways of imagining and living within the ageing body across the life course.

References

Bamberg, M. (2006). Biographic-narrative research, *quo vadis?* A critical review of 'big stories' from the perspective of 'small stories'. In K. Milnes, C. Horrocks, B. Roberts, & D. Robinson (Eds.), *Narrative, memory and knowledge: Representations, aesthetics and contexts* (pp. 63–79). Huddersfield, UK: University of Huddersfield Press.

Bauman, Z. (2005). *Liquid life.* Cambridge, UK: Polity Press.

Blaikie, A. (1999). *Ageing and popular culture.* Cambridge, UK: Cambridge University Press.

Blaxter, M. (2010). *Health* (2nd edition). Cambridge, UK: Polity Press.

Bond, K.A., & Batey, J. (2005). Running for their lives: A qualitative analysis of the exercise experience of female recreational runners. *Women in Sport & Physical Activity Journal, 14*(2), 69–82.

Crombie, I.K., Irvine, L., Williams, B., McGinnis, A.R., Slane, P.W., Alder, E.M., & McMurdo, M.E.T. (2004). Why older people do not participate in leisure time physical activity: A survey of activity levels, beliefs and deterrents. *Age & Ageing, 33,* 287–292.

Denzin, N.K. (1989). *Interpretive interactionism.* Thousand Oaks, CA: Sage.

Dumas, A., & Laberge, S. (2005). Social class and ageing bodies: Understanding physical activity in later life. *Social Theory & Health, 3*(3), 183–205.

Evans, B. (2006). 'I'd feel ashamed': Girls' bodies and sports participation. *Gender, Place & Culture, 13*(5), 547–561.

Fox, N., & Ward, K. (2006). Health identities: From expert patient to resisting consumer. *Health: An Interdisciplinary Journal for the Social Study of Health, Illness & Medicine, 10*(4), 461–479.

Frank, A.W. (1995). *The wounded storyteller: Body, illness, and ethics.* Chicago, IL: University of Chicago Press.

Frank, A.W. (2006). Health stories as connectors and subjectifiers. *Health: An Interdisciplinary Journal for the Social Study of Health, Illness & Medicine, 10*(4), 421–440.

Freeman, M. (2000). When the story's over: Narrative foreclosure and the possibility of self-renewal. In M. Andrews, S. Slater, C. Squire, & A. Treacher (Eds.), *Lines of narrative: Psychosocial perspectives* (pp. 81–91). London, UK: Routledge.

Freeman, M. (2011). Narrative foreclosure in later life: Possibilities and limits. In G. Kenyon, E. Bohlmeijr, & W.L. Randall (Eds.), *Storying later life: Issues, investigations, and interventions in narrative gerontology* (pp. 3–19). New York: Oxford University Press.

Georgakopoulou, A. (2006). Thinking big with small stories in narrative and identity analysis. *Narrative Inquiry, 16*(1), 122–130.

Giddens, A. (1991). *Modernity and self-identity: Self and society in the late modern age.* Cambridge, UK: Polity Press.

Gilleard, C. & Higgs, P. (2005). *Contexts of aging: Class, cohort and community*. Cambridge: Polity.

Grant, B.C. (2001). 'You're never too old': Beliefs about physical activity and playing sport in later life. *Ageing & Society, 21*(6), 777–798.

Green, E. (1998). Flexible work, disappearing leisure? Feminist perspectives on women's leisure as spaces for resistance to gender stereotypes. In C. Aitchison & F. Jordan (Eds.), *Gender, space and identity: Leisure, culture and commerce* (pp. 111–126). Eastbourne: Leisure Studies Association.

Griffin, M. (2010). Setting the scene: Hailing women into a running identity. *Qualitative Research in Sport & Exercise, 2*(2), 153–174.

Gullette, M.M. (2004). *Aged by culture*. Chicago, IL: University of Chicago Press.

Hammersley, M., & Atkinson, P. (2007). *Ethnography: Principles in practice* (3rd edition). London, UK: Routledge.

Haslam, S.A., Jetten, J., Postmes, T., & Haslam, C. (2009). Social identity, health and well-being: An emerging agenda for applied psychology. *Applied Psychology: An International Review, 58*(1), 1–23.

Haughton-McNeill, L., Kreuter, M.W., & Subramanian, S.V. (2006). Social environment and physical activity: A review of concepts and evidence. *Social Science & Medicine, 63*, 1011–1022.

Henderson, K.A. (2003). Women, physical activity, and leisure: Jeopardy or Wheel of Fortune? *Women in Sport & Physical Activity Journal, 12*(1), 113–125.

Heyl, B.S. (2001). Ethnographic interviewing. In P. Atkinson, A. Coffey, S. Delamont, J. Lofland & L. Lofland (Eds.), *Handbook of ethnography* (pp. 369–383). London, UK: Sage.

Higgs, P.F., & Jones, I.R. (2009). *Medical sociology and old age: Towards a sociology of health in later life*. Abingdon, UK: Routledge.

Hinchliff, S., & Gott, M. (2008). Challenging social myths and stereotypes of women and aging: Heterosexual women talk about sex. *Journal of Women & Aging, 20*(1–2), 65–81.

Im, E., Wonshik, C., Hyun-Ju, L., Liu, Y., & Kim, H.K. (2008). Midlife women's attitudes toward physical activity. *Journal of Obstetric, Gynecologic & Neonatal Nursing, 37*(2), 203–213.

Jones, I.R. & Higgs, P.F. (2010). The natural, the normal and the normative: Contested terrains in ageing and old age. *Social Science & Medicine, 71*(8), 1513–1519.

Kirkwood, T. (2001). *The end of age*. London, UK: Profile Books.

Lieblich, A., Tuval-Mashiach, R., & Zilber, T. (1998). *Narrative research: Reading, analysis and interpretation*. Thousand Oaks, CA: Sage.

Little, D.E. (2002). Women and adventure recreation: Reconstructing leisure constraints and adventure experiences to negotiate continuing participation. *Journal of Leisure Research, 34*(2), 157–177.

Lupton, D. (1994). Consumerism, commodity culture and health promotion. *Health Promotion International, 9*(2), 111–118.

McAdams, D. (2006). The role of narrative in personality psychology today. *Narrative Inquiry, 16*(1), 11–18.

Nelson, H.L. (2001). *Damaged identities, narrative repair*. Ithaca, NY: Cornell University Press.

Noland, C.M. (2006). Auto-photography as research practice: Identity and self-esteem research. *Journal of Research Practice, 2*(1), 1–19.

O'Reilly, K. (2005). *Ethnographic methods*. London, UK: Routledge.

Phoenix, C., & Smith, B. (2011). Telling a (good?) counterstory of aging: Natural bodybuilding meets the narrative of decline. *The Journals of Gerontology, Series B, 66*(5), 628–639.

Phoenix, C., & Sparkes, A.C. (2009). Being Fred: Big stories, small stories and the accomplishment of a positive ageing identity. *Journal of Aging Studies, 20*(2), 107–121.

Rail, G., & Beausoleil, N. (2003). Introduction to 'Health panic and women's health'. *Atlantis, 27*(2), 1–11.

Riessman, C.K. (2008). *Narrative methods for the human sciences*. Thousand Oaks, CA: Sage.

Robinson, D. (2002). Using photographs to elicit narrative accounts. In C. Horrocks, K. Milnes, B. Roberts, & D. Robinson (Eds.), *Handbook of ethnography* (pp. 26–38). London, UK: Sage.

Segar, M., Jayaratne, T., Hanlon, J., & Richardson, C.R. (2002). Fitting fitness into women's lives: Effects of a gender-tailored physical activity intervention. *Women's Health Issues, 12*(6), 338–347.

Shapiro, S.B. (1999). *Pedagogy and the politics of the body: A critical praxis*. London, UK: Routledge.

Shaw, S.M. (1994). Gender, leisure, and constraint: Towards a framework for the analysis of women's leisure. *Journal of Leisure Research, 26*(10), 8–22.

Sparkes, A.C., & Smith, B. (2011). Inhabiting different bodies over time: Narrative and pedagogical challenges. *Sport, Education & Society, 16*(3), 357–370.

Stake, R.E. (1995). *The art of case study research*. Thousand Oaks, CA: Sage.

Stake, R.E. (2003). Case studies. In N.K. Denzin & Y.S. Lincoln (Eds.), *Strategies of qualitative inquiry* (2nd edition) (pp. 134–164). Thousand Oaks, CA: Sage.

Tafjel, H. (Ed.) (2010). *Social identity and intergroup relations* (re-issue edition). Cambridge, UK: Cambridge University Press.

Taylor, S. (2006). Narrative as construction and discursive resource. *Narrative Inquiry, 16*(1), 94–102.

Thomson, R., Bell, R., Holland, J., Henderson, S., McGrellis, S., & Sharpe, S. (2002). Critical moments: Choice, chance and opportunity in young people's narratives of transition. *Sociology, 36*(2), 335–354.

Tulle, E. (2008). *Ageing, the body and social change: Running in later life*. Basingstoke: Palgrave Macmillan.

Tulle-Winton, E. (2000). Old bodies. In P. Hancock, E. Hughes, E. Jagger, K. Paterson, R. Russell, E. Tulle-Winton, & M. Tyler (Eds.), *The body, culture and society: An introduction* (pp. 64–84). Buckingham, UK: Open University Press.

Vertinsky, P. (1991). Old age, gender and physical activity: The biomedicalization of aging. *Journal of Sport History, 18*(2), 64–80.

Vertinsky, P. (1998). Run, Jane, run: Central tensions in the current debate about enhancing women's health through physical activity. *Women & Health, 27*(4), 81–112.

Vertinsky, P. (2000). A woman's p(l)ace in the marathon of life: Feminist perspectives on physical activity and aging. *Journal of Aging & Physical Activity, 8*, 386–406.

Vertinsky, P. (2002). Sporting women in the public gaze: Shattering the master narratives of aging female bodies. *Canadian Woman Studies/le cahiers de la femme, 21*(3), 58–63.

Wiley, C.G., Shaw, S.M., & Havitz, M.E. (2000). Men's and women's involvement in sports: An examination of the gendered aspects of leisure involvement. *Leisure Sciences, 22*(1), 19–31.

WSFF. (2007). It's time: Future forecasts for women's participation in sport and exercise. Report produced by The Women's Sport and Fitness Foundation. Retrieved from www.wsff.org.uk/resources/how-women-experience-sport-and-fitness/its-time-future-forecasts-for-womens-par [last accessed 30 May 2015].

Yarnal, C.M., Hutchinson, S., & Chow, H. (2006). 'I could probably run a marathon right now': Embodiment, space, and young women's leisure experience. *Leisure Sciences, 28*(2), 133–161.

Chapter 7

The suffering and loneliness of the fell runner

An ethnographic foray

Michael Atkinson

A decade ago, Ian Wilkinson (2004) rekindled a sociological interest in, and theorizing about, social suffering. Whilst too few have squarely accepted Wilkinson's challenge to reframe the discipline along lines of suffering (that is, outside of the sociology of medicine), one might actually argue that the vast majority of sociologists of sport and physical culture already empirically account for and theoretically scrutinize the nature of human suffering within particular historical moments, structural contexts, cultural and ideological webs, and micro situations of embodied experience. Inasmuch, the analysis of human suffering has been, and continues to be, one of the overarching sociological questions in sport studies, and in particular, ethnographies of sport. In this chapter, I address the unique and richly layered substantive and theoretical contributions an embodied, ethnographic physical cultural studies offers to the sociology of suffering, especially with respect to the performance of voluntary suffering and physical ordeals in the case of fell running. Mainstream sociologists and sociologists of sport both under-study and theoretically downplay the trans-cultural and nearly metaphysical human desire to suffer through a range of play forms (Caillois, 1967). In this chapter, I reflect on an embodied ethnography of 'the [suffering] limit' I conducted on fell running in the United Kingdom over a three-year period. I examine the complex interrelationship between physical, mental, emotional, and social suffering common amongst participants within the physical culture. In the discussion, I underscore the trans-contextual nature of suffering in physical cultures, set an agenda for embodied, ethnographic investigations of suffering, and describe suffering as one of the cornerstone foci of the physical cultural studies *oeuvre*.[1]

To think, let alone write, about the connection between so-called athletics and existential pleasure through physical suffering is almost antithetical in academic work. I speak quite regularly with colleagues in sport and exercise science programs who unabashedly admit that elite, amateur or 'serious leisure' (Stebbins, 2006) sports bear little resemblance to the pursuit of physical health, or the experience of a full range of emotional pleasures (that is, other than those stirred from vanquishing an opponent). Sport/athletic cultures are typically characterized by the containment of all but a tight band of human emotions and existential experiences, and one in which suffering is embraced at times, but most often desperately avoided (Kerr, 2004). But authors document how people engage the willful abandonment of personal control through intense 'sport-like' physicality, and the purposeful placement of oneself in athletic contexts that stir doubt, uncertainty, thrill of the unknown and personal anxiety. The literature on so-called risk or 'edge' sport clearly attests to the psychological benefits and pleasures of adventure-based athletic practices (i.e., the experience of physical pleasure and emotional release through dangerous athletic activities). But few inside or outside of the academy examine many of the run-of-the-mill sports or athletic pastimes as potential zones of personal self-discovery through edge experiences. Stated differently, I am puzzled as to why theorists of physical cultures so rarely refer to authors like Caillois (1967), who, quite some time ago, clearly articulated the benefits of experiencing the simultaneous thrills and suffering produced by *voluptuous panic* in fields of sport, leisure and play.

In the late 2000s, I started researching the physical culture of British fell running as one partially organized around the playful pursuit of suffering, such as the experience of vertigo, dizziness, uncertainty and personal disruption (Atkinson, 2010a). What is fell running? Picture yourself as a typical road-running enthusiast, and then conjure up a mental image of running in the worst spatial and climatic conditions possible. That is fell running. Fell running is typically undertaken in expansive, rugged, inclement highland or mountain areas by people from the British upper working classes or middle-classes, who range in age from 13 to (well over) 60 years old. The term 'fell' is a derivation of the Norse word *fjall* (meaning, mountain), and generally refers to mountainous or hilly terrain. A typical fell run (either recreational or as an organized, competitive race) traverses meadows, crosses rivers or waterfalls, shoots up and down steep hills, staggers across rocky terrain, lumbers through thickets, meanders over bogs, and occasionally dodges animal herds. Fell runs vary in format and length, but normally range from 2 miles to (in excess of) 40 or 50 miles. Fell runners remain a small lot in the burgeoning global running community, and as such tend to maintain rather close (sub)cultural ties within local counties in Britain. I came to study fell running after being introduced to it by a road running clubmate of mine in Loughborough (Leicestershire, UK) and approached it at first as a training supplement (and then absolute alternative) to road running.

What became evident quite early on in the fell running study is the range of suffering experiences faced by enthusiasts. While the physical and psychological ordeals associated with any running or distance sport culture are noteworthy (Atkinson, 2008), amongst the most interesting aspects of suffering in fell running practices is the pleasurable loneliness one often experiences on runs. The runs often take place in remote areas in which one spends quite some time sojourning alone or in small packs of two or three. In addition, one's sense of personal smallness or existential insignificance is often starkly noted and felt when running within or against the bigger, bolder and sometimes daunting scenery of mountains, rocky hills, dales, rivers, forests, and grasslands one traverses. In being decisively cut away from, or out of, heavily socialized and humanized urban spaces, one can become rather lonely on a run. As I argue in this chapter, such a pleasing sense of suffering comes to be embraced by many, but not all, fell running enthusiasts as a pleasurable experience in which one is at first forced to 'let go' of oneself and then begins to seek out the experience of existentially unplugging through fell running. This occurs by first grappling with the physical ordeal of fell learning and then learning to embrace the practice as a personal technique of self-exploration through 'limit experiences' that are replete with self-direction forms of suffering.

Theoretically locating suffering in physical cultural studies

The sociology of sport and physical culture is not openly marked as the study of physicality as means of better understanding and theorizing the forms, contexts, and contours of human suffering. Nevertheless, the study of sport in society is heavily influenced by the parent discipline emphasis on the social bases of suffering in society and their impacts on human movement, expression, and agency. Within the past five years, there has been a renewed, and certainly contested, argument that the research act in the sociology of sport must become more 'politically and socially engaged' (vis-à-vis the attention to, and work toward the alleviation of, human suffering) to retain its utility. Such an argument, coming perhaps most openly from advocates of physical cultural studies as a contender to the sociology of sport throne (Atkinson, 2011b; Giardina & Newman, 2011; Silk & Andrews, 2011), or proponents of a more public sociology of sport, hinges upon the premise that theoretically-driven sociological research on sport offers much insight into a spectrum of social problems pertaining to human suffering. Donnelly et al. (2011) argue that the traditional sociology of sport runs the very real risk of routinely resting on its own intellectual laurels – emerging far too often as an exercise in the philosophical reading of sport, physical culture, power within social formations, or hegemonic representations of moving bodies and identities, and too infrequently as a concerted and unapologetic ritual of transformative praxis. Critical sociological theories and related research, in their most spirited manifestation, attend to and underscore the politics, problems and possibilities of research as a lever of engaged praxis in the process of attending to and proposing solutions related to patterns in human suffering (Atkinson & De Lisio, 2014).

A forward-thinking sociology of sport and physical culture, one that sees human suffering as a (if not the) core sociological subject, is essentially the study of social life manifesting into and engaging with, as Burawoy writes (2005), the possibility/existence of 'better worlds'. It requires sociologists of sport to break new ground, transgress disciplinary boundaries, pursue theoretically driven research with much vigor, and research beyond the comfortable subjects so regularly studied. It may require, only as a small list of possible topics, an invested and concerted interest in matters of sport and physical activity for/as social development; movement cultures as potential solutions to broad gauge social problems; human rights in sport and leisure contexts; visions of democratic humanism across physical cultures; physical cultural 'pastimes'; post-sport physical cultures; issues in bioethics and technology; youth development through mainstream and non-mainstream physical activities; experiences of health, wellness, varied (dis)abilities, and illness as/in physical culture; global sport, leisure and recreation management; and the sensual aspects of physical culture. It also may require, as discussed in the remainder of this chapter, and somewhat ironically given the mandate of physical cultural studies described above, envisioning forms and instances of social and personal suffering from different theoretical perspectives, including those that interpret and categorize human suffering from so-called positive perspectives.

On fell running

I studied the physical culture of British fell running after moving to England in the winter of 2007 after being introduced to this physically exhausting and mentally trying amalgam of cross-country, trail, mountain, and—at times— wilderness running by a road-running clubmate of mine. Not long into the fieldwork, I came to appreciate what many fell runners know: the unique way in which vertigo, self-exploration, and a connection to the specific time and place become focal points of the sport. Between 2007 and 2009, I spent several hundred hours running fells with other enthusiasts, participating in local races, speaking with fell runners during runs and socializing with them afterwards.

Contemporary fell running is physically intense and most often structured like a typical road-running race. Races, or even leisure runs, require participants to venture from point X to point Y as fast as possible. For some races, there is an official route runners must follow between points X and Y, while for others, participants are told to run from X to Y using any route they choose (which normally involves first orienting the runners to the local terrain). Races can involve only a handful of local residents, a small number of officials and spectators, and a pittance to enter; or they can be national in scope— and even include international 'championships'—attracting participants and spectators from around the world.

Although these leisure runs, races, and 'rounds' (classic fell runs) may look like modernist adventure races and eco-challenges, fell runners insist their sport does not share the same ethos or logic. Fell runs and 'rounds'—even organized fell races (which boast only minimal administrative apparatuses)—are not like adventure races staged against the backdrop of a city, or a newly constructed estate or subdivision, or along some urban-area faux forest or green space. Instead, fell-running events place people in the 'raw' contexts of culturally undetermined terrain—what Lyotard (1989) calls a *scapeland*, where the dominant or preferred cultural maps of meaning offer no understanding of what a runner might 'do' there. The ethos of fell runners does not call for the achievement of dominance over others in order to enjoy the events. Here, participants relish—one might suggest almost atavistically—simply getting stuck in the mud. To them, part of the exciting significance of this veritably pre-modern sport stems from the sweaty camaraderie its players enjoy through their collective communion with nature (Atkinson, 2010b, 2011a).

The adjective *scrambling* perhaps best captures the feel of a fell run, its true ethos. Given the terrain one normally traverses in a run, a runner's body gets taken up, down, and even sideways at different times. The runner's speed changes almost meter by meter as they struggle up almost impossible ascents, get pulled down equally daunting descents, slog through mud, and shuffle through rolling terrain. The range of the runner's limb motion expands and contracts throughout the course; they fear falling, getting lacerated, losing direction, straying off course, and becoming physical exhausted. Obdurate, sometimes seemingly unforgiving, elements—like the sun, the wind, the rain, the earth, big rocks—everywhere confront the runner. Indeed, a good fell run assaults the runner's body with a constant disorientation, and one's normal perceptions of space, time, mind, and body get thrown into disarray. This, to a fell runner, is fun; it is gritty play; it is pleasure (Atkinson, 2010b, 2011a).

In short, then, fell running is and always has been, about suffering and pushing the body into suffering experiences in wilderness contexts. Quite simply, one cannot avoid suffering in the physical practice. Most fell running courses or routes are intentionally treatises on suffering. Hills are steep, rivers are cold and wet, mud is sloppy, trees and bracken and fences lacerate the skin, and the wind pushes one's legs backward at almost every juncture of the event. But as a friend of mine named Darrin, and longtime fell runner once told me, "You'll never like it, until you like that [the suffering]. That's the secret. You can be a fell runner, or be comfortable, but you can't be both." The sociological literature on pain and injury in sport underscores how athletes generally avoid, disavow or privately manage such forms of suffering in the throes of athleticism (Young, 2004). While the ability to withstand and inflict pain as a *competitive strategy* is lauded in particular sport settings (Atkinson & Young, 2008a, 2008b; Dunning, 1999), few people enter into recreational activity or games with the expressed purpose to physically, emotionally and psychologically hurt. But participants in the physical culture of fell running often derive intense social and emotional stimulation through 'suffering' athletically; and indeed, not knowing when one or how one is going to hurt during a typical fell run is part of the allure. Even for the most seasoned fell runner, a garden-variety run involves a substantial amount of physical and psychological stress over an hour or several hours of continuous activity. But participants frequently articulate the array of positive experiences accompanying suffering and agony.

Suffering, loneliness and the fells

Within a mutually identified community of participants, the ability to withstand and relish in athletic suffering is embraced as a form of group bonding. In Putnam's (1995) terms, the ability to withstand and enjoy suffering in and over the fells is a form of social capital that members value as a marker of their collective identity. As such, fell runners learned penchants for self-imposed agony in the leisure sphere binds them together as a rather unique social conglomerate, one I refer to elsewhere in the study of triathlon, as a *pain community* (Atkinson, 2008). Second, and akin to Turner's (1969) description of liminal experiences (i.e., in which a person enters into a ritual not knowing how the body, self or mind will be affected in the process), fell running sessions provide participants with ordered contexts for self-exploration through the suffering process. Fell runners who come to relish intense physical and cognitive agony in the sport indeed share a socially learned personality structure, or *habitus* (Bourdieu, 1984; Elias, 2002), that configures instances of voluntary suffering in athletics as exciting and personally significant.

Given the above, Caillois' (1967) description of the importance of form over content in play-based (*qua* athletic) performances resonates in the first stages of reading of fell running culture. For many of the fell runners I know, it is the *form* of athletic experience, in the first instance, and the pleasurable suffering it brings that allures. The hills, the rivers, the exhaustion produced by traversing them are relished. While there are clearly elements of ritualism and aspects of the sacred associated with fell running, akin to how Caillois (1967) describes the ritual and the sacred in games, enthusiasts quite regularly point to the appreciation of moments of unscripted suffering during runs as a central feature of the physical culture. It is amongst the strongest ideological ties that bind them together in the pain community. Charles (age 34) told me,

> I used to run road races, and that [competition running] is charted and scheduled and robotic. Competing in a [race] series comes to be like a job. You train, you eat, you train some more, and clock the progress by numbers and PBs [personal bests] ... When I started fell running, I gave up that lark. Fell running is not clockwork. It's experiencing the moment,

yeah. Chest heaving, legs buckling down the hill, fear of toppling and just getting stuck in for the hell of it ... then we all have a good laugh in the car park talking about the ride [emotional thrill].

For Charles and others, the suffering and existential experiences associated with fell running partly relate to what Caillois (1967) outlines as the social and personal features of play. Caillois' definition of play is comprised of six elements: it is, to him, (1) free—that is, nonobligatory; (2) separate—cut off from, in degrees, the rest of one's social life; (3) uncertain—in the sense that the results are not known beforehand; (4) unproductive—non-instrumental on a strictly material basis; (5) not entirely rule bound; and, (6) fictive—it is, "accompanied by a special awareness of a second reality or of a free unreality, as against real life" (1967, pp. 9–10). All aspects of Caillois' (1967) understanding of play are relevant to the deciphering of fell running as meaningful.

I became especially interested, given the sixth criterion in Caillois (1967) typology, in how fell runners may come to question core truths about the nature of existence and one's essence (an alternative reality than that experienced in everyday life) through playful athletics. Clearly, this is not standard for all fell runners who engage with the practice. Running the fells can provide enthusiasts with the brand of free unreality Caillois (1967) describes. Enthusiasts often venture into fell running and explore what multiple truths may lay beneath/within their culturally-institutionally-discursive framed selves; and as such, describe a collective desire to tap alternative knowledge of themselves (or their bodies) through dizzying suffering experiences which precedes, and cannot be wholly assembled through, the ascribed and achieved social roles, responsibilities and identities they inhabit in the course of everyday life. Even though they exist in a mutually recognized pain community, the loneliness and individuality of doing fell runs forces, to degrees, a confrontation of the self. "Out there," describes Tom (age 42), "I'm not a dad or a businessman. I'm just running and hurting, just trudging, carrying on and breathing. While struggling to make it [through the race], I'm never at more peace with myself because I'm not in my head." Fell running, from this perspective, is a form of athletic play designed to extract the enthusiast from everyday life (and its social trappings), to isolate one from others, and explore physical cultural and emotional experiences such as self-driven and controlled suffering not often accessible to them elsewhere in heavily ritualized (i.e., family, work, school, or other institutional) zones. Finn (age 40) describes the process as,

part of learning when not to care about how to understand or rationalize something, and just live in the moment of running. If you just let go, hours whizz past like minutes ... It starts with making the body hurt, and making your mind focus on that, so everything else disappears.

Fell runners like Finn argue that in such contexts, the social, cognitive, rational self is temporary abandoned so that a pleasurable emptiness is created. Here, loneliness, isolation and physical pain allow one to 'let go'. Whereas emptiness in other contexts of life may signal one's alienation, disenfranchisement or anomie, when deliberately sought out through play, it can be a vehicle for personal release and discovery in fell running. Their practices curiously resemble, at times, a late modern and secular brand of playful *self-mortification*.

The painful and exhaustive ritual of fell running can remind practitioners how physical and emotional suffering can be a vehicle for self-discovery. Le Breton (2000), like Lyng (2008), documents how alternative sport enthusiasts seek out symbolic death experiences in high-risk adventure pursuits as playful forms of symbolic self-annihilation. By using intense forms of physical movement (climbing, tumbling, and slogging through inhospitable terrain) which often involve risk, anxiety, pain and injury, fell runners may temporarily destabilize the socially ascribed self to which they have been heretofore attached, and they often believe, limited by in everyday life; that is, the social self makes them suffer in unpleasant ways. Their sense of athletic play is remarkable in this respect, as they search for alternative aesthetics, pleasures and bio-pedagogies of truth through physical cultural practices like fell running. Again, Caillois (1967) might argue that fell runners' quest to experience this brand of *puissance* (Pronger, 1998, 2002) through self-mortification is a definitive a type of play involving the overloading of the senses that people find exhilarating.

Yet how is the above specifically achieved? Fell runners often articulate that when one learns to let go of external desire and the social self (ways of rationalizing sport/play as a form of competitive play peppered with an element of chance), one's body feels different: flexible, energized, relaxed and vital. A crucial part of this process is allowing oneself to simply move with (or against) the terrain one encounters; that is, to experience a sense of existential loneliness against the terrain. To embrace a slow climb, find joy in the panic of a steep descent, or desire to tramp through mud (rather than avoid it) and immerse oneself in the water one encounters, may require one to relish the physically uncomfortable and even strange sensation of each. Fell runners correspondingly describe tapping the feeling of *ecstasis* (Heidegger, 1977) during a particular run.

In addition to all of the above, to fully appreciate the gravitas of Caillois' (1967) treatise on play and games and its capacity to shed light on the role of suffering in fell cultures, one needs to deconstruct how the notion of encountering and suffering, self-exploration, and competition over terrain can become personally thrilling. It is precisely here where Caillois' (1967, 2003) understanding of humans' drives toward acts of mimicry are important. In "Mimicry and Legendary Psychasthenia" (2003), Caillois argues that humans, like non-human animals, often adopt the guise of (or mimic) other 'things' not as a mode of personal survival but as an act of self-indulgence. Caillois (2003, p. 110) refers to this drive as an instinct of abandonment, or the temporary slippage out of one's everyday roles and identities into an alternative mode of being.

I started thinking about mimicry in the context of fell running one afternoon as I watched a group of runners navigate their way up a daunting hill. They formed a perfect line, were hunched over grasping at the ground for extra leverage and appeared animal-like in their movement. From that day forward, I came to consider the act of fell running as a form of mimicry in Caillois' (1967, 2003) conceptualization: as the temporary slippage of people into a non-human, animal-like form of embodiment where one scurries up, over, down, through, and across 'natural' terrain in the act of losing one's everyday self. To do this, fell runners may encounter running as a deliberate act in which they hurtle their bodies around the course in varying ways in order to be, at least for a moment, like non-human animals inhabiting those spaces. Animal mimicry in this case is achieved not only in the act of running in relatively 'untamed' spaces as detours from the structures (and identities) of their everyday lives, but also, then, through the ways by which they run in animal-like forms. Important is that the runners physically and emotionally encounter the terrain in manners totally dissimilar to their physical and emotional regimens in other material, social and cultural environments. Here, they describe the importance of moving up, moving down, getting stuck, being windswept, becoming soaked, getting bloodied and bruised. Oliver (age 26) says, "I mean you cannot deny it. We march up hills like ants in a line, flail around in water like fish, scurry through the brush like foxes, and jump off rocks [large boulders] like rams. In that mindset, you feel almost animalistic, too, and it's in that mental space where possibilities for not thinking like a proper runner [road racer] are made." The animal mimicry in fell running spaces is important, then, in the performance of the physical culture as moving 'wildly' (and suffering through the task of moving in atypical manners) stimulates the ability to think and feel as non-rational, non-calculating subjects.

Take it to the limit (one more time)

As a result of the above, I became particularly interested in Bataille's (1988) writings on the notion of the 'limit' as they might apply to fell running. The limit experience is a demandingly visceral and sensual event that dislodges the rational subject and decentralizes identity—here, movements involving suffering and animal-like movements in so-called wild spaces are critical in fell running. Cliff (age 26) says, "Getting at the top of a fell or a mountain and seeing animals up there is very cool. It helps me remember how easy running and climbing is for them, and how it could be for me if I moved like them." The emotionally and physically intense, self-isolating limit-experience can push one's sense of subjectivity to the margins, as it exposes and eclipses the cultural limits and parameters of the possible in one's mind. According to Fromm (1973), the limit-seeker carries a deep-seated frustration with heavily circumscribed modalities of late modern life, to the extent that a desire to ritually de-center the socially dominated and confined self (which, of course, enframes one's learned sense of the possible) stirs and is mobilized through seemingly self-sadistic activities. In *America* (1998, p. 38), Baudrillard describes the limit-experience of the runner who hurtles forward in agony as a means of self-escape, and as an emblem of postmodern isolation:

> Decidedly, joggers are the true Latter Day Saints and the protagonists of an easy-does-it Apocalypse. Nothing evokes the end of the world more than a man running straight ahead on a beach, swathed in the sounds of his Walkman, cocooned in the solitary sacrifice of his energy, indifferent even to catastrophes since he expects destruction to come only as the fruit of his own efforts, from exhausting the energy of a body that has in his own eyes become useless. Primitives, when in despair, would commit suicide by swimming out to sea until they could swim no longer. The jogger commits suicide by running up and down the beach. His eyes are wild, saliva drips from his mouth. Do not stop him. He will either hit you or simply carry on dancing around in front of you like a man possessed.

For Baudrillard and others, the limit experience is categorized by the pleasurable immersion into a grey zone of self-identification where one encounters possibilities of the self. In this case, Caillois (2003) was incredibly perceptive with respect to his understanding of how mimicry in play facilitates *liminality*. Liminal activities, in van Gennep's (1909/2004) and Turner's (1969) descriptions, are socio-cultural rituals in which one's body, self or mind are either temporarily or permanently altered (in unanticipated ways) through the events. In fell running, liminality is the space between the beginning and end of a single, or many, running session(s). Dean (age 34) said to me, "I'm the very same person on the job day in and out. I have to be, or I'm sacked. But with running, it's a new adventure, and a new set of possibilities every go. You never know what's headed your way." The liminal state is characterized by ambiguity, openness, and indeterminacy. One's sense of identity dissolves to some extent, bringing about a temporary disorientation. Liminality is a process of transition where normal limits to thought, self-understanding and behaviour are relaxed—a situation that can lead to new perspectives on reality (or at least, existential experiences).

Over the course of time, I learned that for many of the fell runners I studied, their physical practices are quite routinely anchored by the pursuit of liminality. As but one example, during fell running, normally accepted social boundary differences between the participants, such as gender, race, social class, physical ability and others are almost completely de-emphasized or ignored. A cultural feeling develops in training, racing and socialization of common humanity and equality rather than recognized hierarchy (so common in modernist sports cultures that exacerbate rather than dismantle rigid hierarchies of social identity). Ian (age 25) said to me, "I suppose I don't really give a toss how old someone is, or if they are a bloke or not." Interesting, then, are the ways in which fell running activities may serve to, albeit temporarily in many cases, erase or negate socially achieved and ascribed roles participants hold away from running contexts. Sorcha (age 29) says, "What I love about it [fell running] is how for the day of the run I'm not anything ... I am free to be a just someone totally barking [mad] out running up and down some hills."

In a recent review of Caillois' contribution to play, games and leisure theory, Henricks (2010) describes how the pursuit of suffering-based forms of play is relatively rare in late market capitalist societies. Considering when Caillois wrote *Man, Play and Games* (1967), this observation makes empirical sense. But much has changed since the first publication of *Man, Play and Games*. The rise of alternative, lifestyle or otherwise 'resistant' forms of play and games smacks with a late modern desire shared amongst participants to explore a kind of existential suffering not found anywhere else in everyday life (Atkinson & Young, 2008a; Rinehart & Sydnor, 2003; Wheaton, 2004). Indeed, the growing interest in alternative forms of athletics in the leisure sphere (embodied with a distinct play ethos) potentially signals a burgeoning disaffection with the sorts of meritocratic and competitive games so commonly valued in the high age of Western modernity. Many of the fell runners I studied have come to see the incompleteness of experience provided by sport, games and leisure saturated with a middle-class work ethic, and experiment with, in greater numbers, physical cultures allowing for suffering, isolation and loneliness, flow, voluptuous panic and a peppering of serious play. According to Sian (age 28),

> I reckon [fell running] adds a sort of stimulation in my life I don't get anywhere else. I don't come up to [fell running] like work or like the footy [soccer] I played as a lad. The courses, the other blokes in the races aren't there for me to beat them. We're a bunch of lads out there trying to feel alive.

What particularly struck me about some fell running enthusiasts' construction of this adventure sport is how decisively dissimilar it can be to other forms of games, play and sport in the adventure or outdoor sphere. To be sure, when considering the gamut of alternative, whiz, extreme or edge sport, one must ask how 'resistant' many of these subcultures are along modernist, rationalizing, middle-class competitive lines. Le Breton (2000) and Atkinson and Young (2008a, 2008b) describe the full panorama of alternative, adventure or physical cultures from the 1970s onward as not so resistant to dominant social constructions of identity (or play, or emotions, or bodies) inside or outside of sport at all. In fact, since as far back as the mid-1800s, wilderness and adventure sports (the North American pre-cursors to contemporary subcultural risk sports) have been theorized as places where modernist ideologies and identities are the unspoken norm and exist largely without opposition (Erickson, 2005).

Ray (2009) illustrates how the very essence of most adventure, risk or otherwise alternative physical cultures deeply extol long-standing middle-class constructions of sport, physical activity and leisure as only a pseudo time-out from work; and further, a place of tightly controlled and rationalized adventurism, an opportunity to build social capital among others 'like me', as a site of moral character development, as a context for testing one's ability to take risks (in the wilderness, on water, in the sky, and in urban spaces) in the pursuit of honing one's skills in personal, spatial and social mastery. She argues, as does Nash (1967) in his study of 19th- and 20th-century American wilderness cultures, that outdoor, alternative physical cultures retain an early 1900s Progressive Era sentiment of the need to develop personal character through risk-based athletic pursuits. As such, alternative/lifestyle sports subcultures have long been associated with the need for people to 'test themselves' and publicly demonstrate social character in meritocratic manners. Indeed, fell runners replicate this model of nature/self/sport identification in particular times and in situated contexts of competitive racing. Simply put, the pursuit of edgework (Lyng, 2008) has long been a boundary for members of the middle class to evidence their ability to be social leaders. Again, while there are scores of fell runners in the United Kingdom and elsewhere who utilize the practice as a means of reproducing the achieved social identities with very modernist sensibilities regarding sport, play and games, others (as discussed in this chapter) represent an entirely different faction of the overall physical culture.

Final thoughts

Fell running is perhaps best categorized as a burgeoning 'post-sport' play/game physical culture in the UK and elsewhere. Brian Pronger (1998, 2002) first outlined the promise of a utopian 'post-sport' physical culture, wherein the traditional boundary-maintaining sports are replaced with athletic practices underpinned by aesthetic, moral and play-based values. Pronger's (2002) call for post-sport became attached to his critique of mainstream power and performance sports cultures, and, how they purport beliefs that vital body energies, desires and sources of pleasure are negated as a sport participant's body/mind/self in sport is colonized by the rationalist, technological, dominating and socially stratifying discourses prevalent in most games. Pronger (2002) contends that modern sport is an exogenously determined social terrain, contoured more by educational logics, market capitalist discourses, military doctrines, scientific philosophies and State health agendas than organic and humanistic uses of/for sport. Here, and as evidenced by fell runners' logics in this chapter, there are incredible similarities between the pursuit of suffering in physical cultures like fell running and Pronger's analysis of post-sport physical cultures.

A post-sport physical culture like fell running is, then, one in which modernist ideologies and practices are not celebrated outright, and in which corporeal dichotomies between the sacred and profane, the raw and the cooked, the athletic and uncontrolled body are challenged through various forms of athletic suffering. Whereas traditional sports practices tend to contain, discipline and enframe physical bodies as resources to be deployed toward the attainment of external goals and fulfilment of cultural-institutional discourses, post-sport/play practices like fell running eschew the strict body-as-resource schematic. Temporary moments of dizziness, panic, suffering, and letting go through athletics can become the primary focus of fell running for its participants—as Caillois (1967) might have suggested some time ago. Post-sport physical cultures like fell running may often adorn the guise of mainstream sports forms and competitive techniques of play (e.g., running, and running collectively in organized races)—what Wheaton (2004) describes as the "residual elements" of modernist sport—but their individual or collective engagement and experience can bear little similarity at times. A post-sport physical culture like fell running often values human spiritual, physical and emotional experience (or rather, realization) 'in the round' through play-based (and indeed competitive at times) forms of athleticism, beyond medical-technical or power and performance terms. Few have written about or explored what an existential post-sport, sociology of sport might look like or how it might be theorized. In this spirit, I suggest we return to authors like Caillois (1967) and examine the theoretical possibilities for conceptualizing their embodied practices as worthy of new attention.

Note

1   Arguments offered here are extensions and re-interpretations of fell running first made in Atkinson (2011a).

References

Atkinson, M. (2008). Triathlon, suffering and exciting significance. *Leisure Studies,* *27*, 165–180.

Atkinson, M. (2010a). Entering scapeland: Yoga, fell and post-sport physical cultures. *Sport in Society, 13*, 1249–1267.

Atkinson, M. (2010b). Fell running in post-sport territories. *Qualitative Research in Sport and Exercise, 2*, 109–132.

Atkinson, M. (2011a). Fell running and voluptuous panic. *American Journal of Play, 4*, 111–132.

Atkinson, M. (2011b). Physical cultural studies [redux]. *Sociology of Sport Journal*, *28*, 135–144.

Atkinson, M., & De Lisio, A. (2014). Mega events, sport legacies and sociologically informed impact assessment. In C. Okada & K. Young (Eds.), *Sport, social development and peace* (pp. 291–243). London: Elsevier.

Atkinson, M., & Young, K. (2008a). *Deviance and social control in sport*. Champaign: Human Kinetics.

Atkinson, M., & Young, K. (2008b). *Tribal play: Subcultural journeys through sport*. London: Emerald.

Bataille, G. (1988). *Inner experience*. Albany: SUNY Press.

Baudrillard, J. (1988). *America*. London: Verso.

Bourdieu, P. (1984). *Distinction: A social critique of the judgement of taste*. Cambridge: Harvard University Press.

Burawoy, M. (2005). 2004 American Sociological Association presidential address: For public sociology. *British Journal of Sociology*, *56*, 260–290.

Caillois, R. (1967). *Les jeux et les hommes: Le masque et le vertige*. Paris: Gallimard.

Caillois, R. (2003). *The edge of surrealism: A Roger Caillois reader*. Durham, NC: Duke University Press.

Donnelly, P., Atkinson, M., Boyle, S., & Szto, C. (2011). Sport for development and peace: A public sociology perspective. *Third World Quarterly*, *32*, 589–601.

Dunning, E. (1999). *Sport matters: Sociological studies of sport, violence, and civilization*. London: Routledge.

Elias, N. (2002). *The civilizing process: Sociogenetic and psychogenetic investigations*. Oxford: Basil Blackwell.

Erickson, B. (2005). Style matters: Explorations of bodies, whiteness and identity in rock climbing. *Sociology of Sport Journal*, *22*, 373–396.

Fromm, E. (1973). *Anatomy of human destructiveness*. New York: Henry Holt.

Giardina, M., & Newman, J. (2011). What is the 'physical' in physical cultural studies? *Sociology of Sport Journal*, *28*, 36–63.

Heidegger, M. (1954/1977). The question concerning technology. In D. Krell (Ed.), *Martin Heidegger: Basic writings* (pp. 307–342). New York: Harper and Row.

Henricks, T. (2010). Caillois's 'Man, play, and games': An appreciation and evaluation. *American Journal of Play*, *3*, 157–185.

Kerr, J. (2004). *Rethinking violence and aggression in sport*. New York: Routledge.

Le Breton, D. (2000). Playing symbolically with death in extreme sports. *Body & Society*, *6*, 1–11.

Lyng, S. (2008). Risk-taking in sport: Edgework and reflexive community. In M. Atkinson & K. Young (Eds.), *Tribal play: Subcultural journeys through sport* (pp. 89–115). London: Emerald.

Lyotard, J.-F. (1989). Scapeland. In A. Benjamin (Ed.), *The Lyotard reader* (pp. 182–190). Oxford: Basil Blackwell.

Nash, R. (1967). *Wilderness and the American mind*. New Haven: Yale University Press.

Pronger, B. (1998). Post-sport: Transgressing boundaries in physical culture. In G. Rail (Ed.), *Sport and postmodern times: Culture, gender, sexuality, the body and sport* (pp. 277–301). Albany: SUNY.

Pronger, B. (2002). *Body fascism: Salvation in the technology of physical fitness*. Toronto: University of Toronto Press.

Putnam, R. (1995). *Bowling alone: America's declining social capital.* New York: Simon & Schuster.

Ray, S. (2009). Risking bodies in the wild: The 'corporeal unconscious' of American adventure culture. *Journal of Sport & Social Issues, 33*, 257–284.

Rinehart, R., & Sydnor, S. (2003). *To the extreme: Alternative sports, inside and out.* Albany: SUNY Press.

Silk, M., & Andrews, D. (2011). Toward a physical cultural studies. *Sociology of Sport Journal, 28*, 4–35.

Stebbins, R. (2006). *Serious leisure: A perspective for our time.* New Brunswick: Transaction.

Turner, V. (1969). *The ritual process: Structure and anti-structure.* New York: Penguin.

Van Gennep, A. (2004). *The rites of passage.* London: Routledge.

Wheaton, B. (2004). *Understanding lifestyle sport: Consumption, identity and difference.* London: Routledge.

Wilkinson, I. (2004). *Suffering: A sociological introduction.* Cambridge: Polity.

Young, K. (2004). *Sporting bodies, damaged selves.* London: Elsevier.

Chapter 8

The boxer in the mirror

The ethnographic-self as a resource while conducting insider research among professional boxers

Alex Stewart

In present times there are any number of ethnographic modes of inquiry at the disposal of a researcher interested in studying sport and physical activity cultures with often contested epistemological assumptions about how theoretical knowledge is best generated (Sparkes, 2002; Andrews et al., 2005; Young & Atkinson, 2012). The family of ethnographic approaches now encapsulates modes grounded in scientific realism and the quest to seek out objective representations of social and cultural life, to more recent orientations influenced by what Atkinson (2012) calls a "progressive scepticism regarding an ethnographer's ability to merely represent the 'objective' aspects of social/cultural life via a textual account of others" (p. 29). The upshot of such developments has meant a growing interest in the self of the ethnographer unavoidably influencing both the events and relationships developed within the field and the ways culture is finally represented in written form (Collins & Gallinat, 2010). It is far more readily acknowledged that the ethnographer can never be an entirely neutral 'device' for describing, explaining and representing social and cultural life. To do so would imply the ethnographic researcher to be a 'transcendental subject' whereby s/he possesses the ability to become invisible during the research process itself, and intellectually detached during analysis of data and when producing the final written representations of culture (DeGaris, 1999). To acknowledge the impossibility of such ethnographic conjuring brings to the fore the thorny issue of the researchers' subjectivity and the need to confront the unavoidable and perhaps uncomfortable fact that as ethnographic researchers we are always reflexively implicated in the field and the ways we choose to represent our cultural understandings (Coffey, 1999; Collins & Gallinat, 2010; Davida, 2012). The impact of the researcher-self upon both the process and product of ethnographic research is perhaps most apparent in modes of enquiry termed 'insider ethnography', or 'ethnography at home'. Both terms are commonly used to identify ethnographic fieldwork carried out in cultural settings intimately familiar to the ethnographer (Hammersley & Atkinson, 2007; O'Reilly, 2009).

Kirsten Hastrup (1987) argues that ethnographers may harness their subjectivity to cultivate a truly privileged standpoint through which to interpret culture. She uses the analogy of the mirror to explain the fieldwork-as-reflexive process; like the mirror, the ethnographer develops the third person capacity to see oneself at the same time as seeing others:

> It is not solely a matter of both participating (assuming the role of you) and observing (keeping my professional aims intact), but also, and more importantly, to let go of both and live, feel, and experience from the position of the third person.
> (Hastrup 1987, p. 105 cited in O'Reilly 2009, p. 117)

To achieve such an ambitious third-person awareness, the insider ethnographer must balance being intimately attached with a familiar group, or at least a group of social actors subscribing to a familiar way of life, while doing (thus 'living') the same day-to-day practices for an extended period of time. Simultaneously, through theoretical contemplation and analysis, the insider ethnographer seeks to understand her 'fellow-other' in the field through abstracted and as such somewhat detached and thus objective social-scientific standpoints of analysis. The reality of 'letting go' to reflexively examine and understand the contours of social life engulfing our own and others' sense-making capacities is far more complex and arduous than many methodological texts tend to suggest (Coffey, 1999).

For the purpose of this discussion I draw upon my own 'insider' ethnographic journey as a competitive boxer and doctoral researcher conducting fieldwork among amateur and professional boxers based in Luton and London, England, over a five-year period (Stewart, 2008), to offer concrete methodological insights regarding the processes entailed for achieving the somewhat illusive third-person standpoint of analysis. In the spirit of a methodological 'confession' (Sparkes, 2002; Smith & Waddington, 2014; Van Maanen, 2011) my discussion seeks to evoke something of the perpetually messy and physically, emotionally and intellectually draining labour experienced in 'becoming' ethnographic in order to investigate the boxing-world practices and cultural norms that, in both obvious and rather more hidden ways, informed my own subjectivity. Having reflexively grappled with the field in this way to successfully submit my PhD thesis, and with the benefit of retrospective hindsight gained in the intervening years, I assert that it is possible to view the 'internal' ethnographic-self as a valuable resource, one that may be harnessed in epistemologically productive ways to investigate sport and physical activity cultures. As documented below, inherent to my third-person (self)awareness was an epistemological recognition and subsequent articulation of the subtle and barely conscious subplot of my identity transformation from 'boxing-insider' to 'researcher' by way of the ethnographic process and the way that contributed to my cultural (re)interpretations.

Entering the field: 'the boxer'

The holy grail of the insider ethnographer remains the same as for all ethnographers; it is to hone the necessary intuition to connect with and intellectually explain how the subtle yet incredibly powerful cultural forces serving to organise social life provide what Raymond Williams (1977) describes the 'maps of meaning' for people to make sense of their life-circumstances. Paul Willis (2000) suggests that optimal understanding of culture as a collective and intersubjective experience requires the researcher to engage in the temporal, symbolic and sensuous dimensions entailed. He thus favours ethnography for conducting cultural explorations as:

> the ethnographic impulse is to be so moved with curiosity about a social puzzle...that you are seized to go and look for yourself, to see 'what's going on' as bound up with 'how they go on'. Physical and sensuous presence then allows observation and witness and the use of five sense channels for recording data relating to social atmosphere, emotional colour and unspoken assumptions
>
> (Willis 2000, p. xiii).

Having clocked many years of competitive boxing experience prior to commencement of the research my strategy for cultivating the ethnographic understanding espoused by Willis was premised upon my (self)perceived ability to adopt a research role as a 'real' (i.e. competitive) boxing-world insider prior to the start of fieldwork. As an 'open class' amateur boxer (i.e. eligible to participate in international level competition) I was in a position to be granted a professional boxing licence by the British Boxing Board of Control (BBBC). Having passed the procedural interview with Robert Smith, the assistant General Secretary of the BBBC, I undertook the required medical procedures and signed a standard Boxer–Manager agreement with 'Jim' (a pseudonym) that enabled me to acquire a professional boxer's licence and by definition access to the 'real' world of professional boxing in England. I assumed at that time that my membership among the boxing fraternity offered an authentic ethnographic vantage that had been earned, and thus was legitimized, through bona-fide corporeal engagement within the front and backstages of the boxing universe – the elevated boxing ring taking center-stage in an assortment of competitive venues and boxing gymnasiums and the fraternity dealings and goings-on taking place in the backstage changing room and medical areas.

As such, I had fully lived and shared a myriad of the realities experienced by other professional boxers, including: the tranquillity of early morning 'roadwork'; the exhilaration of arriving at peak fitness; the monastic discipline of 'making weight'; the camaraderie exchanged among professional boxers while preparing in the gymnasium during the weeks and days before a scheduled fight; the uncle-like words of advice received from the coach and the emotional roller-coaster of self-doubt, exhilaration and fear when contemplating 'the fight' in the days, hours and minutes before the event; the tension-fuelled bravado enacted and near overwhelming emotional intensity experienced when undertaking the short yet very public ring-walk to finally and intimately become acquainted with your adversary for the next few minutes; the physically exhausting experience of the fight itself; the effortless motion of a scoring punch delivered 'just right' and its instant appraisal as it inscribes the adversaries bodily and spiritual demeanour; conversely the sharp intake of breath and ting of pain as the opponent's well-timed punch connects to 'spark' retaliation or retreat; the joy at having one's hand raised and being announced the winner; the deflation and awkward silence accompanying 'a loss' while getting changed back into civilian clothes. As such, I could readily identify and empathise with the "...sensorial and emotional pedagogy" (Wacquant, 2004, p. 15) of 'real' boxing as a participant sport geared towards self-discipline, craftsmanship, 'honorary' respect for others as for self, self-denial and differed gratification, the glorification of an autonomously 'heroic' masculinity manifesting as an adventurous risk-orientated spirit (see Sugden, 1996; Wacquant, 2004).

I thus ventured into my ethnographic project believing that as an insider who could not only 'talk the talk' but also 'walk the walk' it would be possible to viscerally and symbolically locate the social and cultural basis defining the rewards, seductions and contestations experienced by other boxing-practitioners inside and outside the squared ring. This kinesthetic learning process would be the 'black-box' to inform my fieldwork interpretations and ultimately guide my academically informed (thus objective) yet empathetic critical evaluations to add nuanced, privileged even, perspectives to existing scholarly discourse. Whatever suppositions I may have harboured at that time, however, I can now more readily acknowledge that my investigative vigour was, in fact, rather naïve. As a neophyte researcher I had little, if any, appreciation of the intellectual terrain necessarily to be navigated in order to achieve the 'third-person' capacity to simultaneously be able to interpret *my* boxer-self while endeavouring to 'see' other boxing-practitioners through the various social-scientific lenses engaged with when adopting a more scholastic orientation away from the action. As a self-proclaimed 'boxing-insider' saturated in the normative belief systems of what boxing intuitively was and was not, I became increasingly (and frustratingly) aware of the methodological requirement to exercise a balance between personal involvement and detachment. In reading and re-reading the body of social-scientific and methodological literature necessary to add analytical detail and sociologically informed depth to my insider fieldwork experiences, I was forced to acknowledge the inevitable impact of my subjectivity upon the research. As I shall discuss below this 'awareness' became manifest as an embodied way of life; the tension sensed and felt (as much as logically inferred) was never really absent.

'In the blue corner...'

In this section I incorporate narrative description of a 'focal event' (Brewer, 2000) of the professional boxing universe in England, that is replicated on a regular basis in and around many post-industrial urban landscapes. Advertised as a 'Gentleman's Evening of Professional Boxing' this event was staged in a hotel function room located next to a major motorway linking the South of England with its Northern regions. An audience consisting of several hundred men all wearing tuxedos were seated comfortably around tables draped in immaculate white linen. The central focal point of this space was an elevated platform structure, laid with a padded canvas and squared by sprung ropes supported by four posts in each corner set back behind padded protective leather screens. The ropes of the ring formed the boundary between observation and participation, effectively separating audience from the ring interior. My 'insider' role was prominently displayed on the posters advertising the evening's entertainment on offer: four professional boxing contests, the performance of a stand-up comedian, hospitality food, free-flowing alcohol, gambling, fraternisation of a business nature and an auction of sport memorabilia in support of various charities.

By the point of entrée into my narrative I had contested the eight rounds and had just been declared loser (points decision). As a direct consequence of my efforts I had acquired six stitches courtesy of my opponent's propensity to make use of his head as well as his fists and had become £800 richer (minus the one-third 'cut' owed to my manager and trainer). Through evoking, in written form, my insider vantage of lived experience during this instance in time and space, I seek to evoke something of the felt, sensed, heard and observed patterns of meaning and social interaction through which I endeavored to engage my ethnographic imagination:

> The MC has just declared the winner to a loud chorus of cheers and whistles as my victorious opponent raises both arms in salute of his supporters. The MC continues *"...a round of applause for a very gallant and sporting loser, ladies and gentlemen in the blue corner a fine boxer, Luton's Alex Stewart..."* of which follows a smattering of barely audible appreciation for my efforts. I duck underneath the ring ropes to exit centre-stage only to be instructed by 'Coach' to lay on a makeshift stretcher consisting of two dining tables prised together and positioned immediately to the side of the elevated ring. Self-consciously I lie on the tables. To the periphery of my vision I can see waitresses rapidly clearing unwanted plates and filling empty glasses. As I seek to compose myself the 'banter' directed at my expense from a well-inebriated voice somewhere to my left catches my attention, *"aye, aye... thee should 'ave ducked lad... [laughing] ...you lost me five-hundred quid blue corner...you should have used that right hand more kid...serves thee right for getting a wallop 'int*

eye [more laughing]". In a mixed state of contemplation, fatigue and endorphin-induced stress-relief I am content to let the comments pass by, remaining muted as I await the resident British Medical Association doctor to inspect my injury. Unlike many who have found themselves in a like situation, I uncontrollably become submerged in a thought process through which I seek to, (or perhaps I'm forced to), interpret my embodied perceptions by way of scholarly analysis. A number of sociological debates concerning the social significance of boxing flash through my mind: *'If this is "theatre with blood" am I well and truly being exploited right now? By definition have I just offered up my body for the pleasure and amusement of these strangers…much as a human commodity of the sport-entertainment business?'* The here and now takes primacy, however, and as I more fully feel the impact of defeat on my bruised and blood-stained features I eschew the intrusion of such rather abstracted, fuzzy and negative (?) thoughts. I'm resigned to feeling frustrated with my somewhat lacklustre performance and I become increasingly agitated by my surroundings. By way of reasserting some kind of control over my current predicament my thoughts prioritise a concern along the lines of *'let's get paid and let's get out of here…'*

The 'doc' appears in my line of vision and proceeds to inspect the injury. Over the years I have heard many yarns of doctors subsumed in the hospitality on offer barely able to stand let alone focus on the intricate job of inserting stitches into someone's (my) eyebrow. I fix into his gaze in the hope that a study of assiduous concentration will be reflected back. To my relief his focus is clear and he skilfully executes the job at hand. Six stitches later 'doc' advises me on the appropriate course of care and paternalistically bids me farewell…

Having retreated from centre-stage to the solitude of the changing rooms, the gloom of defeat hangs in the air. Peering at my bruised and still flesh-raw eyebrow 'Jim' (my Manager) breaks the silence to quip, *"You should have had that…you deserved a draw at least. He never got near you apart from the early rounds. Perhaps if you had not done the spaghetti dance the judges would have given you the nod! Never mind I will be able to match you with less bother for the next one. He were a good lad you know, threw bombs and did his bit with the head, lots of experience. Anyway, let's get paid!"* While counting the wad of cash passed on to me in a brown envelope, my mind once again drifts into analytical (self)enquiry, *'what have I just experienced and how does this emotionally perceived and physically felt lived experience relate to the still rather fuzzy wider frames of reference which, I'm led to believe, will offer sociological coherence?'* The immediacy of boxing reality effortlessly takes precedence once again, however, and I become absorbed by the conversation at hand, *"I found the eight-round distance no bother really, especially after I found my rhythm. Quite honestly, as a technician he wasn't that good. Most of the boys I fought in the amateur ranks were far sharper. He was a tough cookie though, strong as an ox and had real power..."*

It was in the early hours of the morning when I was finally driving back along the motorway, homebound. I dropped 'Coach' off at his house so he could get at least a couple of hours sleep before getting back on the motorway again to do a day's work *"laying bricks on a posh estate just North of London"*. In a subdued mood he bade me farewell and scarred eyebrows frowning ruminated, *"another day another dollar I guess son, eh? I'll see you back at the gym..."* Customarily I found it impossible to sleep immediately post-contest so I stayed up all night replaying the video recording of 'the fight' with the commentary on and then off, thinking and analysing. Next morning I opted for different scenery and drove to the nearby cathedral town of St Albans. Strolling through the centre of this historically picturesque and affluent social landscape I tried to ignore the inquisitive (or were they horrified?) stares directed at the 'marks of battle' stitched into my bruised features from passers-by, before settling for a quiet and less public spot in a local cafe. With critical scrutiny in mind I made a record of the recent experiences gained in and through the professional boxing 'fight game'...

(Fieldnotes [amended] December 2000)

Fieldwork embodied

What had just transpired and was later recorded in written form as data was my insider experience in, and subjective understanding of, the patterns of meaning defining the social interactions and practices through which the culture of 'pro' boxing is (re)produced in its modern-day incarnation. My authorial voice clearly demonstrates the ethnographer to be a breathing, sentient and visceral research instrument unavoidably influencing knowledge production and its representation. Having experienced, by way of embodiment, the 'realities' of professional boxing as described above I was in a position to gauge the sensual, symbolic and emotional dimensions shared by professional boxing-practitioners in time and through space. As Amanda Coffey (1999) asserts, fieldwork is necessarily an embodied activity: "our body and the bodies of others are central to the practical accomplishment of fieldwork" (p. 59). Fieldwork experiences are as such unavoidably lived by and experienced through bodies and thus, as participant members, researchers' scholarly endeavours cannot be divorced from the necessarily subjective and visceral reality of 'being' in the field (Coffey, 1999; Madden, 2010). For ethnographic research within sporting and physical activity cultural worlds in particular, the competence of bodies – their physicality, positioning, visibility, status and performance – are readily apparent as not only material and observable entities but also symbolic, interactional and intersubjective signifiers necessary for negotiating the spatial and cultural contexts of those particular fields.

If ethnographies are bodily and intellectual enterprises, therefore, there is recognition that given interpretations of culture are unavoidably constructs of human choice, desire, capability and/or comprehension as to what, whom and how to investigate particular facets of social life. The act of acquiring embodied cultural insight is thus openly acknowledged as being inherently biased, be it from the researchers' biographical subjectivity, the social relationships established throughout the research process, the nature of the actions experienced, or the adoption and interpretation of various theoretical standpoints through which to make analytic judgments.

As a self-defined 'real' boxer I beheld an awareness of the game that was defined through my ability to recall or incite memory of personal experience. As Collins (2010) argues, the ethnographer's self and his/her memory are centrally involved in all human interaction and so cannot be excluded from one small part of it; that is fieldwork. As such, my understandings of boxing as experienced and observed within the field and shared among other boxing-practitioners were implicated in the processes of my multiple, socially embedded and emergent biographic-self who has learned, become, experienced, remembered and, in fact, forgotten (Coleman, 2010). Furthermore, following Spry (2001), such biographically situated insider boxing impressions were embodied, that is, felt directly rather than understood cognitively (see Collins & Gallinat, 2010, p. 12).

Insider (mis)understandings

Immediately after my losing contest narrated above I was happy to declare boxing as my sport of choice, one that I felt proud to be associated with. Even so, it is not difficult to discern the felt and sensed contradictions, tensions and ambiguities informing my subjective voice. Although at that time barely conscious of this, I was crafting a scholarly worldview that, over time, allowed me to locate my socialisation in and through boxing and wider society within theoretical and philosophical discussions about the nature of knowledge and consequent representations of reality made by ethnographic researchers – what has been referred to as the 'double crisis' of legitimation and representation (see Brewer, 2000; Denzin & Lincoln, 2003; Hammersley & Atkinson, 2007). For insider sport and physical activity ethnographers in particular, the very real concern is that because of socialisation into and through a given sporting code they will fail to recognise, or perhaps even refuse to honestly acknowledge, in analytical terms, the rather less enchanting, overly (self)cherished and/or self-serving understandings and workings of the culture investigated (O'Reilly, 2009). For instance, when contemplating Joyce Carol Oates's (1987) observation that, "Impoverished people prostitute themselves in ways available to them, and boxing offers an opportunity for men to make a living of a kind" (p. 34), I shook my head in disbelief at the comparison of boxing with prostitution – 'What is she on? How can anyone not declare boxing the one sport that all other sports aspire to be?' Equally, I stubbornly rejected the dominant discourse that boxing was somehow an affliction of societies divided by privilege and dispossession, wealth and poverty (Sugden, 1996; Wacquant, 2004; Woodward, 2008). Nonetheless, as I peered into the mirror wondering how visible my newly acquired scar tissue was likely to be, at that fleeting instance, it was difficult to claim a sense of fulfilment and empowerment from my most recent episode with the 'Noble Art'. The internal dialogue of the meanings I and other professional boxers attached to our 'chosen' athletic identities, behaviours and relationships, took another turn. As I came to realise, this formative ethnographic process manifested feelings, impulses and ideas through which I was *forced* to objectify the field. In essence, I was, at least partially, becoming reflexively detached from the life-word forces defining my ethnographic presence in the field as a 'real' boxer. Moreover, I grew to better acknowledge my own ontological complicity – as a heterosexual male of Anglo-Greek heritage embarking on intellectual discovery among predominantly working-class social actors – in assuming a somehow privileged insider vantage of examination to make sense of my own and other boxing-practitioners' realities. In particular, the embodied tension subjected *upon* and *within* my ethnographic-self indicated the contingent nature of the, albeit co-produced, processes of ethnographic interaction and knowledge production. This 'interrogation of situadedness' (Woodward, 2008 p. 547) – although for much of my research journey only implicitly felt and sensed rather than logically deduced – enabled me to both reflect upon the partial nature of knowledge that emerged from my recorded fieldnotes and interviews and, in turn, situate such knowledge as being grounded in complex social and cultural factors related to the sport ethic, commercialization, gender ideology and social class. This process of (self)discovery was intellectually disorientating, emotionally draining, physically numbing and symbolically disenchanting.

'The boxer' in crisis

The analytical mind-set adopted (of a critical disposition) imposed what felt like an 'objective' force impeding my 'subjective' desire to 'go at it'. As time wore on I (as 'the professional boxer') became increasingly disgruntled and, rather more tellingly, harboured a nagging intuition that *'this just does not feel right'*. When doing my 'road work' in the early hours of the day while the rest of the world slept, it was usual for fresh ideas and thoughts assimilated during an uninhibited sleep-state to converge in floods as I listened to the music playing on my personal stereo. The 'pro' boxer met the fledgling academic, in this sense, in a bid to conceptualise and contextualise 'objective' understandings of boxing as an athletic experience and as a social practice. What are the differences between 'amateur' and 'professional' boxing? Do I feel different when shadowboxing in a 'pro' gymnasium? If so, why is this? Should I do 'it' (i.e. boxing and my research) this way, act in such a way or even allow myself to think such thoughts? How do other boxers perceive their own actions, interpret my actions and understand this or that value orientation, relationship or practice? Is my identity as 'the boxer' perceived to be mutual among other professional boxing practitioners, as a mutual-outsider with perhaps a degree of status, or in fact merely a 'dreamer who's got no chance'? Is boxing really the sporting equivalent of prostitution? Am I simply inventing academic absurdities and contemplating too much?

As the research journey evolved I lost much of my appetite for training and in a 'burned-out' manner steadily retreated from the rigours of competitive professional boxing. In what felt at that time like 'paralysis by analysis' my motivation to train with the verve and dedication I had cultivated over many years steadily declined. As I lurched into a kind of apathetic rendition of my previous 'boxer-self', I increasingly entertained doubts when estimating the intentions of those round me while questioning cultural truths and moral codes of boxing per se. When overhearing the sentiments of a world-renowned champion professional boxer while shaking his head wearily with an air of resignation in the changing room of a London gymnasium that, "I'm just sick and tired of being punched on all the time...too much give and take mate...too much give and take...boom-boom, day in, day out...[grinning wearily]...I need to chill out and return to normality...", I too had begun to acknowledge, 'logically' perceive and thus question the brutal physicality and emotional labour of boxing training and competition. As time wore on, I perceived boxing from a somewhat detached and disembodied standpoint rather than that of a focused and necessarily self-centred athlete submerged in the viscerally fuelled tunnel-vision of 'real' boxing competition. Following Ellis and Bochner (2000), I had come to more readily acknowledge the multiple layers of boxing reality that, like many of the boxers I had cast my insider analytical gaze upon, included somewhat veiled yet ever-present impulses towards vulnerability and value conflict.

This process of identity transformation was physically and emotionally draining yet vital for, in the first instance seeing, and thereafter evaluating, the cultural dimensions informing my own and other boxers' interpretative logic. With the benefit of hindsight some years on from that period I can see that the life forces fuelling my identity as the boxer had been torn asunder as I steadily succumbed to the inevitably introspective and physically passive library-based musings demanded of ethnographic scholarship. As I delved deeper into academic enquiry, I re-evaluated my own symbolic attachment to the 'pro' code and as such viewed afresh the truths upheld among other boxing-practitioners. By doing so, I was forced to cast a critical outlook upon the cultural norms, rituals and values through which I had forged relationships and value attachments through the practice of boxing. Over the five-year period of ethnographic fieldwork the symbolic heroism through which I enchanted my own and other boxing-practitioners' boxer-identities was dulled and I lost much of my appetite for the 'real thing' – competing as a professional boxer. Boxing-practitioners compare the process leading towards retirement from competitive boxing to the withdrawal a heroin addict is subjected to (Wacquant, 2004) – the disorientating uncertainty of this experience cannot be over-emphasised. Nonetheless, by having persisted with the research to eventually documenting the embodied processes leading to my identity transformation it became possible to begin to perceive the layers of reflexivity informing old truths held and new academic vistas emerging. This process of identity and consciousness transformation can be understood as ethnographically 'being' and 'becoming' culturally sensitised to the patterns of the social world engulfing us, which have profound implications on how we create order and meaning to our lives (Ballantine & Roberts, 2010).

Going academic

As the research journey evolved, try as I could, my endeavours to formulate somehow precise and fully theorised 'findings' were at best haphazard. Moreover, for much of the five-year period of fieldwork I agonised at my inability to formulate understandings that appeared to be coherent enough to contribute to the existing pool of academic knowledge. As I grappled with various methodological debates and theoretical stances to guide my library-based musings on boxing as experienced 'out there', in the 'real' world. Van Maanen's insightful observation resonated with my own experience and as such proved an unexpected source of comfort:

> Without mentors or cohorts, our appreciation and understanding of ethnography comes like a mist that creeps slowly over us while in the library and lingers with us while in the field. This lack of tutoring is perhaps most telling at that still point in our studies when we have returned from the field and sit before the blank page that must eventually carry the story of what we have presumably learned. Aid, comfort, and confidence may be difficult to come by at this lonely and sometimes terrible stage.
>
> (Van Maanen, 2011, p. xvi)

With little ethnographic foresight, intuition and expertise to draw upon, the embodied tension I experienced as 'the boxer' conducting fieldwork persisted. Following years of such messy fieldwork, and when sitting in the rather more reclusive environ of the library, I grew to appreciate that this tension experienced as a way of life during the research journey was not a problem that needed resolving, but rather it became a productive force I had to learn to confront (Madden, 2010). Over much time I realised that the embodied tension had, in fact, informed my evolving awareness of both the field and the dialogue with existing literature. The realities of achieving such an esoteric and reflexive awareness to (potentially) awaken and enhance cultural interpretation and analysis is, however, far from a straightforward and somehow linear journey of (self)discovery leading to progressive enlightenment (as I hope has been demonstrated in this discussion). Following Coffey (1999), acknowledging that the self lies at the heart of any given ethnographic enterprise reciprocally entails the recognition that insider cultural interpretations are crafted in response to the interactional processes enacted and role identities negotiated, accomplished and contested between researcher and researched and between researcher and her reflexive grapple with the literature. The realities of ethnography are such that a researcher's insider or outsider status cannot ever be (self)defined in static and somehow essentialist terms. Rather, it must be recognised that the ethnographic-self is reflexively and dynamically crafted in response to the web of interactional and often contingent processes that, it should never be forgotten, take place both within and beyond the research field (including the academic field).

The final round ... confessions and insider impressions

Having retreated from the field to write up the final representation of my 'findings', and fully aware of impending deadlines I was expected to meet by my academic paymasters, the feeling of disorientation as to how I was supposed to convey the cultural dimensions experienced and understood – as much through sensed, felt and emotionally conceived embodied intuition and tension as by logico-deductive reflection – persisted. My lingering suspicion was that academic convention insisted that I articulate a final representation of knowledge through demonstrating the capacity to coherently write 'about' the boxing fields examined through linearly structured and authoritative prose. I did this as I could, choosing to instil my 'In the Field' chapter – an essentially descriptive account of data collection methods and procedures – in the appendices of the thesis, mindful of the necessity to provide some proof that the ethnography had, in fact, been undertaken with the necessary rigour.

The thesis and I were examined. Upon receiving mainly positive remarks regarding my ethnographic thick descriptions, I was urged to consider repositioning my methodological discussion more prominently in the thesis structure. Left pondering as to what my two examiners could see in regard to my methodology that could add value to both my research and my competence as a researcher/academic, I re-engaged the literature. In due course I adopted a rhetorical convention referred to as the 'confessional' (Sparkes, 2002; Van Maanen, 2011). Rather than pursuing an "...author-evacuated and methodologically silent" (Sparkes, 2002, p. 57) representational style to write about the research, the confessional makes explicit the research process from start to finish. The intention is to be open about the messy and problematic experience of fieldwork and bring to the fore the many methodological and ethical dilemmas encountered. By foregrounding the relations "...between the author, the object of analysis and the final constructed text" (Wheaton, 2002, p. 249), the tension-fuelled procedures of data collection and analysis become in themselves topics of research. Moreover, as Sparkes (2002) points out, by recording the perils and pitfalls of the research experience as a hermeneutic process, the community of sport scholars benefits through raising, "...a host of ethical and methodological questions about the basis of ethnographic authority – how we come to know about ourselves and others via our research activities" (p. 71). Of course, from a more pragmatic standpoint, the research experience documented in this way may also provide the basis for relevant guidance for future research (Fleming, 1992).

So, rather than 'writing about' the field of inquiry, as best I could, I attempted to account for the tension and unanticipated consequences reflexively experienced throughout the research journey. Consequently I am, as 'the boxer' and 'the researcher', "...written into, and not out of, the text" (Sparkes, 2002, p. 17). As Ellis and Bochner (2000) remark, the fieldwork tales written for final readership make explicit the inevitable conversations that have taken place with ourselves as we struggled to make sense of our ethnographic experiences and inevitably changed over time as a consequence. By doing so, the multiple and often uncertain and emotionally conflictual layers of social and cultural experience may be acknowledged and ultimately accounted for as a constituent force defining and informing the final ethnographic representations. Following Sugden and Tomlinson (2002), I argue that my ethnographic (self)representations of boxing-practitioners' cultural practices can be understood as being analogous to the representations of reality conveyed through impressionistic art:

> The impressionist painting...is constructed over time and incorporates the various dimensions of the artist's gaze and what is known about the places and people that are painted. It also leaves room for interpretation by those who view the work in the gallery. Thus, what is produced is not reality per se, but an informed *impression* of that reality. The artist then offers the painting for public appraisal, acclaim or ridicule, implicitly challenging other artists to depict the chosen scene differently (p. 18).

Much like an impressionist painter's canvas, my ethnographic journey into and through the world of professional boxing is conveyed with a sense of lived and necessarily subjective texture that seeks to openly and honestly convey both the embodied and intellectual tensions through which cultural (self)discovery was arrived at, both within the field and beyond. The appraisal of the always messy, disorientating and fundamentally life-changing methodological praxis on offer can then be publicly acclaimed or ridiculed. Either way, the potential is there to creatively engage with, and account for, the inevitable tension of being 'inside-out' in the field and thus subsequently learn about, and offer interpretations of, sport and physical activity cultures and experiences with a touch more nuance, if not much more.

References

Andrews, D., Mason, D., & Silk, M. (2005). *Qualitative methods in sports studies.* Oxford and New York: Berg.

Atkinson, M. (2012).The empirical strikes back: Doing realist ethnography. In K. Young & M. Atkinson (Eds), *Qualitative research on sport and physical culture* (pp. 23–50). Bingley: Emerald.

Ballantine, J.A. & Roberts, K.A. (2010). *Our social world: Introduction to sociology* (3rd edition). London: Sage.

Brewer, J.D. (2000). *Ethnography.* Buckingham: Open University Press.

Coffey, A. (1999). *The ethnographic self: Fieldwork and the representation of identity.* London: Sage.

Coleman, S. (2010). On remembering and forgetting in writing and fieldwork. In P. Collins & A. Gallinat (Eds), *The ethnographic self as resource: Writing memory and experience into ethnography* (pp. 215–227). Oxford: Bergham Books.

Collins, P. (2010). The ethnograpic self as a resource? In P. Collins & A. Gallinat (Eds), *The ethnographic self as resource: Writing memory and experience into ethnography* (pp. 228–245). New York / Oxford: Bergham Books.

Collins, P., & Gallinat, A. (Eds) (2010). *The ethnographic self as resource: Writing memory and experience into ethnography.* Oxford: Bergham Books.

Davida, D. (2012). *Fields in motion: Ethnography in the worlds of dance.* Waterloo, ON: Wilfrid Laurier University Press.

DeGaris, L. (1999). Experiments in pro wrestling: Toward a performative and sensuous sport ethnography. *Sociology of Sport Journal, 16,* 65–74.

Denzin, N.K., & Lincoln, Y.S. (2003). *The landscape of qualitative research: Theories and issues.* London: Sage.

Ellis, C., & Bochner, A.P. (2000). Autoethnography, personal narrative, reflexivity: Researcher as subject. In N. Denzin & Y. Lincoln (Eds), *Handbook of qualitative research* (2nd edition) (pp. 733–768). London: Sage.

Fleming, S. (1992). *Sport and South Asian male youth* (Unpublished PhD Dissertation). University of Brighton, Brighton, UK.

Hammersley, M., & Atkinson, P. (2007). *Ethnography: Principles in practice* (3rd edition). London: Routledge.

Madden, R. (2010). *Being ethnographic: A guide to the theory and practice of ethnography.* London: Sage.

Oates, J.C. (1987). *On boxing.* New York: Harper Collins.

O'Reilly, K. (2009). *Key concepts in ethnography.* London: Sage.

Smith, A., & Waddington, I. (Eds) (2014). *Doing real world research in sports studies.* London: Routledge.

Sparkes, A. (2002). *Telling tales in sport and physical activity: A qualitative journey.* Champaign IL: Human Kinetics.

Spry, T. (2001). Performing autoethnography: An embodied methodological praxis. *Qualitative Inquiry, 7*(6), 706–732.

Stewart, A. (2008). *From the boxer's point of view: A study of cultural production and athletic development among amateur and professional boxers in England* (Unpublished PhD dissertation). University of Luton, Luton, UK.

Sugden, J. (1996). *Boxing and society: An international analysis.* Manchester, UK: Manchester University Press.

Sugden, J., & Tomlinson, A. (Eds) (2002). *Power games: A critical sociology of sport.* London: Routledge.

Van Maanen, J. (2011). *Tales of the field: On writing ethnography* (2nd edition). Chicago: University of Chicago Press.

Wacquant, L. (2004). *Body and soul: Notebooks of an apprentice boxer.* Oxford: Oxford University Press.

Wheaton, B. (2002). Babes on the beach, women in the surf: Researching gender, power and difference in the windsurfing culture. In J. Sugden & A. Tomlinson (Eds), *Power games: A critical sociology of sport* (pp. 240–266). London: Routledge.

Williams, R. (1977). *Marxism and literature.* Oxford: University of Oxford Press.

Willis, P. (2000). *The ethnographic imagination.* Cambridge: Polity.

Woodward, K (2007). *Boxing, masculinity and identity.* London: Routledge

Woodward, K. (2008). Hanging out and hanging about: Insider/outsider research in the sport of boxing. *Ethnography, 9*, 536–560.

Young, K. & Atkinson, M. (2012). *Qualitative research on sport and physical culture.* Bingley: Emerald.

Chapter 9

Considering micropolitical (under)'currents'

Reflections on fieldwork within an elite men's rowing programme

Laura G. Purdy

Journal entry

Jake stood up and pointed me out in the group, "She's here." I froze. Everyone looked at me. I felt my face heat up so I quickly turned my gaze towards the floor. I had worked so hard to show them that I was not a threat and I thought that things were going well, but Jake's comment suggested otherwise. By reminding people of my role as a researcher, will they change their behaviour, will they guard their comments? Could Jake's comment undo all the work that I have done to make people more comfortable with the study?... I felt sick... Worst case scenario, people change their behaviour and we start building the rapport again, but is there enough time remaining in the programme to do that? If not, do I have enough data to complete the PhD?...

Increasing accountability of academics to produce research that will be favourably judged in respect to national audits of research quality has led researchers to consider more carefully what and who will be investigated and in what context this investigation will take place (Craig, Amernic & Tourish, 2014; Sparkes, 2013). Indeed, identifying and gaining access to a particular setting may, increasingly, have a variety of political ramifications to the researcher, but the fieldwork itself may be used by participants to further or protect their own interests or agendas. As such, it is also worth acknowledging the strategies researchers employ to advance their positions in the research setting in an effort to achieve richer data. In doing so, a micropolitical reading of the varying and/or inconsistent motivations, goals and interests of the researcher and participants could aid novice fieldworkers in better comprehending the nature of the situations that they encounter and a more nuanced understanding of the 'social terrain' of practice (Kelchtermans & Ballet, 2002; Thompson, Potrac & Jones, 2014).

The purpose of this chapter, then, is to draw attention to the micro-political nature of ethnographic research. In particular, this chapter focuses on my work on an elite men's rowing training programme. The data, as evidenced in the excerpt above, are primarily sourced from the reflexive journal[1] I kept over the course of my fieldwork including fieldnotes relating to observations, encounters and conversations, and more personal notes relating to my thoughts, feelings about the experience and the research process. The data were read through a micropolitical lens, with micropolitics broadly understood as the use of power by individuals or groups to pursue their interests in an organisation (Blase, 1991; Hoyle 1982). In this chapter, I draw upon work from education, specifically Kelchtermans and Ballet's (2002) notion of micropolitical literacy, to make sense of my fieldwork experience. This approach was appealing as it focused on the early career experiences of teachers in a new context and their readings of and reactions to the micropolitical landscape in which they worked. Certainly, parallels can be drawn to my experience as a novice to fieldwork and how I became aware of, reacted to, and learned to read the micropolitical landscape of fieldwork. To do so, I have organised the chapter as follows: to begin, I briefly outline my theoretical framework and provide background to the study; the subsequent section includes excerpts from my reflexive journal and discussion in light of the theoretical framework. Similar to Kelchtermans (2009) and Denzin (1989), the data is then organised in light of the critical incidents, phases and people which/who drew my attention to micropolitical activities within the field. I then reflect upon the experience in light of how it prepared me for future projects and conclude by reviewing the main arguments.

Making sense of my experience: theoretical framework

According to Kelchtermans and Ballet (2002), all teachers have beliefs about the working conditions (i.e. material and relational), also known as professional interests, which will best enable them to undertake their professional activities. Teachers attempt to create, and protect, these desired working conditions if/ when they are threatened and re-establish them if/when they are removed (Kelchtermans & Ballet, 2002). Central to these desired working conditions are people's understandings of their professional selves which include their beliefs about themselves as teachers, their professional self-esteem and task perceptions. To clarify, a teacher's professional self-esteem refers to the individual's appreciation of his/her job performance with a positive self-esteem being viewed as fundamental in beginning teachers' identity politics (Kelchtermans & Ballet, 2002, p. 111). Closely linked to self-esteem are self-image and task perception. Here, self-image refers to how individuals typify themselves as teachers (Kelchtermans, 2009). This self-image is strongly influenced by how the teacher is perceived by others as well as the teacher's task perception: essentially, his/her idea of the tasks and duties that constitute doing a 'good job' (Kelchtermans, 2009). As such, professional self-esteem, self-image and task perception are prominent in a person's interpretive framework.

In the process of creating, protecting and re-establishing these desired working conditions, if teachers' identities, professional self-esteem or task perceptions are threatened by their working context, self-interests emerge (Kelchtermans & Ballet, 2002). This increase in self-interests may result in micropolitical activity such as individuals seeking self-affirmation, coping with feelings of vulnerability and striving for visibility in the job (Kelchtermans & Ballet, 2002). The latter point is particularly important as being recognised by significant others within the workplace has been identified as an essential source of beginning teachers' positive self-esteem (Kelchtermans & Ballet, 2002).

Similar to beginning, researchers enter the field with the agenda of generating rich data will have beliefs about the task that will be undertaken and the conditions (i.e. material and relational) which will best enable him/her to undertake his/her professional activities. Should the working conditions challenge the researcher's expectations, identity, professional self-esteem or task perceptions, self-interests emerge. Upon the emergence of self-interests, the researcher may respond by employing strategies to protect or enhance his/her working conditions in an effort to collect data. Some of these strategies are outlined in the subsequent sections.

Background to the study

The study was undertaken to fulfil the requirements of a PhD. To do so, I received a scholarship which enabled me to relocate from Canada to pursue my studies in New Zealand. With limited, but manageable funding and a visa which was dependent upon student status, there was an omnipresent pressure to keep my doctoral work to a reasonable timeline (i.e. 3–4 years). Prior to the start of this project, I had some experience with data collection (from undergraduate and MSc studies), but little experience with ethnography. Consequently, I was entering the field not only feeling pressure to 'find' interesting data, but my lack of experience made me uncertain about the process and unsure of my professional (research) self.

The aim of the project I was undertaking was to explore the climate of an elite men's rowing programme and the participants' (i.e. coaches, athletes and administrators) interpretation of this climate. Specifically, I wanted to study the factors/influences which were perceived to enable and/or constrain the development of a productive climate. For the purpose of this project, climate was viewed as the result of the interaction between the coach, athletes and environment: that which both influences and 'houses' coaching. To achieve this, I relied upon ethnographic methods (e.g. interviews, observations and note taking) to acquire a 'thick description' (Geertz, 1973) of the behaviour of the administrators, coaches and athletes in the programme and, more importantly, how such behaviour was interpreted by these constituent parties. This involved spending five months in the field as a participant-observer during the participants' preparation for selection trials to upcoming significant international competitions.

Fifteen participants were involved in the programme. The coaching and administration team (i.e. coaches, administrators and athletes) was comprised of a programme coordinator, two full-time coaches and two technical experts. The ten athletes involved in the programme ranged in experience from this being their first experience with the elite level to those who had been involved for several international campaigns. Training sessions were held on a minimum of five days a week, comprising between one and three training sessions per day and racing on weekends. When the athletes trained in the eight (i.e. a boat comprising eight rowers), I served as coxswain (i.e. a person who, located in the boat, directs the crew). I attended meetings between the administrators and coaches, coaches and athletes, athletes and administrators. I observed the athletes' sessions with the sport psychologist and bio-mechanists and was present or participated in regattas attended by the crew. Outside of the training environment, I assisted administrators, coaches and athletes with various jobs which provided an ideal opportunity to discuss their feelings about the programme.

A critical incident: a rocky start

Given that the fieldwork would be undertaken in a high-performance programme, one of the main issues to consider early in the development of the project was that of access. Because the competitive nature of high-performance programmes and the related financial investment would make the context sensitive and restrictive (Kelly, 2008; Lyle, 1999; Treadwell, 1986), there was no guarantee that I would gain access to the environment. As the project took shape, I sought official permission from the highest levels of the organisation, who, to my surprise, quickly approved it. Nearer to my entry into the field I visited the organisation and provided prospective participants with information about the study. Everyone seemed happy and keen to be involved. However, unbeknownst to me, during the few months that had passed between my initial request and entering the field for the data collection, the structure of the organisation had changed. Those who had approved my project were no longer involved in the organisation and new coaches, athletes and administrators who were unaware of the project had been introduced to the programme while those who had agreed to be involved were released. Unaware of these changes in personnel, I assumed that all parties were aware of the project and were happy for me to enter the field. This, however, was not the case. Prior to relocating to my new environment, I realised that things were not going to be as seamless as I had hoped and, for my study to be a success, I was going to need to quickly learn, and respond to, the micropolitical landscape of the context and how to 'write' myself into it.

Journal entry

Where do I begin? The people who had approved the project are no longer involved in the organisation. BIG PROBLEM. Now I don't know if they approved the project knowing that they would not be involved or if they genuinely didn't know that their time in the organisation was limited. The ones who are currently running the show knew nothing about the project and are a bit worried, however, on a positive note, they do feel as though they need to know more (re: project) and haven't shut it down yet. I found this out because one of the administrators (John) who works part-time with the programme phoned my supervisor. He seems really angry about the project. I feel terrible because it is partly my fault. I should have made sure that the organisation had informed all stakeholders or should have checked to see that the same people were involved. Anyway, he has told the coaches that I am evaluating them (even though I'm not) which has concerned some. I feel sick – my stomach is turning and I can't concentrate. I don't know what to do. I should have known better and covered my basis more securely than I did. #learningcurve. I spoke to my supervisor and we got advice from the university about an embargo which will clearly outline the terms of my involvement and the data that can be published. This might make the organisation feel a bit more comfortable, but what if they still say no? What will I do? I can't think about it without panicking. I may need to start over, but then I won't meet the deadline for my scholarship and my current student debt will be doubled with the cost of international fees. This is a major reality check, there's a chance that the project may be over before it even begins...

Journal entry

Things are moving fast, which is good. There's no time to be waiting around. The programme formally starts in a couple of days. I think the possibility of an embargo has made me more optimistic about the project, but there are no guarantees and that makes me worry.

The BIG meeting was today. I was very nervous. I felt like I was walking into a courtroom to be sentenced for a serious crime I didn't know I had committed. I didn't know how to act or what to say. Only two of the coaches (Dean and Ernie) and John, the administrator, attended. I answered all their questions, clarifying everything. Interesting Dean was the one who talked most. Perhaps John stirred up the concerns, but these were not shared? He kept asking me questions like 'where do I locate myself in this study?', 'which paradigm?' and telling me that my methodology was limiting. Ernie was concerned with how he could coach 'properly' if I was around, so he seemed to support John, but I don't think Dean did (he could be an ally!). At the end of the meeting, when we were outlining the 'rules' around the data collection, I made it clear that I would need to be present as much as possible, to get a real sense of the experience. I mentioned this might make participants feel more comfortable as opposed to me dropping in and out, I'd be able to see consistencies rather than focusing on a 'bad' day. Dean agreed and said that would be the best approach as "the more you are here, the less you are noticed". I told them I was happy to help the organisation out as much as possible – they liked that as they wanted something in return. We agreed the terms of the embargo which not only put restrictions on what data could be published but also the timeframe around it; subsequently I got all participation. Phew. What a relief – I now feel like I am walking on clouds! I am not really sure what this will mean for my future as I won't be able to publish as much or as quickly, but the clock is ticking and I can't afford (time and $$$) to start a new project. This might work out in my favour though as it shows that I won't settle for an easy option, however universities want publications and I'm not sure that I will be very marketable.

Although the introduction of an embargo alleviated many of the participants' initial concerns, John's discontent still bothered me. John was not a fan of the study and, as he was more established in the programme, I wondered if he would encourage the others to stop the project. However, the meeting revealed a potential ally in Dean, suggesting that not everyone shared John's views. As such, I knew that my project was not over yet, but I would need to pursue a course of action that could advance my position in the setting (Ball, 1987). To be successful, I would need to gain the strong support of the other participants, making it more difficult for John to turn them against me. In other words, I needed to employ political actions which would allow me to gain social recognition as well as to ensure my new workplace conditions were suitable so that I could undertake a 'good' performance (Kelchtermans, 1996) and generate rich data.

A critical phase with critical people: being seen and feeling vulnerable

As the position of researcher was new (and, for some, controversial) to the programme and its participants, for the first couple of weeks, I concentrated on not 'rocking the boat'. This choice of political strategy was in keeping with my previous experience (Kelchtermans & Ballet, 2002) with the research process and preparatory reading which suggested the less disruption I caused, the less attention I would bring upon myself. Ideally, such an approach would ease the transition and help the participants adjust to and feel more comfortable with my presence. To me, this low profile was important. Given the concerns voiced by John and Ernie in the initial meeting, I could not afford to be viewed as a threat. As such, I tried to be as supportive as possible, reminding participants that I was not there to judge.

Journal entry

Every time Ernie says something when I'm around, he justifies it to me. Despite telling him at the outset of the project that it wasn't my intention, he must still think I'm evaluating him. It was really uncomfortable. I don't want him to worry about having me around, he has enough to worry about in trying to get the boats up to speed. I also don't think I could handle five months of awkwardness. I have to put his mind at ease. This week I've been casually trying to challenge the notion of a 'right' way to coach. I want him to feel more comfortable around me and to know that I am not evaluating him. I think it has worked as today he seemed more open to talking in the coach boat.

Given that the presence of a researcher was novel to the context, it was unsurprising that in the initial stages of the data collection the participants granted me a high degree of visibility. During this time, I witnessed the rowers, coaches, and administrators observing and commenting upon my actions as they tried to "place or locate the ethnographer within their experience" (Hammersley & Atkinson, 1983, p. 77). In essence, I was "working in a fishbowl" (Blase, 1988, p. 135), with the surveillance having consequences on how I adjusted to and made sense of my new role.

Journal entry

My initial idea when entering the field was to downplay the project as much as possible so that people don't feel disrupted or consider it to be a big change in their 'normal' routine. However, the athletes keep asking about the study, so I guess they are trying to make sense of my presence. I think they are surprised (and flattered?) that someone wants to study them. In return, I am trying to 'act' like a researcher by asking questions, conducting formal interviews after the sessions and nodding when they suggest that I should write something down. I am writing everything from descriptions of meeting rooms to conversations I hear! Is that right? It's what we talked about in research methods modules, but is this what it 'looks like' in the field? I don't want to mess this up. It doesn't help that everyone is watching me and I don't really know if I'm doing this right.

My previous experience as a coxswain was crucial at this juncture as I was familiar with the sport and had often raced against several of the participants. This knowledge aided my transition into the field as I was familiar with the people, rules, routines and language of the sport. However, I was entering the field as a researcher, not a coxswain and, consequently, I was unsure of how to behave. To help me settle into my role, I used the participants' feedback to partially inform how I acted. At this point in the project my understanding of my professional self was strongly related to how I was perceived by others (Kelchtermans & Ballet, 2002: Kelchtermans, 2009). Comments such as: *"If training was boring for us today, it must have been worse for you – you had to look interested!" "Where's your notepad? How are you going to remember THAT session?" "Write that [incident] down, it will take up a whole chapter!" "It is nice that you are interested in this but do you actually think this study will change anything?"* helped me better understand their expectations of my position and the project so I wrote my researcher role and script accordingly.

While most participants were supportive of the project and helped me find my way in the field, there were others who I perceived as threats to my position and evoked concern. From the outset of the project, it was apparent that I lacked support from two key players (i.e. John and Ernie) who could stop the study easily. Already uncertain about the fieldwork and concerned about my scholarship and visa, the vulnerable nature of my position added to my anxiety. These feelings were unsurprising as previous work has suggested that when social recognition is threatened, uncertainty and vulnerability result (Kelchtermans, 1996). Remembering the early discussions with the programme team which emphasised that I needed to 'earn my place', and hoping it would help alleviate the vulnerability that I felt, I tried to create a role for myself: baking, cleaning, coaching and cooking at the intensive camps. These acts not only met the organisation's expectations which were outlined at the outset of the study, but also contributed to writing me into the scene in a productive way (Kelchtermans & Ballet, 2002, p. 105).

Journal entry

> Ernie complained that I never go in his coach boat when I make cookies! I've been baking most mornings and today my food was much needed as a 20+km row was on the agenda. The coaches and rowers inhaled the food when we reached the half-way point and it was rated as the highlight of the session (the training we were doing was VERY boring). On another note, Ernie referred to me as the coxswain today!!! That's great because it means I am no longer known as 'the researcher'! I noticed that the guys are treating me 'normally' now (well, how I would be treated at any other rowing club when I am not a 'researcher') and Tito made a similar comment. This morning Chad was (literally) pushing me around.

While assisting with extra tasks helped me become more comfortable in the setting and viewed as less of an outsider, it also helped me to fulfil a micropolitical agenda of being viewed as competent, creative and hardworking

(Kelchtermans & Ballet, 2002). This, I believed, provided me with more security in the context as, given my positive contribution, it would be harder for John or Ernie to accuse me of hindering the programme. Furthermore, assisting also allowed me to "advertise [my] professional competence" (Kelchtermans & Ballet, 2002, p. 113) which not only was advantageous to the stakeholders, but also bolstered my esteem as 'I was being useful' and I was doing a 'good job', thereby achieving the working conditions that I desired. Consequently, I felt more secure and confident as I believed I had gathered data that was of interest given my research questions as well as developed a positive reputation as a researcher. I was also exhausted!

There were times, however, during the data collection when these working conditions were threatened, causing me to "take stock… re-evaluate, revise, resee and rejudge" (Strauss, 1962, p. 65) my position.

Journal entry

> I saw John at the session today and I got nervous. I was very uncomfortable and did not know how to act. While I understand his reasons for raising the issues at the start of the study, I am worried that he is not finished with me yet. Yes, he can always withdraw from the study, but I am still concerned that he will try to convince everyone to drop out. I guess if that happens now it will be okay, not ideal, but workable. It isn't as bad as it was at the start of the project because at least now I have data, but I'd like to see this through to the end. There's some interesting stuff happening and I don't want to walk away yet. Therefore, I pretended nothing had happened and made small talk with him, but tried to avoid him as much as possible. How else am I supposed to handle this?

Although I had worked hard to write myself into the context and felt I now had the support of the athletes and coaches, I was not confident that I had the full support of the organisation. There was still a chance that if John was unhappy with my presence in the programme, the organisation's managers might support him. I responded by undertaking extra efforts to help the organisation. This strategy was based on the positive reaction I had received at the initial stages of the project and the belief that the backing of the organisation would be stronger than any disruption caused by John. To do this, I started to visit the main office, aware that they were understaffed, and offered additional help.

Journal entry

> Between rows I helped the office staff do some data entry. I will see if there is extra work to do so that I can make myself a bit more useful to them. While at the start of the project I was helping to keep my place,

I now feel as though I owe them. They've been so generous to let me stay. It is so hard – I need the data for my PhD, but they need to benefit as well. It's really bugging me. What do other researchers do in these situations? There's no session this afternoon so I'm going to the local university library to read about reciprocity...

While assisting the organisation strongly contributed to the maintenance of my desired working conditions, as my involvement in extra tasks increased, I began to struggle. The extra work was starting to interfere with the time I could have or felt that I *should* have spent in the coach boat. On the other hand, helping out appeared to enhance my security in the context as well as contributed towards my desire for reciprocity.

Journal entry

I have been coaching a secondary school girls' crew as a favour to one of the elite coaches. The coach needed more help with the number of girls interested in the sport, so asked if I would help out. After being in the field for a few weeks, I can appreciate the pressures and workload of these elite coaches so I am happy to help in any way possible. I've been working with a crew between rows or on rest days, however, there's an opportunity to go to an intensive camp and with racing, I'll need to spend more time with them. However, as this happens, I'll also need to be around the boatshed with the elites. I know the girls need a coach and I enjoy working with them, but I feel as though I am getting distracted from my 'real' job. I'm also getting really tired. How can I focus on the fieldwork and also help out – how much is enough???

As mentioned above, as the fieldwork evolved so did my interpretation of the working conditions that would 'best' enable me to meet my professional interests as a researcher. I felt torn between my academic role which necessitated analysing the context for data-collection purposes and my desire to develop a positive standing within the organisation as a volunteer. My reputation with the organisation was very important to me as a bad word about me could ensure I would not have access to similar environments again. I also felt that I 'owed' them. They had granted me access to a context into which very few researchers are allowed and I was grateful. Consequently, I continued to help the organisation which, at the time, I believed might have been to the detriment of the initial data collection. After reflecting on the situation whilst writing this chapter and revisiting the related reflexive journal, I believe that assisting the participants/organisation may not have been as detrimental to the data collection as I had thought. Rather, undertaking various roles offered me new insights into the daily lives/events of the participants and, as such, contributed to the 'thick description' that I intended to construct.

While my micropolitical actions may have helped me achieve more security in the context, similar actions of others (i.e. John) impacted my feelings of insecurity. As mentioned above, these feelings led me to undertake strategies to restore and protect my desired working conditions. I was not alone in my actions. It became apparent that, in addition to John, other participants were also employing micropolitical strategies to achieve their desired ends.

Journal entry

Robert led the talk this morning. We had all gathered in the clubhouse for the pre-race chat. He was going on about the usual race plan but then started to say something unflattering about another rower – my ears perked up, this might be an interesting bit of data!! But before Robert could divulge the information, Jake stood up and pointed me out in the group, "She's here." I froze. Everyone looked at me. I felt my face heat up so I quickly turned my gaze towards the floor. I had worked so hard to show them that I was not a threat: baking cookies, babysitting, helping around the club. I thought that things were going well, but Jake's comment suggested otherwise... I felt sick. I needed these data for my PhD, but by highlighting my presence, by reminding people of my role as a researcher, will they change their behaviour, will they guard their comments? Could Jake's comment undo all the work that I have done? Why didn't he buy into my performance? What have I done wrong? Much to my surprise, Robert carried on, not changing the topic. The rest of the day people seemed to be acting 'normally', so maybe no one took notice of Jake's comment... As I write this I feel guilty. I had entered the programme as a researcher and expected people to have forgotten my initial purpose. More recently I have felt like a member of the group, like I fit in and belong. Perhaps I've been distracted by all of my other roles that I've forgotten my purpose! Arg, what does this say about me as a researcher?!

Due to the short nature of the fieldwork (i.e. five months), I was naïve to believe that the participants had forgotten my main purpose in the programme; however, Jake's revelation still left a sting. Why hadn't Jake bought into my performance? I had worked so hard to 'blend' into the context, but he hadn't forgotten why I was there. How was this possible? As the fieldwork had progressed I had become more confident with my knowledge and skills as a researcher. I thought I was doing a 'good' job, after all, I had plenty of data (i.e. numerous interview transcripts and several thick notebooks filled with observations, notes from informal conversations and personal reflections). I was operating within my desired working conditions. However, Jake's reluctance to engage in the same way as the others challenged my professional self (Kelchtermans & Ballet, 2002). Was I wrong when I thought I had been doing a good job?

I began my final weeks in the field with Jake's outburst playing in my mind. Given the programme was nearing completion, I felt that I did not have time to employ additional strategies that might encourage Jake to 'buy into' my performance. Consequently, I reluctantly accepted his position and, instead, invested my energies with those who were willing to engage in the manner that I desired. Several years after the fieldwork, Jake and I were reminiscing about the project.

Journal entry (after the fieldwork)

I spoke to Jake today – it's been a while since I've seen him. I asked him if he remembered the fieldwork and the events of that season. It surprised me with the amount he could recall. He remembered the session with Robert when he warned him that 'the researcher' was present. I told him that it had been bothering me for ages! He recognised that I had tried very hard to blend in and he recalled my attendance at every session so that my presence wasn't 'out of the norm'. He recalled his reaction to Robert's 'pep' talk. He said he was trying to protect Robert and himself. He didn't want anything (no matter how trivial) or anyone to interfere with his international selection.

The conversation with Jake highlighted that I was not the only one employing strategies to pursue my self-interests; rather, participants were also acting upon their own motivations, goals and interests, which may have conflicted with mine (Kelchtermans & Ballet, 2002). The incident provided a catalyst for me to consider the (in)significance of my influence as a researcher in this context.

What this experience has taught me

In writing this chapter I have had to reflect on my initial experience of fieldwork through the contents of my reflexive journal. During this process, I have been questioning whether I would behave differently if given another opportunity to undertake fieldwork. While the student loan might no longer be a pressing issue, funding pressures have not disappeared nor has the importance of collecting rich data to ensure there are quality publications for various institutional and national research audits. What has improved however, is my micropolitical literacy (i.e. how I read the micropolitical landscape in which I operate and how I write myself into it) (Kelchtermans & Ballet, 2002). As mentioned in the chapter, this was far from a passive process; it was both interactive and interpretive (Kelchtermans & Ballet, 2002). From the outset, I was challenged to consider whether it was 'worth it' to try to conduct fieldwork in a restrictive context knowing that the embargo may affect my 'marketability' as an academic. Consistent with the teachers interviewed by Kelchtermans and Ballet (2002), "getting and keeping a job" (p. 113) was a concern, but I had a few months of my scholarship left before it would be a necessity. It was only until I was faced with resistance from John that I realised that I had been quite naïve to think such a project could be unproblematic and the fieldwork that I had read about did not look like the reality I was experiencing. In response, I drew upon strategies that had worked for me in other contexts to help reduce my vulnerability and create the working conditions that I desired. Helping the organisation and the participants with various tasks inside and outside of the study's context allowed me to 'write' myself into the landscape as well as attain the level of reciprocity that I desired. Additionally, the roles I created also gave me more insight into the context that I was studying as I was able to experience the daily pressures and demands that were placed upon the various stakeholders, adding a new layer to the data collection.

It must be noted that, at the time, I was not sure how to read the landscape in which I was operating; however, upon reflection, it was these interactions and layers that added richness to the project and, I argue, contributed to a more informed, reflexive and insightful approach to subsequent projects. While the project was memorable as it marked my introduction to fieldwork and was important in the development of my self-confidence as a researcher (Kelchtermans & Ballet, 2002), it also prepared me for future projects by highlighting that the research process, particularly the data collection, involves appreciating and navigating various, sometimes conflicting, motivations, ideologies and goals. As such, an appreciation of the micropolitical nature of the research process will be beneficial in preparing for and undertaking future projects as it is these 'hidden' agendas that provide a more nuanced and interesting account of the context and of the research process itself.

Conclusion

The purpose of this chapter was to draw attention to the micropolitical nature of fieldwork. In doing so, I drew upon my, a novice researcher's, reflexive journal which documented my journey in an elite men's rowing programme as I attempted to write myself into the field. Although each fieldwork context is unique and brings to light its own challenges, lessons can be learned from my experience. Far from being a passive process of objectively recording events, I have drawn attention to the strategies I employed to develop and maintain 'security' in the field, fostering relationships that were constantly being negotiated between the participants and myself. As such, the value of this work lies in encouraging a dialogue regarding the micropolitical processes of fieldwork. Such discussions would be of use to encourage novice and experienced researchers to consider their own vulnerability, sensitivities and sensibilities as they embark in the research process as well as to encourage reflection on subsequent wider methodological issues relating to fieldwork.

Sharing our 'realities' of the research process and the emotions inherent in fieldwork encourages us to consider the 'thinking' and 'feeling' aspects of the research process (Campbell, 2002) with the resultant work providing an insightful conduit to knowledge (Lupton, 1998).

Note

1 For ethical reasons, information that might reveal the participants' identities (i.e. names, dates, locations) has been modified or excluded from this chapter.

References

Ball, S.J. (1987). *The micro-politics of the school: Towards a theory of school organization.* London: Methuen.

Blase, J. (1988). The everyday political perspectives of teachers: vulnerability and conservatism. *International Journal of Qualitative Studies in Education, 1*(2), 125–142.

Blase, J. (1991). *The politics of life in schools: Power, conflict and co-operation.* Newbury Park, CA: Sage.

Campbell, R. (2002). *Emotionally involved: The impact of researching rape.* New York: Routledge.

Craig, R., Amernic, J., & Tourish, D. (2014). Perverse audit culture and accountability of the modern public university. *Financial Accountability & Management, 30*(1), 1–24.

Denzin, N. (1989). *Interpretive biography.* Newbury Park, CA: Sage.

Geertz, C. (1973). Thick description: Toward an interpretive theory of culture. In C. Geertz (Ed.), *The interpretation of culture* (pp. 3–30). New York: Basic Books.

Hammersley, M., & Atkinson, P. (1983). *Ethnography: Principles in practice.* New York: Tavistock Publications.

Hoyle, E. (1982). Micro-politics of educational organisations. *Educational Management Administration & Leadership, 10,* 87–98.

Kelchtermans, G. (1996). Teacher vulnerability: Understanding its moral and political roots. *Cambridge Journal of Education, 26*(3), 307–323.

Kelchtermans, G. (2009). Career stories as gateway to understanding teacher development. In M. Bayer, U. Brinkkjaer, H. Plauborg & S. Rolls (Eds.), *Teachers' career trajectories and work lives* (pp. 29–47). London: Springer.

Kelchtermans, G., & Ballet, K. (2002). Micro-political literacy: Reconstructing a neglected dimension in teacher development. *International Journal of Educational Research, 37,* 755–767.

Kelly, S. (2008). Understanding the role of the football manager in Britain and Ireland: A Weberian approach. *European Sport Management Quarterly, 8*(4), 399–419.

Lupton, D. (1998). *The emotional self.* London: Sage.

Lyle, J.W.B. (1999). The coaching process: An overview. In N. Cross & J. Lyle (Eds.), *The coaching process: Principles and practice for sport* (pp. 3–24). Oxford: Butterworth-Heineman.

Sparkes, A.C. (2013). Qualitative research in sport, exercise and health in the era of neoliberalism, audit and New Public Management: understanding the conditions for the (im)possibilities of a new paradigm dialogue. *Qualitative Research in Sport, Exercise and Health, 5*(3), 440–459.

Strauss, A. (1962). Transformations of identity. In A.M. Rose (Ed.), *Human behaviour and social processes: An interactionists approach* (pp. 63–85). London, UK: Routledge & Kegan Paul.

Thompson, A., Potrac, P., & Jones, R.L. (2014). 'I found out the hard way': Micro-political workings in professional football. *Sport, Education and Society.* DOI:10.1 080/13573322.2013.862786.

Treadwell, P.J. (1986). British coaching: How do we begin to move towards a profession? In *Proceedings of the VIII Commonwealth and International Conference on Sport, Physical Education, Dance, Recreation and Health* (pp. 322–327). London: F.N. Spon.

Chapter 10

Reflecting on the 'perils of ethnography'

A case study of football fan rivalry in Birmingham

Adam Benkwitz

In this chapter I offer some reflections on what Sugden (1996) called the "perils of ethnography"; focusing on the challenges faced during my ethnographic study. This is by no means an attempt to discourage researchers from adopting an approach that I have found to be challenging, rewarding, enjoyable and a robust and detailed methodology. Instead, this chapter is a cautionary tale; for whilst ethnographic work is rich, critical and rewarding, it can come at a cost. Extreme examples are the dangers of disease in tropical locations (for instance, Clifford Geertz (1973) catching malaria) or, as Hobbs (2001) lamented, the murder of the sociologist and ethnographer, Ken Pryce, during his extended study of Jamaican organised crime. Subsequent to some initial contextual information on my study of fan rivalry, the following reflections and vignettes aim to both inform the practice of future researchers as well as contribute to the existing empirical transparency that was so beneficial to this study.

Exploring football fan rivalry in Birmingham

Academic literature on fandom, in particular football fandom, has shifted focus in recent decades from 'exceptional' fans to exploring the 'ordinary and everyday' fans and their experiences. In particular, the rivalry-related aspect of football fandom has been given growing attention. Gradually increasing literature has demonstrated that rivalries are unique and complex (Giulianotti, 1999; Thompson, 2001), underpinned by social, historical and/or cultural factors (Armstrong & Giulianotti, 2001). Therefore, each rivalry must be studied in-depth in order to understand the underlying factors which shape oppositions and social identities. One such football fan rivalry that has previously received no academic attention is Aston Villa and Birmingham City, despite these two being the main clubs in Birmingham, England's second largest city, with a long history of intra-city rivalry. Since the first fixture between the two clubs in 1879, a strong, distinct and often violent rivalry has developed, based on its own unique and idiosyncratic social, historical and cultural factors.

Previous literature demonstrated that one of the most effective ways to explore and interpret football fan (sub)cultures has been through ethnography (for example, Armstrong, 1998; Clarke, 2006; Giulianotti, 1995; Hallinan et al., 2007; Weed, 2006). Participant observation was conducted at nineteen football matches involving Aston Villa (known as Villa) and Birmingham City (known as Blues), including matches when the two played each other, as the aim was to observe where the imagined communities (Anderson, 2006) of fans come together and interact. During the fifteen months of the data collection, participant observation was also conducted in other locations, such as bars, restaurants and, when an opportunity presented itself, in fans' homes, in order to further develop a sense of the fans' lived experiences. In addition to participant observation, semi-structured interviews were conducted with twelve fans of both Aston Villa and Birmingham City. Participants were recruited for interviews either during participant observation (the majority were fans that I had struck up a conversation with in the field) or sometimes via 'snowballing' (Giulianotti, 1995). These interviews were interwoven with participant observation, as one of the strengths of ethnography is that the flexibility of the research process enables interviews to provide further insight to and clarification on themes and lived experiences that may have been identified during participant observation (Bryman, 2008).

'Perils of ethnography'

Previous candid accounts based on fieldwork by Klein (1993), Sugden (1996), Bourgois (2002) and Venkatesh (2008) have discussed not only the theoretical underpinnings of ethnography, but also the formal and informal practical aspects of actual self-immersion in a subculture. This chapter builds upon and contributes to this discussion around the "perils of ethnography" (Sugden, 1996) by reflecting on some of the ethical dilemmas and physical risks involved in the fieldwork. This ethnographic project may not have been based in the cut-throat milieu of US ghettos with high rates of crime, neither was I involved in high-speed, high-adrenalin car chases and bloodcurdling shoot-outs (similar to several of the above studies), but there were potentially dangerous episodes in some of the less salubrious parts of Birmingham where personal safety was a genuine concern on several occasions. Sands (2002) drew on Sugden's (1996) experiences to highlight how for an ethnographer it can be a risk to simply step outside of their predictable daily patterns to even a small extent, as being in a different social and political context immediately means their cultural mastery is limited, and, thus, risk is increased. Therefore, the following reflections aim to elucidate some of the challenges relating to physical risks, witnessing illegal acts, and emotional distress, as well as some of the more commonplace difficulties of this approach as experienced by a novice ethnographer.

One night in Small Heath

On one particular night during the fieldwork, when Blues hosted Villa in a League Cup quarter final at St Andrews, I had my first 'real scare'. The following excerpts are taken from fieldnotes:

> Due to fan violence in the preceding years, all league matches between the two clubs are played at midday on Sundays, in order to discourage drinking (and, apparently, therefore violence)... As this was a League Cup match it had to be played during the week so was an evening kick-off, at the start of December, which meant darkness, drinking and a lively atmosphere; on the sort of cold night when you can see your breath in the air...
>
> Tomorrow they are deciding who will host the World Cup in 2018, and the authorities are worried that fan trouble at this match will damage England's bid – so the police are out in force... Despite the overt police presence, there were clashes between rival fans in the city centre before and after the game, as well as in and around the ground...
>
> But it was at the final whistle that things went riot; as hundreds of Birmingham City fans ran onto the pitch towards the Villa supporters. With only a line of police between the fan groups, there was a fifteen-minute spell when missiles, seats, flares, and anything else people could find, were thrown between the fans... Due to being given a complimentary ticket at late notice, I was in the 'away' end amongst the Villa fans (when the two teams play each other I usually just buy a ticket in whichever part of the ground is cheapest). I chose to stay back away from the pitch, as I had already been hit by a coin thrown earlier in the evening. (As I was entering the ground alongside other Villa fans, I felt sudden pressure on the top of my head. It was caused by a coin presumably thrown by a Blues fan. Fortunately, due to the cold weather, I had a thick, woolly hat on which helped the coin bounce off the top of my head without causing any lasting damage. Another fan saw the flying coin, picked it up, handed it to me and said "There you go, mate, you've made 20p".) The police were not allowing any of the Villa fans to leave in order to 'maintain safety'. The irony was that many fans *were* being injured, and also the police between the fans were in danger... Due to the seating allocation in the stadium, there were also Birmingham City fans located in the tier above the Villa fans – which meant that they were also throwing things down onto the away supporters – myself included. A large advertising board landed a matter of feet from me, in addition to a glass tomato ketchup bottle (presumably smuggled into the ground from catering vans outside) landing 'safely' in the aisle...
>
> Eventually the police relented and let the away supporters out... only for us to find that the police had created a holding area by parking police

riot vans close together just outside the away section of the ground. So I was being held amongst hundreds of Villa fans, whilst the rival fans continued to throw things at each other – rocks, bottles and even a mop bucket... In the gaps between the riot vans some rival fans could 'get at' each other, and were quite clearly trading punches, despite the police being in close proximity. One Villa fan was even being pulled back by a police officer holding his left arm, whilst punching a Birmingham City fan with his right arm, before being dragged away and presumably arrested...

I asked one of the police officers (who was standing back away from the vans) 'What is the plan, how are we going to get out of here?', and he replied that he had 'No idea, there's been silence on the radios for a while now'. The police clearly weren't in control, and I was very much concerned for my well-being, so I followed some other fans through a small hole in a fence, scrambling through some mud and then jogged through a housing estate back towards the city centre. Participant observation was important, but given the opportunity I'd have happily left the ground early and watched the trouble on the news later at home... As it turned out, I did get a little bit dirty and a little bit bloody that night, but that was from squeezing through a fence trying to get away!

This match did feel different to others I had attended. I felt wary all evening as there was a palpable tension and animosity in the air from the outset. Thanks to social media, it seemed to be fairly common knowledge that some fans had already clashed in and around the city centre prior to kick-off, which only fuelled the atmosphere further, with a certain inevitability that things would boil over. Whilst it was productive to be at the centre of the fan rivalry, and the fieldnotes, photos and videos that I was able to collect were certainly valuable, I could quite easily have been injured. As suggested by Silk (2005), just because the physical danger may not have been as real as it was perceived, it did not mean that I was prepared for the adrenaline, fear and emotion of the situation.

Having been to many matches between the two sides, and been in the vicinity of plenty of 'trouble', there was undoubtedly something different about this match. Speaking to fans in the days and weeks after the event, they expressed similar views, with some stating that they did not feel that they would go to another derby, as 'it wasn't worth the risk'. So perhaps that particular evening was my 'rite of passage' as an ethnographer. However, it was important to gain this experience and collect data, whilst also being provided with a reminder (not that one was actually needed) of the intensity and hatred involved in this football rivalry, and that I had to constantly reassess how close I wanted to get to the action.

There were also four separate, and similar, occasions at matches when fights broke out within the stadium amongst fans in close proximity to me (which, incidentally, goes against the discourse that football stadiums post-The Taylor

Report (1990) are sanitised and safe). On each occasion the stewards and police were too slow to react, and the culprits escaped by either moving to different seats (with the help of other fans to attempt to conceal them) or by casually exiting the stadium at their leisure. Witnessing ongoing illegal acts presented a further peril to negotiate. I, similar to countless other fans that witnessed each fracas, could have informed the authorities and pointed out those individuals, but to do so would have been against the subcultural rules of the field, and would have opened up the very real possibility of some form of reprisal for being a 'grass' or a 'snitch'. So I remained quiet and carried on making notes for the sake of personal safety.

Being in a situation that was potentially dangerous was something that was anticipated prior to entering the field. However, I had not envisaged witnessing illegal acts on the scale that I did – certainly not in such close proximity. To follow Sugden's (1996, p. 207) advice, the ethical rule of thumb I obeyed here was that "although I witnessed an illegal event, I did not take part in it and, as such, my presence in the field did not contribute to that act". Giulianotti (1995) drew on Albritton's (1991) work to make a similar point; though on reflection it remains a judgement call for the researcher, and there are grey areas. For instance, if there was a genuinely life-threatening situation unfolding, would I stand by and avoid intervening or seeking help from elsewhere? Though I was not faced with that decision, it is recognised that there are situations for which Sugden's simple rule of thumb would not suffice. Nevertheless, there cannot be a clear guide of how to behave in the field. Murphy and Dingwall (2001, p. 342) instead placed emphasis on the "moral sense of the researcher and their ability to make reasoned decisions in the field", rather than seeking a prescriptive code of practice or procedure. With regard to the incidents and confrontations I did witness, they would certainly have occurred without me being in the vicinity, and as I felt that there were copious numbers of police present (a fact that did not seem to bother those fans that were fighting), and no doubt CCTV, the authorities had ample opportunity to follow up on any incidents. Judging by the subsequent media reports, the police did just that, as numerous arrests were made, in addition to several people being hospitalised during these episodes (Kendrick, 2010), but for the fans this appeared to be normal and even quite mundane.

The lowest point

I was also helpless to do anything at another match between Blues and Villa, as missiles were again thrown between rival fans. As a consequence of artillery-like combat tactics, a young girl (probably around thirteen years old) sitting two seats away from me was hit in the face by a coin:

> The scene had become increasingly chaotic and extremely loud, as the rival fans in the corners of the two adjacent stands had seemingly whipped

each other up into a frenzy during the second half, despite nothing in the match itself sparking off any disorder or frustration... As well as hurling abuse, it seemed people were throwing anything that they could get their hands on, though mostly coins and cigarette lighters. I was watching on whilst also trying to cover my face as missiles zipped past me, bouncing off people and seating all around, only to be picked up and launched again in the opposite direction...

Then I saw it happen, a coin bouncing off the girl's face – she immediately put her hand to her eye but she did not scream or shout. It was like she was in shock. Her father did begin shouting; 'Let me see! Let me see!' That's when I was able to take a glimpse at the damage inflicted, as the blood was pouring from around her eye. As the stewards were busy attempting to prevent the troubles, it was not possible to get their attention to come and assist with first aid, despite more and more of us around the girl shouting for help... The father quickly gave up waiting, and the girl's eye was still bleeding as he carried her down the steps and out of the stadium.

I had no way to ascertain whether the girl made a full recovery, and during the course of the participant observation this was the incident that I found most distressing. I found it frustrating and difficult to comprehend that a young girl had gone to watch football with her dad, and left the stadium with a bloody gash over her eye. Sands (2002) is one of the relatively few ethnographers to write extensively on the *emotional* distress and risk of fieldwork (though he focused predominantly on the emotions of being an injured athlete), and whilst this was a difficult incident to reconcile in my mind, it helped me to read the reflections of other ethnographers and realise that I was not alone in finding some aspects of fieldwork emotionally challenging. As Goffman (1989) highlighted, in addition to contributing to the rich accounts of the fieldwork, including the emotions of the ethnographer is beneficial to the overall account as these responses to certain events may well mirror those that occur naturally in the field. Judging from the reactions of many fans around the girl on that particular Sunday match, it seemed like my discomfort and frustration were indeed shared by others. Though this event was ethically problematic, there was no way to envisage that this would have happened, especially, again, with me being in such close proximity, so it is felt that it would have been impossible to safeguard against (certainly at a micro- or inter-personal level). This did not deter me from writing strongly worded letters to both the club (Birmingham City on this occasion) and the West Midlands Police, criticising them for their (mis) handling of the (broader) situation and pleading for further measures to be implemented to ensure fan safety. After many months, I'm still awaiting a response from either...

Perils, or par for the course?

It is also acknowledged that the more practical, commonplace (or mundane) problems with adopting an ethnographic approach that are usually highlighted (see Bryman, 2008; Smith & Caddick, 2012) were certainly evident during this study. Two inter-related benefits of ethnography also provided major challenges in the research process: the time allowed to conduct research and also the flexibility. A criticism of the (albeit, limited) existing research on football fan rivalries is that previous studies lacked a clear and transparent methodological approach (Benkwitz & Molnar, 2012), with little or no evidence of researchers actually engaging with fans and experiencing any rivalry. In Birmingham, the ethnographic study provided time and flexibility to become immersed in the subculture and engage with fans, allowing the research to be led by their thoughts, opinions and experiences. Not only did this enable 'thick description',[1] but the long-term flexible nature facilitated numerous opportunities to gain clarification on significant or contentious issues (Sugden, 1996) that related to the phenomenon or to 'dig deeper' in relation to certain aspects of participants' lived experiences when required (Sands, 2002).

Nevertheless, the time that is actually required for this is extensive. The actual time spent being a participant observer depends on many factors, though in my case it was fifteen months. Then there is the time it takes to write up fieldnotes, then to re-write or 'polish' the fieldnotes into a more coherent format (Emerson et al., 2001), plus (in my case) lengthy tasks of interviewing and transcription (Clarke, 2006); all combined with the painstaking, on-going analysis. Add to that the unexpected (and frustrating) amount of time wasted, for instance, there were two separate occasions when I had spent time recruiting interviewees and then travelled to meet with them only to find that they did not show up and ceased all correspondence, giving no reason or apology. This was seemingly unavoidable, but it led me to try (where possible) to group together a couple of interviews in one day, and combine trips to the stadia or library, in order to reduce the number of 'wasted' journeys. Additionally, as Smith (2001) highlighted, researchers rarely articulate the challenges of how personal life – moving house, change of job, family upheavals and bereavements, financial concerns, and so on – can shape the conduct of the research process, and ultimately impact on either the time spent in the field or the time the whole project takes to complete. Or, certainly in my case, both.

Notwithstanding, to reiterate, it was only by spending this time and having the flexibility to keep returning to the field and interviewing fans that I was able to gain an understanding of the complex and often very subtle interactions involved, as rival fans battled for power in a variety of ways. The flexibility of ethnography enables a study to extend the boundaries and limitations where necessary (Cresswell, 2007). So, for instance, when a fan referred to a particular pub being a 'Blues' pub in an interview, and discussed its significance as part of the fans' match-day ritual and experience, it was then possible to visit the pub on the subsequent Saturday and experience it for myself. Similarly, as the histories of the two clubs emerged as being especially significant for fans (and to the rivalry), the length of the project and the flexibility meant I could explore the historical context further – not only of the clubs, but also the city – by traversing the local libraries and archives and learning more about what the fans felt was important, often on a Saturday morning before later going to a match. So this flexibility of the inductive project led me in different directions, and therefore utilised more of my time and resources; but it was all to benefit the study. Another potential peril linked to spending so much time within a subculture is developing 'over-rapport' with participants (Hammersley & Atkinson, 2007), though it is more commonly known as 'going native' (Armstrong, 1993).

Going native

Whilst it is advantageous to become immersed in these contexts and environments, researchers must remain reflexive and keep a balance between engaging too much or not enough. Ethnographers must guard against the mistake of assuming that 'just being there' actually gives one the opportunity to understand and analyse cultures (Hargreaves & Tomlinson, 1992), as immersion into the field requires us to relinquish our comfortable position on the verandah (Malinowski, 1922) and get close enough to the social actors involved for long periods of time (Emerson et al., 2001) in order to gain a rich, thick description (Geertz, 1973). However, critics of ethnography have argued that researchers may get too close, too immersed in the field and cease to think as academics (Rock, 2001). The researcher is said to lose sight of their position as a researcher and "therefore find it difficult to develop a social scientific angle on the collection and analysis of data" (Bryman, 2008, p. 412). Consequently, it is the ethnographer's task to embrace this sensitive balancing act to get close enough to the action without ever being totally incorporated within it and thereby losing sight of their own position (Sugden & Tomlinson, 2002).

During this study, 'going native' was avoided through a number of means. Firstly, due to having to travel 35 minutes to Birmingham for each 'period' of participant observation, it was possible (and necessary due to living arrangements) to withdraw from the field – which then enabled the writing up of fieldnotes and the on-going interplay between theory and data. So whilst travelling added to the time and resources expended, it did also offer benefits to the process. Secondly, not living within the field, and therefore not being totally immersed, there was very little chance of 'over-rapport' with any specific participants – especially when compared with the type and degree of immersion of studies like those of Burawoy (1979), Bourgois (2002) or

Venkatesh (2008) who lived amongst participants for several years. The third mechanism to avoid going native was through constantly engaging in reflexive thinking (Etherington, 2004) and consideration upon 'retreating' from the field, and discussing progress with experienced researchers and supervisors whenever possible.

Further challenges

There were also several additional, inter-related problems which are pertinent to address. Firstly, though access to participants was not necessarily an issue, actually getting them to take part in an interview was far more difficult than expected, as it was (naïvely) considered that with so many thousands of fans it would be a straightforward task. I exchanged countless emails and text messages with participants in order to arrange an interview, with so many coming to nothing due to various factors. In retrospect, I delayed organising participants to interview during the early stages of data collection, as I thought that I had a great deal of time and many potential participants, and that people would willingly give up their time to be interviewed. This meant it was more difficult to arrange interviews when the time came. On reflection, it is vital to identify possible participants and build a rapport early in the research process. Secondly, financial costs also inhibited the progress made at various points – both in terms of buying tickets in order to attend matches for participant observation and also in terms of travel. Whilst these issues may not have necessarily altered the study, they certainly resulted in many challenges and headaches, and numerous small, personal sacrifices had to be made along the way. Therefore, speaking from experience, when previous researchers and supervisors inform you that this type of data collection will be very time-consuming and challenging, that advice must be fully taken on board.

The final challenge to reflect on was unanticipated and happened at the outset of my fieldwork. Prior to entering the field, I had read all I could on the more technical components of ethnography as a methodological approach. However, it was only when I actually went out into the field for the first time that it dawned on me that I was not sure exactly how to go about collecting data. What should I observe? What do I take note of? Who should I try and talk to? I had been going to football matches all my life, but suddenly I was unsure of my surroundings and what I was required to do. It seemed surprisingly overwhelming. So, with Geertz's (1973) notion of 'thick description' fresh in my mind from the countless weeks of reading, during those early periods in the field I took note of everything I possibly could. I used my smart phone to take notes, pictures, videos and sound recordings – trying to describe everything around me in minute detail – often whilst also trying to pretend that I was actually talking to someone on the other end of the phone to avoid being too conspicuous. Although hindsight might suggest that I was wasting precious time with this level of data collection, I felt far more assured once I got into this participant observation as it felt like I was doing 'real' ethnography. I felt like a 'proper' researcher, if not quite following in the distant footsteps of Malinowski (1922) and Geertz (1973) by exploring exotic, foreign cultures, then certainly gaining confidence from 'getting out there' and trying to 'make the familiar foreign' after so many months sat at my desk. However, a setback was around the corner.

As this final, brief vignette aims to demonstrate, my eagerness to 'jump right in' and gather data wherever and however possible led me into a potentially treacherous situation within the first few weeks of fieldwork. Having struck up a conversation with 'Dave' at a match (I had bought a ticket alone and he was in the seat next to me), I was invited to go for a drink afterwards with a group of his friends at a well-known pub near the stadium, as I had already disclosed that I was a researcher and he seemed keen to express his views on various matters. For a couple of hours we discussed all things around football, and I was really positive that I had been initially welcomed into this small group, especially as they spent a great deal of time openly discussing the Birmingham rivalry and recounting entertaining anecdotes. Then they declared that it was time to 'move on' to another bar in a part of the city I did not know at all, and having initially declined their offer to join them, against my better judgement I was soon in a speeding, unlicensed taxi heading to what turned out to be a slightly shabby and seedy bar:

> As soon as we walked in I had a feeling that something was not right. It struck me as surprising that such a run-down bar would be so popular, as people were packed in tight... The group headed over to what I was told was 'their' booth, in the far corner where it emerged two more of their friends were seated, and after getting a bottle of beer I ended up sitting squashed in the corner of the booth... The dynamics of the group had instantly changed in here. Not only was there no talk of football, there was no talking to me, either, it seemed. Previously, Dave had not left my side all evening, but now it looked like he was chatting away to every person that passed our booth, most of whom were heading to the toilet, which was a matter of feet away from us – and, strangely, half the time Dave popped into the toilet with them. Being slightly naïve, and a bit tired at this point, it took me some time to realise what was going on. It eventually dawned on me that my 'new friend' Dave was involved in selling drugs. In fact, he seemed to be the ring-leader of the whole set-up, with the other group members standing guard at the toilet door. Though I never actually saw anything change hands, presumably Dave's 'stash' was hidden away in the toilets somewhere. I immediately started to panic, and felt trapped in the corner. Frenzied thoughts began to run through my mind; if the police burst in now would I be considered an accomplice? Had I seen too much? Are they going to let me leave?...

Thankfully, as their initial interest in me had long since worn off, I waited for Dave to head into the toilets again and pretended I had a phone call to take outside, and then got away from the bar as quick as I possibly could, jogging back towards the bright lights of the city centre for at least fifteen minutes before flagging down a taxi.

This episode, coming so early on in the fieldwork, really shook my emerging confidence. I thought it would be straightforward that people would just want to talk to me and everything would run smoothly. Instead, I became cagey about going anywhere with fans/potential interviewees, and this probably contributed to the previously mentioned delay in the recruitment of participants, as I was reluctant to end up in a situation like this, which for many people I'm sure would be fairly commonplace, but for me it was extremely troubling.

On reflection, it emerged that my apprenticeship with the requisite research methods textbooks had been too sanitised, too technical. I felt something was missing. The turning point was reading the likes of Klein (1993), Sugden (1996), Armstrong (1998), Bourgois (2002) and Venkatesh (2008) following these very early stages of being in the field, as they opened my eyes to what 'real' fieldwork is like, and especially how there is not a clear set of instructions for how to conduct this type of research. These all too rare candid and transparent narratives gave me confidence and helped me to realise that it is OK if things get slightly messy at times, and just how challenging some of the perils of ethnography can be.

These candid texts and my early challenges also highlighted how much of 'negotiating the field' was based on judgement calls, often between seeking data and the 'spirit' of ethnography, versus the alarm bells ringing in my head. Reflecting now, being in a slightly different position, I have to reconcile in my own mind the potential conflict in the future in my continuing role as a research supervisor, with the knowledge of what can occur and all the unpredictable perils that can arise. Many ethnographers reflect with bravado on their 'rites of passage' (Giulianotti, 1995; Sugden, 1996), much as I have done here, perhaps. But the question remains, am I happy to send students and researchers out into their chosen field, knowing that it is almost inevitable that they will have to negotiate a perilous rite of passage themselves? There is, of course, always an ethical clearance process in place, but all the examples that have been highlighted in this chapter have passed through such rigorous procedures, yet the risks and perils remain.

Concluding thoughts

It has been previously highlighted that critics of reflexive texts feel that they are too messy, subjective and open ended (see Etherington, 2004) or that they are too verbose when focusing on *our* field experiences, which diverts ethnographies away from their prime purpose of making sense of *other people's* realities (see Crang & Cook, 2007). The response to this by advocates of reflexivity has been to explain fully and justify their own philosophical approach (Coffey, 1999), especially in terms of subjectivist research and actually valuing the subjectivities of the researcher (Lincoln, 1990). With this notion in mind, this chapter aimed to offer up a reflexive and unashamedly subjective explanation of some of the challenges faced, in order to provide a candid account in the hope that future researchers might benefit from the experiences and transparency.

Sands (2002, p. 97) stated that "part of doing good ethnography is deciding what level of risk to bear", which is all well and good for an experienced researcher; but for the neophyte it is problematic when you are caught between wanting to immerse oneself and being too naïve to recognise the risk, or even to just feel confident as an ethnographer generally. And that is not to mention the pressure that can be put on an academic trying to combine personal life with research, lecturing and gaining qualifications within designated timeframes. My reflection on this (extended) period does not offer solutions or pearls of wisdom on how to manage this fairly common juggling act; all I would offer is that time must be managed and prioritised, and that tough decisions and sacrifices are thrust upon the researcher throughout. It is hoped that at least an expectation of this may benefit the neophyte ethnographer prior to entering the field. These aspects are central to the ethnographic methodology, however they are often omitted from current literature, therefore it is argued here that this sort of transparency is vital not only for individual projects but also for future growth and progress in this area.

Note

1   Bryman (2008) described thick description as a concept used by Geertz (1973) which refers to detailed accounts of social settings that can form the basis for the creation of general statements regarding a culture and its significance in people's lives. Further, Kvale and Brinkmann (2009) viewed it as the ability to see and describe events in their value-laden contexts, and interpret appropriately.

References

Albritton, J.S. (1991). Professor/policeman: Reflections on a practicum in policing. *Wisconsin Sociologist, 28*(1), 47–56.

Anderson, B. (2006). *Imagined communities: Reflections on the origin and spread of nationalism,* London: Verso.

Armstrong, G. (1993). Like that Desmond Morris? In D. Hobbs & T. May (Eds.), *Interpreting the field: Accounts of ethnography* (pp. 3–43). Oxford: Oxford University Press.

Armstrong, G. (1998). *Football hooligans: Knowing the score.* Oxford: Berg.

Armstrong, G., & Giulianotti, R. (2001). Afterword: Constructing social identities: Exploring the structured relations of football rivalries. In G. Armstrong & R. Giulianotti (Eds.), *Fear and loathing in world football* (pp. 267–279). Oxford: Berg.

Benkwitz, A., & Molnar, G. (2012). Interpreting and exploring football fan rivalries: An overview. *Soccer and Society, 13*(4), 479–494.

Bourgois, P. (2002). *In search of respect: Selling crack in El Barrio.* Cambridge: Cambridge University Press.

Bryman, A. (2008). *Social research methods* (3rd edition). Oxford: Oxford University Press.

Burawoy, M. (1979). *Manufacturing consent: Changes in the labour process under monopoly capitalism.* Chicago: University of Chicago Press.

Clarke, A. (2006). Qualitative interviewing: Encountering ethical issues and challenges. *Nurse Researcher, 13*(4), 19–29.

Coffey, A. (1999). *The ethnographic self: Fieldwork and the representation of identity.* London: SAGE.

Crang, M., & Cook, I. (2007). *Doing ethnographies,* London: SAGE.

Cresswell, J.W. (2007). *Qualitative inquiry and research design: Choosing among five approaches* (2nd edition). London: SAGE.

Emerson, R.M., Fretz, R.I., & Shaw, L.L. (2001). Participant observation and fieldnotes. In P. Atkinson, A. Coffey, S. Delamont, J. Lofland, & L. Lofland (Eds.), *Handbook of ethnography* (pp. 352–383). London: SAGE.

Etherington, K. (2004). *Becoming a reflexive researcher.* London: Jessica Kingsley Publishers.

Geertz, C. (1973). *The interpretation of cultures.* New York: Basic Books.

Giulianotti, R. (1995). Participant observation and research into football hooliganism: reflections on the problems of entrée and everyday risks. *Sociology of Sport Journal, 12*(1), 1–20.

Giulianotti, R. (1999). *Football: A sociology of the global game.* Cambridge: Polity.

Goffman, E. (1989). On fieldwork. *Journal of Contemporary Ethnography, 18*(1), 123–132.

Hallinan, C.J., Hughson, J.E., & Burke, M. (2007). Supporting the 'World Game' in Australia: A case study of fandom at national and club level. *Soccer and Society, 8*(2/3), 283–297.

Hammersley, M., & Atkinson, P. (2007). *Ethnography: Principles in practice,* London: Routledge.

Hargreaves, J., & Tomlinson, A. (1992). Getting there: Cultural theory and the sociological analysis of sport in Britain. *Sociology of Sport Journal, 9*(1), 207–219.

Hobbs, D. (2001). Ethnography and the study of deviance. In P. Atkinson, A. Coffey, S. Delamont, J. Lofland, & L. Lofland (Eds.), *Handbook of ethnography* (pp. 204–219). London: SAGE.

Kendrick, M. (2010). Mat Kendrick reflects on Birmingham City defeat. *Birmingham Mail.* Online. Retrieved from www.birminghammail.co.uk/sport/football/football-news/aston-villa-writer-mat-kendrick-136623 [last accessed 30 May 2015].

Klein, A.M. (1993). *Little big men: Bodybuilding subculture and gender construction.* Albany: State University of New York Press.

Kvale, S., & Brinkmann, S. (2009). *Interviews: Learning the craft of qualitative research interviewing,* London: SAGE.

Lincoln, Y.S. (1990). The making of a constructivist: A remembrance of transformations past. In E.G. Guba (Ed.), *The paradigm dialog* (pp. 67–87). California: Sage.

Malinowski, B. (1922). *Argonauts of the Western Pacific*. London: Routledge and Kegan Paul.

Murphy, E., & Dingwall, R. (2001). The ethics of ethnography. In P. Atkinson, A. Coffey, S. Delamont, J. Lofland, & L. Lofland (Eds.), *Handbook of ethnography* (pp. 339–351). London: SAGE.

Rock, P. (2001). Symbolic interactionism and ethnography. In P. Atkinson, A. Coffey, S. Delamont, J. Lofland, & L. Lofland (Eds.), *Handbook of ethnography* (pp. 26–38). London: SAGE.

Sands, R.R. (2002). *Sport ethnography*. Leeds: Human Kinetics.

Silk, M.L. (2005). Sporting ethnography: Philosophy, methodology and reflection. In D.L. Andrews, D.S. Mason, & M.L. Silk (Eds.), *Qualitative methods in sports studies*, (pp. 65–103). Oxford: Berg.

Smith, B., & Caddick, N. (2012). Qualitative methods in sport: A concise overview for guiding social scientific sport research. *Asia Pacific Journal of Sport and Social Science*, *1*(1), 60–73.

Smith, V. (2001). Ethnographies of work and the work of ethnographers. In P. Atkinson, A. Coffey, S. Delamont, J. Lofland, & L. Lofland (Eds.), *Handbook of ethnography* (pp. 220–233). London: SAGE.

Sugden, J. (1996). *Boxing and society: An international analysis*, Manchester: Manchester University Press.

Sugden, J., & Tomlinson, A. (2002). Theory and method for a critical sociology of sport. In J. Sugden, & A. Tomlinson (Eds.) *Power games: A critical sociology of sport*, (pp. 3–21). London: Routledge.

Taylor, P. Lord Justice. (1990). *Inquiry into the Hillsborough Stadium disaster: Final report*. London: HMSO.

Thompson, W.R. (2001). Identifying rivals and rivalries in world politics. *International Studies Quarterly*, *45*(4), 557–586.

Venkatesh, S. (2008). *Gang leader for a day: A rogue sociologist crosses the line*. London: Penguin Books.

Weed, M. (2006). The story of an ethnography: The experience of watching the 2002 World Cup in the pub. *Soccer and Society*, *7*(1), 76–95.

Chapter 11

The legitimacy of ethnographic film

Literary thoughts and practical realities

Christian Edwards and Robyn L. Jones

Despite the advent of qualitative means and methods within sports coaching research, it has recently been argued that such work remains relatively starved of contextual considerations (Jones, Edwards, & Viotto Filho, in press). The claim here relates to investigations being somewhat hollow in terms of appreciating the complexities and contestation of situated action (Jones, Bowes, & Kingston, 2010). This extends to more than a simple critique of reductionism (which has been done extensively elsewhere), to a critical appraisal of what often appears as 'snapshot' research. Consequently, although producing insightful, in-depth accounts of human organisations and subcultures has been sought, such work has largely ignored the social beyond the interactional. Notwithstanding a few exceptions (e.g., Cushion & Jones, 2006, 2014; Purdy & Jones, 2011), the production of context-rich ethnographic work into the social logic and enacted craft of sports coaching remains conspicuous by its absence.

The aim of this chapter is to suggest how visual representation, through ethnographic film, can provide an additional means to augment understanding (and presentation) of coaches' on-going existential challenges. The point, however, is not to further link ethnography to realist assumptions of 'evidenced' recorded events and of 'being there'. Rather, it is to make the case that recorded images have the ability to enrich the building blocks of a narrative argument through accepting that "images are much more than the sum of their material traces" (Stanczak, 2007, p. 11). In the words of Stanczak (2007, p. 9), the general purpose is to "help us to ask what we know about the social world and how we know it." But more of this later.

In terms of structure, we begin by providing a brief insight into the ethnographic concept, highlighting the problematic related issues of data 'collection', construction and interpretation. This is followed by an outline and discussion surrounding the case for ethnographic film, inclusive of given critiques and limitations. Personal reflections are then given by the first author in relation to using ethnographic film as a means of data collection within recently completed fieldwork. Finally, a reflective conclusion summarises the principal points made.

An introduction to ethnographic work

Within the qualitative paradigm there are many ways of conducting research. One particular genre that can be seen as both an analytic perspective and a methodological approach is that of ethnography (Van Maanen, 2011). Ethnography's central premise is to allow researchers to explore and make sense of the social and cultural dynamics of human interaction which, in turn, are understood to be a product of shared meanings. Such an approach requires the ethnographer to adopt a cultural lens through what is called an *emic* perspective. Doing so, it is claimed, allows for more penetrative insights into individuals' lives through providing 'thicker' descriptions of social rules and contextual events (Fetterman, 2010). Ethnography then, is an interpretive craft that focuses on discovering the meaning of an individual's actions and explanation: on the 'how' and 'why' rather than the quantifiable 'how much' or 'how many' (O'Reilly, 2005).

A principal method associated with ethnography has been participant observation. As the name suggests, this involves the researcher becoming a participant or a part of the cultural context being observed. Participant observation rests on the principle of interaction, and the 'reciprocity of perspectives' between social actors (Atkinson & Hammersley, 1994). Thus, such a method is a complex, politicised way of gathering data, involving a variety of problematic issues which include how to enter the context, the constructed and various 'roles' adopted by researchers, as well as the analysis of data. Notwithstanding such concerns, of particular relevance to this chapter is the issue of 'interpretation': that is, what data are included and excluded, and why?

The observations undertaken by researchers using this method are usually recorded through 'fieldnotes'. In its simplest form, this is where researchers write something down in relation to their observations of, or interactions with, the context. These could be an indication of what was said (a direct quote), or some key terms to be elaborated upon later. Such recorded impressions become the ethnographer's data. Wolfinger (2002), in quoting Van Maanen (1988, p. 223) however, reminds us that such a process is not straightforward; that such inexact notes are no less than "the secret papers of social research". In questioning 'where do fieldnotes come from?' Wolfinger's point was that such notes are not taken in a socio-historical vacuum, but are inevitably influenced by an ethnographer's background and biography. This is knowledge that is "seen but unnoticed" (Garfinkel, 1967, p. 118). Another interesting claim here is that ethnographers frequently "choose to record a particular observation because it stands out...because it is deviant" (Wolfinger, 2002, p. 90). This problematises the assumption of 'looking for regularities' in a data set, as, by their very nature, such occurrences are infrequent. The purpose of citing such complexities is to bring to attention that, despite best efforts at reflexivity and self-critique, ethnographers are never able to 'call it as it is', just as 'they see it'. One way in which to overcome problems related to (mis)representation of events is to use a variety of methods. Acknowledging that a neutral, objective observation of the data is not possible, Kawulich (2004) suggests that such an approach allows researchers the means to reflect on data already collected to further consider the nature and 'accuracy' of their interpretations.

The literary case for (and against) ethnographic film

In seeking to expand upon traditional methods associated with interpretivist research, visual means have increasingly been employed (Buckingham, 2009). Although such inquiry has tended to reflect the use of photographic images, other visual representations (e.g., maps, diagrams, sketches, posters, signs and symbols) have also offered ways of enriching what is visible (and affective) about social life (Kluge, Grant, Friend & Glick, 2010). The objective here has been to delve beyond the traditionally dominant talk and text of interviews and fieldnotes (Brown, Dilley & Marshall, 2008), to offer a deeper portrayal and understanding of the multiple meanings embedded within any given culture (Phoenix, 2010). Although visual methods are not new within the qualitative paradigm, the case for visual ethnography remains something of a diverse specialism (O'Reilly, 2012).

One particular form of visual inquiry that holds great promise as a qualitative method is ethnographic film (Pink, 2012): a promise which, in recent years, is being increasingly realised (Pink, 2013). For example, the fields of anthropology, sociology, education, cultural studies and American studies among others, have utilised ethnographic film to redefine epistemological, methodological and representational concepts. Throughout these theoretical 'turns', however, the central purpose of ethnographic film, that is elicitation, has remained the same: elicitation as related to the ability to both frame and deconstruct multi-layered meanings (Phoenix, 2010, p. 94). Doing so, holds the potential to foster an understanding of situational complexity or the sequencing of events (Aull Davies, 2008). Hence, it has been argued that ethnographic film offers the opportunity to provide a more contextual account of *who* people are and *how* they function within any given setting. This is because it allows us to capture, revisit and disambiguate the serendipitous interactions and intangibles of social life in a way that neither words nor still photos can (Basu, 2008). Additionally, when presented back to those under study, such data can evoke reflection in individuals so that they better interpret their experienced worlds. In doing so, *what people do* rather than only *what they say they do* can be reviewed and critiqued (Kluge et al., 2010). Furthermore, through capturing the nuances of meaning embedded in gestures, facial expressions and other visual interactional cues, ethnographic film can act as a powerful tool for deconstructing the sensorial aspects of social research (Dufon, 2002).

The historical roots of ethnographic film lie firmly within anthropology. In fact, an etymological definition of the term suggests that its origins are a sub-gene of the documentary tradition (Basu, 2008). Initially, its usage was a phenomenon of colonialism, to document the primitive lives of the non-western other. Such fieldwork or 'expeditions' were considered to provide a day-to-day snapshot of cultural life, where the camera was used as an instrument to 'freeze' subjects' motions, thus allowing subsequent and considered analysis (Marks, 1995). Such a methodology enabled ethnographers to somewhat preserve the integrity of the cultural context by presenting their data as 'whole acts' and 'whole bodies', hence offering a richer understanding of group interactions (Heider, 2006). It is from this notion of 'whole cultures' that ethnographic film can be somewhat differentiated from documentary film. Subsequently, following Weinberger's (1992) suggestion that as *ethnos* is 'people' and *graphe* is 'a writing, a representation', ethnographic film can be simply deemed as 'a representation of people on film'.

Due to its very nature however, ethnographic film has faced a long battle to legitimise its use as a research genre. Indeed, the critical discourse about ethnographic film has been rife with contentious and opposing viewpoints. Much of this dispute stems from questions surrounding the method's accuracy, fairness and objectivity (Durington & Ruby, 2011). Others (e.g. Rony, 1996) have even debated the ontological nature of ethnographic film itself, in terms of it being based on a positivist objective notion of 'this actually happened'. Consequently, despite its growth, ethnographic film has faced many issues in trying to convince traditional social sciences as to its benefits (Grady, 2008). For example, Fetterman (2010) considered that ethnographic film is only capable of supplementing rather than replacing the written text of ethnography, while others have concluded that what is captured through ethnographic film is more of a rehearsed illustration of events rather than something naturally occurring (Ball & Smith, 2001). Such value-insecurity and critique prompted Henley (1998) to conclude some time ago that, although substantial interest in ethnographic film was and has been evidenced, its credibility as a serious academic activity was yet to be truly established: a situation many believe remains unchanged today.

Of greater substance, however, are the challenges faced by ethnographic film in terms of its epistemology and the realities of its use (Rakic & Chambers, 2009). In relation to the first, Bull and Back (2003) suggested that the genre was insufficiently decisive in its description and analysis: the result of a kind of identity crisis between positivism and interpretivism. The point made engages with the debate encapsulated in the 'realist' assumptions of the data gathered. Although arguments have often been heard supporting the accuracy of the evidenced events 'as they happened', Henley (1998) among others claims that interpretation still has a considerable role to play. Here, he suggests that film is just as exposed to manipulation as the written text, whilst its production is just as subject to interpretation. This quasi-constructivist nature of visual methods was recently discussed by Jones et al. (2013), although more specifically in terms of still photographs than 'moving' film. In steering a line between positivist assumptions and the postmodern turn, Jones et al. quoted Stanczak (2007, p. 7) in stating that although "the camera is susceptible to the selectivity of the operator, it is not selective once the shutter is opened". Such moments as recorded then, can be considered both *decisive* and *decided* (Stanczak, 2007). This was a sentiment echoed by Rakic and Chambers (2009), who argued that what is caught by the camera lens is not so much absolute truth but a fragmented view of reality provided through the guided eye of the cameraman. Consequently, Stanczak (2007) believes that such methods and the images they produce ask us to hold both positions simultaneously. In this respect, they demand that 'this has been', while also questioning subjectivities which can be further scrutinised (Jones et al., 2013). Despite such middle-ground conceptual articulations, this epistemic question remains very much alive.

With regard to practical realities, although possessing the ability to record many contextual events for subsequent re-evaluation, ethnographic film can be critiqued for lacking a connection to what Sparkes (2000) termed an "ethnography of the senses". For instance, while film can capture explicit behaviours and interactions, it fails to contextualise the embodied feelings of the group context. Here, it can be argued that the data captured are devoid of the intimacy and insight derived from hearing, smelling, tasting and touching. The result is a two-dimensional view of situated 'goings on'. Such a reduction of knowledge seriously questions the value of such a method and how it can sufficiently provide a credible 'feel' for the social order under study (Bull & Back, 2003). Somewhat relatedly, questions have also been raised about the ability of ethnographic film to capture deeper and contextual accounts of the field in respect of the authenticity of the data collected (Schuck & Kearney, 2006). This is due to the presumed invasive nature of the camera and its possible influence on group members. In response, however, Gobo (2008) has claimed that although a camera can be initially intrusive, much like other forms of observational research, participants 'acting to' the camera diminishes with familiarity. Hence, the camera, as the research study itself, soon become accepted and integrated into contextual cultural norms.

In giving a personal flavour to the theoretical discussion presented, we now progress this chapter to Christian's reflections of using ethnographic film within his on-going PhD work. To provide some context, the purpose of the project lies in exploring the social significance of humour as a critical component in the negotiation of coaching relationships. More detailed objectives relate to examining (1) the 'power exchanges' between coach and athlete as expressed through humour; (2) what sort of humour is used in coaching, why it is used, and what are its consequences; and (3) how humour contributes to the production of social 'hierarchies' and group identities within a sports coaching context. Not surprisingly, undertaking such critical, ethnographic research required engagement with, and interpretation of, the nuances of individual flourishes within given socio-cultural norms. Consequently, in order to collect related data, it was decided to adopt participant observation as the principal research method. Christian now takes up the story.

My ethnographic reflections: the value (or not) of using film

Due to the nature of my doctoral work, I adopted the unconventional position of occupying the roles of researcher, participant and coach simultaneously. As such, I deliberated on a number of issues when considering my choice of data collection methods. I wanted to grasp the type of humour used within semi-professional football, why it is used, and the effects of such humour on the context in which it occurs. I wanted to capture this as it happened, where it happened. Hence, I needed a means that would portray complex events and situations in language specific to the events themselves.

Having been a contextual insider for many years, capturing implicit, humorous actions would be easy, or so I thought. Entering the 'field', the explicit acts were obvious to see. I 'saw' and identified with the players' actions and language clearly; hence, the process of note writing was not difficult. Yet, each night, when I looked to elaborate on 'loose' findings, my texts appeared limited and vague. They didn't seem to convey what my eyes had seen. Although I thought I could trust my own cultural 'lens', trying to bring the nuance of humorous interaction to life was not easy. My work was transparent, it had no depth; it didn't seem to capture the meaning I wanted it to. There was a missing link between text and experience. Using my supervisor as a critical friend, I frequently asked how my notes should look and what they should portray? Although reassurance was given, I remained unhappy with my recorded words. I wanted to catch more, while my multi-levelled role within the process was an increasing concern in terms of limiting what I could see.

Before undertaking fieldwork, I had naturally read the relevant literature. The texts argued that my ethnographic 'eyes' would be initially frail and the muscles weak. Such was the case. I further read and wrote about reflexivity and how it applied to me, which certainly led me to greater criticality. Nevertheless, the issue of capturing 'everything' within my observations overtook my thoughts; I constantly considered my intentions, and why the events I saw and felt weren't reflected in my notes. In trying to provide sufficient balance between subjectivity and objectivity, my continued frustrations centred on my 'complete member researcher' role (Adler & Adler, 1987). At first, I feared that this 'wrestling' with my notes was due to inexperience. I soon acknowledged, however, that the displeasure felt was due to one principal reason: that of trying to occupy multiple roles within the field. As a result of this endless 'busyness', I had serious concerns regarding the 'richness' of the data collected. For example, jotting down notes at training and at matches were often challenging due to my contextual various commitments. In reading over the initial stages of my fieldwork (3 weeks), I felt the resultant logs provided me with both 'sanitised' and 'dense' data. They were either too simple, or too complex, with little meaning apparent. Of more importance, I was constantly plagued by a fear of 'missing something': something important that I should be seeing and, hence, recording. Although this anxiety stemmed from the normal nervousness of a novice researcher, it was also rooted in my multiple roles within the context. There were too many things to do, and too many things going on. I struggled to contextualise earlier observations, a tussle which led me to consider alternative ethnographic methods. I wanted an agency that evoked deeper reflection on hidden, embedded cultural practices. I had to find another way to become more confident in my data, another means that would allow me to navigate the challenging pathways I encountered, so I could better relate to the problems of 'how to be' in the field (Castellano, 2007).

It was here that I considered using a video camera. Why? Because I thought it would allow me to 'better' observe the inherent interactions in the context. Placed in clearly visible positions in the dressing room, training pitches and facilities, the camera soon became part of daily life. It became a 'social actor' within our culture, and was soon forgotten. What I hoped for was a 'richer' account of individual(s) and group life: one that I could rely on if I 'missed something' in the moment. My purpose then, was to use the film to secure 'accuracy' in my work; to review every night; to ensure I had recorded what I 'should' have done. In this respect, the aim was not to totally replace my fieldnotes but to check them, or enrich them, against a perceived fuller record. The film was to act as a support mechanism or 'refresher' to my notes, enabling considered and enhanced analysis (Harris, 2010). And, indeed, the camera allowed me to move freely around the club to interact with players, coaches and support staff without fearing for the credibility of my work. No doubt, this process also offered cues that elicited personal (and theoretical) reflection, so that my notes became more aesthetic. In this way, the film could be claimed to have helped provide a 'thicker description' of social reality. I became a more 'relaxed' researcher.

However, although a possible convenient location to conclude these reflections, my story or experiment with ethnographic film didn't really stop there. Although initially enabling more considered fieldnotes (from revisiting filmed events), I soon realised that what I was adding from this re-viewing process was ever lessening as the empirical work continued. I thus came to appreciate that what the filmed records provided me with, was not so much additional information, as a reaffirmation of what my developing ethnographic skills had already 'seen'. In short, the film had taken away (or lessened!) anxiety about missing things due to my multiple contextual roles. In turn, this confidence allowed me to work on, and better trust, my observational instincts about what and what not to record. As opposed to relegating or weakening my ethnographic muscles then, the process and related use of film actually enhanced them (without using the film as intended). Although such an explanation may go somewhat against the literary purpose of using ethnographic film, foregrounding the primacy of the research objectives at the expense of purity of method, filming certainly served a very valuable purpose within my work. For me, this was the principal worth and benefit of the film, not so much in terms of expanding my notes, but in giving confidence to focus on events and interactions knowing I could look back and reflect upon in my interpretations at a later time. Without it, I know I would have struggled to 'capture' the nuances and idiosyncrasies of the day's events, in terms of how humour is a ubiquitous feature of coaching life.

Conclusion

Being researchers rooted in the interpretivist paradigm, our initial theoretical engagement with film as a means of data collection was discussed at length between us. This was because, although we believed in its constructivist nature, the purpose of its use in Christian's PhD was rationalised as a 'safety net' of sorts, to ensure capturing of an 'accurate' record of events and happenings as they unfolded. Such a situation resulted from anxiety regarding Christian's multiple roles within the research setting; including being both head coach and researcher: of being a complete participant in context. In order to maximise the opportunity provided by the unique contextual window, to understand the social relationships that manifest themselves through humour in sport, it was principally decided to utilise such a method so that situations could be revisited and retrospectively considered. Any concerns regarding opening up or revisiting a fundamental epistemic debate about the 'objective' nature of the data, however, proved largely groundless. This was because, rather than providing the planned-for safety net in terms of securing data comprehensiveness, the film acted merely to support original 'live' interpretations of events. Indeed, its value lay in developing a degree of researcher confidence in the observations undertaken, thus freeing Christian from a restricting degree of anxiety which initially tended to inhibit what he 'saw'. Hence, rather than trying to focus on everything for fear of missing anything, Christian now felt somewhat liberated to focus on more insightful areas of the data for further analysis, safe in the knowledge that they could be revisited if necessary. The fact that he rarely amended any of his 'live' notes from subsequent film analysis was somewhat ironic. This is not to decry the value of ethnographic film in the 'documentary tradition' or as a means to constantly compare and contrast against 'live' fieldnotes, for which we believe it holds substantial benefits. Rather, it is to somewhat problematise such means' sometimes functional claims by highlighting an unintended, alternative instrumentality from its use, which nevertheless served an important purpose for the research undertaken.

References

Adler, P., & Adler, P. (1987). The past and the future of ethnography, *Journal of Contemporary Ethnography, 18*(1), 4–24.

Atkinson, P., & Hammersley, M. (1994). Ethnography and participant observation. In N.K. Denzin & Y.S. Lincoln (Eds). *Handbook of qualitative research* (pp. 248–260). London: Sage.

Aull Davies, C. (2008). *Reflexive ethnography: A guide to researching selves and others.* London: Routledge.

Ball, M. & Smith, G. (2001). Technologies of realism? Ethnographic uses of photography and film. In P. Atkinson, A. Coffey, S. Delamont, J. Lofland, & L. Lofland (Eds.), *Handbook of ethnography* (pp. 302–319). London: Sage.

Basu, P. (2008). Reframing ethnographic film. In T. Austin & W. de Jong (Eds.), *Rethinking documentary: New perspectives and practices* (pp. 94–106). Open University Press: Maidenhead, UK.

Brown, M.K., Dilley, R., & Marshall, K. (2008). Using a head-mounted video camera to understand social worlds and experiences. *Sociological Research Online, 13*(6), 1.

Buckingham, B. (2009). Creative visual methods in media research: possibilities, problems and proposals. *Media Culture Society, 31*, 633–652.

Bull, M., & Back, L. (2003). Introduction: Into sound. In M. Bull & L. Back (Eds.), *The auditory culture reader* (pp. 1–23). London: Berg.

Castellano, U. (2007). Becoming a non-expert and other strategies for managing fieldwork dilemmas in the criminal justice system. *Journal of Contemporary Ethnography, 36*(6), 704–730.

Cushion, C., & Jones, R.L. (2006). Power, discourse and symbolic violence in professional youth soccer: The case of Albion F.C. *Sociology of Sport Journal, 23*(2), 142–161.

Cushion, C., & Jones, R.L. (2014). A Bourdieusian analysis of cultural reproduction: Socialisation and the hidden curriculum in professional football. *Sport, Education and Society, 19*(3), 276–298.

Dufon, M.A. (2002). Video recording in ethnographic SLA research: Some issues of validity in data collection. *Language Learning & Technology, 6*(1), 40–59.

Durington, M., & Ruby, J. (2011). Ethnographic film. In M. Banks & J. Ruby (Eds.), *Made to be seen: Perspectives on the history of visual anthropology* (pp. 190–208). Chicago: University of Chicago Press.

Fetterman, D.M. (2010). *Ethnography: Step-by-step* (3rd edition). Applied Social Research Methods Series, Vol 17. Los Angeles, CA: Sage.

Garfinkel, H. (1967). *Studies in ethnomethodology.* Oxford: Polity Press.

Gobo, G. (2008). *Doing ethnography.* London: Sage Publications.

Grady, J. (2008). Visual research at the crossroads, *Qualitative Social Research, 9*(3), Art. 38.

Harris, K. (2010). *Enhancing coaches' experiential learning through 'communities of practice'* (Lave & Wenger, 1991) (Published PhD Thesis). University of Wales Institute, Cardiff.

Heider, K. (2006). *Ethnographic film* (2nd edition). Austin, TX: University of Texas Press.

Henley, P. (1998). Film making and ethnographic research. In J. Prosser (Ed.), *Image-based research: A sourcebook for qualitative researchers* (pp. 42–59). London: Falmer Press.

Jones, R.L., Bailey, J., & Santos, S. (2013). Coaching, caring and the politics of touch: A visual exploration. *Sport, Education and Society, 18*(5), 648–662.

Jones, R.L., Bowes, I., & Kingston, K. (2010). Complex practice in coaching: Studying the chaotic nature of coach–athlete interactions. In J. Lyle & C. Cushion (Eds.), *Sports coaching: Professionalism and practice* (pp. 15–26). London: Elsevier.

Jones, R.L., Edwards, C., & Viotto Filho, F. (in press). Activity theory, complexity and sports coaching: An epistemology for a discipline. *Sport, Education and Society.* DOI:101080/13573322.2014.895713.

Kawulich, B.B. (2004). Muscogee women's identity development. In M. Hutler (Ed.), *The family experience: A reader in cultural diversity* (pp. 83–93). Boston: Pearson Education.

Kluge, M.A., Grant, B.C., Friend, L., & Glick, L. (2010). Seeing is believing: telling the 'inside' story of a beginning masters athlete through film, *Qualitative Research in Sport and Exercise, 2*(2), 282–292.

Marks, D. (1995). Ethnography and ethnographic film: From Flaherty to Asch and after, *American Anthropologist, 97*(2), 339–347.

O'Reilly, K. (2005). *Ethnographic methods*. London: Routledge

O'Reilly, K. (2012). *Ethnographic methods* (2nd edition). London: Routledge

Phoenix, C. (2010). Seeing the world of physical culture: the potential of visual methods for qualitative research in sport and exercise. *Qualitative Research in Sport and Exercise, 2*(2), 93–108.

Pink, S. (2012). *Advances in visual methodology*. London: Sage Publications.

Pink, S. (2013). *Doing visual ethnography* (3rd edition). London: Sage Publications.

Purdy, L.G., & Jones, R.L. (2011). Choppy waters: Elite rowers' perceptions of coaching. *Sociology of Sport Journal, 28*(3), 329–346.

Rakic, T., & Chambers, D. (2009). Innovative techniques in tourism research: an exploration of visual methods and academic film making, *International Journal of Tourism Research, 12*(4), 379–389.

Rony, F.T. (1996). *The third eye: Race, cinema, and ethnographic spectacle*. Durham, NC: Duke University Press.

Schuck, S., & Kearney, M. (2006). Using digital video as a research tool: Ethical issues for researchers. *Journal of Educational Multimedia and Hypermedia, 15*(4), 447–463.

Sparkes, A. (2000). Autoethnography and narratives of self. Reflections on criteria in action. *Sociology of Sport Journal, 17,* 21–41.

Stanczak, G.C. (2007). Introduction: Images, methodologies and generating social knowledge. In G.C. Stanczak (Ed.), *Visual research methods: Image, society and representation* (pp. 1–22), Thousand Oaks, CA: Sage.

Van Maanen, J. (1988). *Tales of the field: On writing ethnography*. Chicago: University of Chicago Press.

Van Maanen, J. (2011). *Tales of the field: On writing ethnography* (2nd edition). University of Chicago Press.

Weinberger, E. (1992). The camera people. *Transition, 55,* 24–54.

Wolfinger, N.H. (2002). On writing fieldnotes: Collection strategies and background expectancies. *Qualitative Research, 2*(1), 85–95.

Chapter 12

Traversing ontological dispositions

The intersection between remote Indigenous communities and elite urban-based men's football organisations

Tim Butcher, Chris Hallinan and Barry Judd

> Some methodologies regard the values and beliefs, practices and customs of (indigenous) communities as 'barriers' to research or as exotic customs with which researchers need to be familiar in order to carry out their work without causing offence.
>
> (Tuhiwai Smith, 1999, p. 15)

Linda Tuhiwai Smith's comment serves to succinctly remind ethnographic researchers that the colonial legacy is difficult to dislodge from those interwoven mechanisms and behaviours that guide contemporary practice. It also assists us in introducing the essence of our contribution to this volume. We are in the midst of undertaking a major ethnographic project that places significant emphasis on reconsidering the usual procedural and theoretical dimensions of fieldwork research concerning Australian Indigenous sports participation. Our aims in this chapter are to set out and explain the historical relations between the people of Papunya and sporting organisations; and to convey the research framework to be put in place to conduct an ethnographic investigation of the relationship that has developed between the remote Aboriginal community of Papunya and the Central Australian Football League (CAFL). Our project aims to understand the ontological dispositions and cultural meanings of Australian Football that are syncretically enacted across and between the intersections of sport in a social system in Central Australia. The primary emphasis of this chapter attends to ethnography issues and frameworks implemented when combining Organisation Studies and Australian sports studies. Secondarily, we briefly address and explain paradigmatic shortcomings pervading the contemporary analysis of Aboriginal participation in Australian football.

Emergence of Australian Indigenous sports studies

If the academic interest and output involving ethnographic sports studies is relatively recent, then that of Australian Indigenous sports studies is even more so. Nevertheless, there has been a decided surge of research activity and outputs during the last decade (Hokowhitu, 2013). The initial foray was mostly concerned with descriptive write-ups of Aboriginal games and play. These accounts were constructed by physical educators for the curious Anglo-Australian readers who had no first-hand experience with indigenous Australia. Later, the more in-depth research was driven by historian Colin Tatz's research which documented the centrality of sports and traditional games to Aboriginal communities and both the achievements and experiences of racism of Aboriginal participants in sports (Tatz, 1995), and historian Richard Broome's studies of Aboriginal boxing (Broome, 1980). During the next phase numerous researchers also challenged the positive picture of Australian sport as an institution where Indigenous participation is both welcomed and formally encouraged, and produced studies showing that the relationship, while much improved, remains highly problematic and characterised by ill-informed discourses of race/culture/indigeneity and novel forms of colonial racism (e.g. Gardiner, 1993; Godwell, 2000; Hallinan, Bruce & Coram, 1999; Hallinan & Judd, 2007, 2010, 2012a, 2012b). The field has now developed to such an extent that there are numerous published accounts of research that is primarily field-based and utilising conventional ethnographic-based methods. There are considerable spatial and temporal challenges that limit the extent to which researchers can sufficiently immerse themselves in the various settings. As such, longer-term studies have primarily emanated from PhD studies or sponsored research ventures undertaken by full-time academics. Examples include those of Gorman (2005), Judd (2008), McCoy (2012) and Norman (2012). Our current project is similarly contingent upon the necessary sponsored support to ensure the availability of full-time research assistants during the crucial data collection periods. It extends the body of knowledge in organisation studies, Indigenous studies, and the interplay potential of both.

The remote Aboriginal community of Papunya

The focus of the project is on the remote Indigenous community, Papunya, as an exemplar of the relationships under investigation.

Papunya is a remote Aboriginal community located 240 kilometres northwest of Alice Springs in the Northern Territory (NT). In the 1970s the settlement population peaked at more than 1800 people from mostly the *Pintupi* and *Luritja* language groups who had previously been forced to leave their traditional country situated on the Western Australia – Northern Territory boundary, in the 1930s, a further 290 kilometres west. Today it is home to approximately 418 people, with many *Pintupi* people returning to their traditional country, founding the community of Kintore in the early 1980s ("Community information," 2011; "Our communities", 2014). Poverty and disadvantage have plagued Papunya since at least the 1970s. Poor living conditions, ill-health and tensions between language groups and clans are said to have led to the *Pintupi* migration ("Community information," 2011; Skelton, 2010). Papunya's difficulties perpetuate today.

The Luritja-Pintupi men of Papunya and beyond have played in the CAFL as a combined-communities team – the MacDonnell Districts Football Club since 2008. Elders at Papunya have become increasingly dissatisfied with the terms of their relationship with the Alice Springs-based organisation, the local non-Indigenous member organisation of the Australian Football League of the Northern Territory (AFLNT), which is directly owned and controlled by the Australian Football League (AFL) Commission in Melbourne. Despite Papunya's remote location, the CAFL makes few concessions to the Indigenous footballers that live in that and other remote communities. All matches are played at Traeger Park in Alice Springs. This means McDonnell Districts Football Club is required to frequently travel to and from 'town' during the football season to play, which places significant burdens on the Papunya community, a community that according to almost every measure of social and economic wellbeing suffers extreme disadvantage (after Skelton, 2010). Besides the logistical challenges of bringing the team together in town, Alice Springs is a place where cultures and historical differences converge and numerous liquor-licensed premises offer distractions to people from 'dry' communities. Elders unsurprisingly see Alice Springs as a place of risk, and a threat to the current and future wellbeing of their remote communities. Critically, the question must be asked: why do remote Indigenous people continue to participate in an organised sporting competition that perpetuates non-Indigenous hegemonies? A community response has been to develop an alternative 'on country' football league, the Wilurarra Tjutaku Football League (WTFL).

Importantly, the meaning attached to football in remote Indigenous communities draw on a wellspring of understandings to the effect that the game is an important social practice that transcends non-Indigenous definitions of the sport (Hallinan & Judd, 2012b; McCoy, 2012; Tatz, 2012). Football in such communities is not only a sporting pastime but is also integral to how boys and men now come to engage with and practice aspects of Indigenous law, commonly referred to as 'men's business' (McCoy, 2012). Sports participation might thus be viewed as contemporary hybridisation of the game to enact forms of corroboree (Butcher & Judd, 2015 Hearn Mackinnon & Campbell, 2012; Norman, 2012). Despite the efforts of Indigenous people to participate in non-Indigenous organised sport, such intersections are highly problematic and can lead to ethico-political resistance to Western cultural hegemonies of organisation (after Pullen & Rhodes, 2013; Tengan, 2008). Besnier (2012), for example, demonstrates these features with reference to Tongan players and professional rugby in the corporate leagues of Japan.

One consequence is a particular form of emasculated embodiment. Such Indigenous disempowerment has led, in the past, to anti-colonial forms of resistance and robust cultural assertion, as seen in Māori and Kānaka Maoli contexts (Tengan, 2008). Similarly early Indigenous–settler encounters in Australia took anti-colonial forms (e.g. Shellam, 2009). Yet research into such hegemonic masculinities in Australian remote Indigenous communities has been limited (Wenitong, 2002).

Organisation of football in Central Australia

The AFL and its national, regional and local subsidiaries bring with them the structures, processes and practices of corporate organisation, shaped by commercialisation, economic scale and financial regulation. Organisation is, though, not new to Papunya. From its establishment in the mid-20th century by government officials and Lutheran Church missionaries, this community and others experienced hegemonic organisation imposed by non-Indigenous stewards, designed to bring closely managed social order and assimilation to people from different clan and language groups, arguably through the institutionalisation of a protestant work ethic. With employment available during the working week, they participated in pastimes such as sport at weekends as part of weekly routines culminating in compulsory church attendance on Sunday. Organised sport at that time in Papunya might therefore be viewed as a form of Muscular Christianity (Mangan, 2013). Changing government policies in the 1970s progressively removed localised management to restore Aboriginal self-determination. In 2007, reacting to changing social order, the Federal government imposed new and wide-ranging remote controls in the Northern Territory by policing social practices through intervention (Butcher & Judd, 2015). Complex hybrid social identities have therefore developed in Papunya over time in relation to the proximity of non-Indigenous organisation and external control of the community.

Today, with almost no opportunity for paid employment in Papunya, and government services centralised in distant regional urban centres such as Alice Springs, poverty and disadvantage is endemic and entrenched in this remote community. Hope of self-determination, autonomy and local management by Papunya Elders continues to glimmer, despite repeated and renewed external interventions. The social and cultural significance of Elders is critical to the continuation and growth of their people's languages, heritage, knowledge, practices, and their orthodoxy as a viable 21st century cosmopolitan society. The ontologies handed down to current Elders, and importance of 'country' and its intersections with other peoples must be passed on to future generations to prevent terminal consequences of the eugenics they have perpetually experienced. They continue to struggle to "build [sic] a quality desert lifestyle", as the MacDonnell Regional Council website puts it ("Our community", 2014). Sport is viewed as an avenue to achieving this.

Participation in organised sport is viewed by those Elders as a way to strengthen and enhance a sense of Luritja-Pintupi identity and rediscover the community wellbeing and habitus that was perhaps previously enabled through organised social order (Butcher & Judd, 2015). With CAFL fixtures being played exclusively in Alice Springs, new non-Indigenous hegemonies are enacted. The risks associated with alcohol consumption and tensions with people from other Indigenous and non-Indigenous cultural groups are high, leading to the incarceration of many individuals. Anecdotally, time in the Alice Springs gaol is increasingly experienced as a 'right of passage' for the men of Papunya, not their traditional ceremonies. In collaboration with other remote communities, Papunya Elders initiated an 'on country' football competition in 2012, the WTFL, as an alternative to the CAFL, but not a direct rival to it. The WTFL is organised in the summer months so as not to prevent remote community representative teams from playing in the CAFL through winter (Butcher & Judd, 2015).

Elders' identification with a 'golden era' of community organisation in the 1960s might thus be viewed as similar to nostalgic identity work in post-industrial societies where people long for bygone work organisation and the habitus built around it (Barton & Cairns, 2013; Gabriel, 1993; Strangleman, 2007, 2012). When wilfully employed, such nostalgia becomes ethico-political resistance to social change (Bonnett, 2009; Robertson, 1990; Stauth & Turner, 1988). It evokes symbolism and (re)constructs a sense of belonging to the objects of a self-perceived more stable, more productive, more socially coherent past (Brown & Humphreys, 2002; Butcher, 2013a; Milligan, 2003; Ylijoki, 2005).

Such constructions of identity as resistance to change and power underpin the current debate in Organisation Studies (He & Brown, 2013). Understanding the relationship between Indigenous identity and organisation is though new to that field of research (Jack et al., 2011; Westwood & Jack, 2007). Equally, organisational identity theory is not applied in Australian Indigenous Studies. What is not yet understood in either field of research is how remote Indigenous people participate in organisation, and how and to what extent it influences their specific identities.

Hence this project investigates the cultural complexities of remote Indigenous identity construction through organised sport in Central Australia. It aims to understand the structures and strategies of participation used to enact Indigenous identity and rediscover habitus (after Bourdieu, 2005; Silverstein, 2004). The current sporting culture within many remote Indigenous communities is enmeshed in the convergent historical narratives of community and organisation; questions about it can only be answered through empirical research. The research focuses on past and present sporting encounters through archival and field research methods that bring Indigenous voices to the fore (Butcher, 2013a; Judd, 2008). This requires a transdisciplinary approach, bringing Organisation Studies into an engagement with Australian Indigenous Studies for the first time in a way that directly addresses the national research priority of improving the health and wellbeing of Aboriginal and Torres Strait Islander people.

Prevailing essentialism regarding Aborigines and Australian Football

Our general subject matter of Aboriginal football participation opportunities is not without issue. Australian Football is seen as 'the national game', via a narrative that associates engagement with the sport as enacting national identity (Judd, 2012). The current debate focuses on Australian Football in relation to both its British imperial and Indigenous origins. Specifically, the game is defined as the preserve of non-Indigenous Australia while the dominant organisation is urban-based and associated with the racial politics of white Australian nation building through the late 19th and early 20th centuries (Judd, 2012). These sentiments have been roundly endorsed by sport historians – likewise urban based (see Hallinan & Judd, 2014). This academic sub-group is influential in terms of relative membership numbers but more so because the limited Australian-based sports studies outlets are mostly operated by the Australian Society for Sport History (ASSH). Many of the contributing sport historians appear to have selected AFL as their main interest. Furthermore, the majority sport subject of ASSH publications is AFL. Nevertheless, that in itself is not an issue. The concern and shortcoming with this heavy interest rests with the accompanying and dominating paradigm which serves as the framework for almost all of the publications. The output is not only singularist but also carries a dismissive and authoritative swagger should alternative paradigms be invoked. The most obvious instance concerned the commissioned publication of the history of football and how it dealt with the Aboriginal connections to the sport's origins. We became directly involved with this debate, and while we pressed our contention that the sport may well be a derivative of the Aboriginal game *marngrook*, our principal concern rested with the rigid singular version and the accompanying authoritative tone assumed by proponents of the non-Aboriginal version of sport history. As well, critical scholars from within the sports history community (e.g. Booth, 2006; Phillips, 2006), although significantly outnumbered, have railed against the prevailing essentialist view built around a singularist view of reality embedded within the publications of ASSH and similar outlets. The essence of this sentiment was expressed at the height of the debate:

> For those of us in Indigenous Studies, the cultural formations of essentialist research are connected to the historic processes of imperialism and colonialism.

> (Hallinan & Judd 2014, p. 70)

Our current research engages with theories of colonialism, anti-colonialism, post-colonial identity, organisational identity and business ethics to examine the *structures* and *strategies* of engagement between remote Aboriginal communities and the AFL, and the cross-cultural tensions this creates. It thus unifies two current yet largely disparate debates, namely that of Aboriginal identity in sport, and that of organisation enacted as neo-colonialism and the consequent business ethics. A narrative inquiry, the project focuses on *past* and *present* encounters between the remote Aboriginal community of Papunya in Central Australia and the local and national administration of organised sporting competition through archival and ethnographic methods.

Decolonising Western research assumptions and practices

We abide with the view that "ethnographies offer the most accessible means of getting to the heart of the questions about why and how groups of people do what they do in particular social contexts and settings" (Hallinan & Hughson 2001, p. 3). However, several authors have confronted the standard (Western) research principles and methods taken for granted over time when researching Aborigines and Aboriginal communities. In fact, these sentiments are re-affirmed and take central place in our own research in general and the Papunya project in particular. Linda Tuhiwai Smith (1999) advocates that research in Indigenous communities requires it be decolonised, embrace cultural understanding, respect, the ability to build, maintain and nurture relationships, and a positive connectivity and legacy. Though not specifically directed at ethnographers, the issues inevitably concern ethnographic research. Moreton-Robinson and Walter (2009) suggest some key principles: recognition of distinctive worldviews and knowledges, respect for Aboriginal mores, and inclusion of Aboriginal voices and experiences. Thus, in seeking to conduct our research, it is necessary that the study confronts the central issue affecting research with indigenous communities.

Designing and organising the framework

The following key research questions direct this project: (i) What are the past and present structures and strategies of remote Indigenous community participation in organised sport? (ii) How have these structures and associated strategies developed over time? (iii) What are the problems and successes with the approaches adopted?

The project has three key sub-aims to investigate Indigenous understandings of football in Central Australia. These are: (1) to rediscover the history of relations between remote Indigenous people (of Papunya, NT) and organised sport; (2) to make sense of Papunya's present participation in organised sport; (3) to understand cultural meanings of football to remote Indigenous people (in Papunya).

Implementing the research plan

The research is an in-depth historical and empirical investigation of the relationship that has developed between the remote Indigenous community (Papunya) and organised sport. It therefore employs an innovative conceptual framework that understands and explains the hybrid constructions of what football has meant and means to Indigenous identity. Hence structures and strategies of engagement at the past and present intersection(s) where community and sports organisation meet are examined through archival narratives of organised sporting competitions and community stories of participation in them (after Boje, 2001; Bourdieu, 2005).

As a starting point, this project acknowledges that Indigenous identity and Western notions of social belonging are problematic and contested (Stokes, 2002; Sullivan, 2011; Yuval-Davis, 2011). Although Indigenous sporting participation is uncritically discussed in popular Australian discourse as exemplary reconciliatory engagements that bridge binary and incompatible opposites, this project understands them as reflecting highly complex ways of living in which Indigenous and settler identities have become entangled through organisation in ways that have often given rise to new formations of identity that can be described as being hybrid, third-space or in-between (Bhabha, 2004; Frenkel & Shenhav, 2006; James et al., 2012; Povinelli, 2001).

We have carefully prepared for the project in an incremental way. We attended the annual general meeting of the MacDonnell District Sporting and Social Club Corporation (MDSSCC) (ORIC number 7169) at Papunya on 24th September 2011. Reciprocally, we convened a research symposium, Wellbeing not Winning, in 2012 to draw out past and present issues that face Indigenous people at their intersections with sporting organisations. These preliminary discussions brought to light the key features of each organisational setting and enabled the identification of the research trajectory for this project.

Three separate but convergent research streams aligned to the three key sub-aims above are used to understand the Indigenous meanings of organised football in this context across the past and the present, the remote and the urban. The first stream examines archival community and organisational records to rediscover historical relations as documented between Papunya and sporting organisations. The second stream focuses on the past and present meanings of football as told by the people of Papunya and observed at CAFL and WTFL football matches. The third stream conducts a narrative analysis of the data and brings the findings together so that the research questions are addressed. This overall approach follows and extends the methodology used by Judd (2008) in researching shared football histories in Australia, combining it with the methods used by Butcher (2013a; 2013b) to understand organisational nostalgia and belonging.

Research plan

The research is based on three inter-related and co-joined periods of data generation, data capture and analysis across a three-year project period. The fieldwork in Central Australia is planned to coincide with the league schedules of the CAFL and WTFL in order to observe the day-to-day intersections of football and life in that context. The research streams that comprise the research agenda are as follows.

Stream 1: historical research

Using archival methods to rediscover past encounters between Papunya and forms of sporting organisation, we undertake historical research at the Lutheran Church of Australia archives in Adelaide to identify records that document the development of Papunya as a remote settlement from the 1950s. This archival work investigates the central role played by the Finke River Mission in Central Australia in the organisation of community and the emergence of football culture among the Luritja and Pintupi peoples who came to settle at Papunya. It retraces how football was first introduced, organised and played at Papunya.

We also conduct archival research at the CAFL local office in Alice Springs to catalogue and read records that retrace the expansion of organised football in Central Australia during approximately the same period and how league structures engaged with or disengaged from Indigenous people, particularly those living on remote settlements such as Papunya.

The methods employed in this stream of the research are developed in accordance with contemporary historical research approaches used in the field of Australian Indigenous Studies (e.g. Attwood, 2005; Clark, 1994; Curthoys & McGrath, 2001; Moses, 2004; Reynolds, 1987; Shellam, 2009). These approaches make explicit the disciplinary abilities of history to know the colonial past in a way capable of capturing Indigenous perspectives. The archival research in this stream of the project is therefore conducted in a way that acknowledges that the past, as reconstructed from documentary archives, and overwhelmingly documents non-Indigenous histories that are characterised by the subjective political agendas of non-Indigenous organisations and the power relations that have shaped their engagements with Indigenous peoples in colonial and post-colonial contexts.

Documentary materials provide the basis of a history of organised football in Papunya. In keeping with widely used historical research methods employed within Australian Indigenous Studies, the non-Indigenous history to emerge from the archive materials is cross-checked against the fieldwork materials that document the same past arising from the oral histories of the Papunya Elders to be collated in stream 2 (Tuhiwai Smith, 1999).

Stream 2: the organisational and cultural study of Papunya

First, community conversations (after James et al., 2012) at Papunya are used to negotiate access, clarify and document the research relationship in a signed and witnessed 'Elders Agreement', including what the project will and will *not* offer the community (James et al., 2012). These conversations and the documentation of them will follow a de-colonising research approach (Tuhiwai Smith, 1999; Tengan, 2008) following AIATSIS ethical guidelines and be convened through the MDSSCC, which nominates research participants and grants consent for audio recordings.

Second, fieldwork is scheduled to coincide with football matches of both the WTFL (played in the summer months) and the CAFL (played in the winter months) with the researchers travelling with the Papunya football team to and from matches. Two data collection methods are employed:

- *Strategic conversations* involve interviewing nominated groups of participants representing a broad cross-section of the community (James et al., 2012). Interview audio is recorded, and fieldnotes are kept (cf. protocols in Emerson et al., 1995). Strategic conversations are planned to elicit shared cultural meanings of football in each of the two leagues.
- *Listening to stories* of participants in and around football matches ethically invokes Indigenous oral traditions (Tuhiwai Smith, 1999) to contextualise the strategic conversations data.

This research is planned to be iterative. During and after each fieldwork stage, the *presenting back* of researchers' notes, transcripts and findings to participants is on-going to ensure a reflexive engagement with the participants in relation to the data (AIATSIS, 2012; James et al., 2012). The second stage begins with discussion of the outcomes of the first, and the third stage will refer back to the second, and so on. Most fundamentally, it is designed to understand and explain the organisational form and cultural relevance of football in the past and present of community life.

Stream 3: data analysis

This stream of the research develops the narrative analysis of the data collected in streams 1 and 2. The archival materials, transcribed audio data, and other collected documents are cleaned and coded when the researchers return from the field (Bazeley, 2007; Richards 2009). A research narrative is written to present the analysis in terms of the places, people and voices of football in Central Australia through time. The purpose is to generate Indigenous meanings of football and frame the effects of organisation on identity in that space (Boje, 2001; Bruner, 1991; Cunliffe & Coupland, 2012; Pink, 2008).

Concluding remarks

The need for improved men's health and wellbeing is more pressing than ever in remote communities such as Papunya (Wenitong, 2002). In such communities the achievement of good health is a prerequisite to their social and economic strengthening set within their sociological imagination (cf. Mills, 1959) of the colonial and post-colonial violences of their past and present. The move to initiate the WTFL is most fundamentally about community sustainability. While it is important for Indigenous communities to maintain good relations with the CAFL, the demands that the organisation places on the people of Papunya are inconsistent with strengthening the remote community's social and economic fabric. There is a long history to the problem that we do not yet fully understand, and contemporary perspectives are equally complex and demand investigation. In identifying and comparing the historical and present intersection that is the football ground, this project assists the people of Papunya and the AFL to identify sustainable modes of engagement that reconcile the requirements of the community *and* the organisation. We seek to understand and explain meaningful ways in which Aboriginal men can actively engage with sporting organisations whilst fulfilling kinship and community obligations. More fundamentally, this can be done in a way that retains and nurtures their now hybridised ontologies and spiritual connection to Country.

The shared ontological dispositions of remote Indigenous peoples in Central Australia are a consequence of their past and present encounters with Western imperialists and colonisers – those who have sought to either isolate and eradicate them, or those more recently who have sought to offer them self-determination through 'community engagement' and 'social inclusion'. Their intersections with Western forms of organisation have been both productive and unproductive, in that, on the one hand, their communities have had opportunities for education, access to health care, investment in infrastructure, and political engagements beyond their community boundaries. However, these have been sporadic at best, due to changing political ideologies and sudden shifts in government policies. Having known seemingly better times during the 1970s and 1980s, current Elders know how they would rather their community be, but wish to learn how to return to their preferred ways of life; this is to some extent, their identity struggle. They do not necessarily want to return to times before colonisation, but do seek opportunities to engage with their current and future social realities on 'a level playing field'.

This research aims, in part, to assist them in their (intergenerational) odyssey. Sport holds deep performative and symbolic meanings in all societies. The Elders of Papunya recognise this. We contest that the AFL either do not understand this, or they are losing sight of it, in their neo-imperial quest to identify Australian Football as the game that is most distinctly Australian.

Our consideration is how football is practised *across* the intersections of communities and organisations, which separately contain ontological formations that are widely misconstrued into a "Great Divide" *between* ways of living. What the people of Papunya show us is that their sporting intersection is not one in which 'customary' or 'traditional' culture meets 'modern' society and organisation. The use of 'modernity' as an epoch and a dominant ontology is indeed problematic. Viewed though as layers of the social, those different ontologies are mere reflexive modalities of everyday life, in which ways of being in one layer can play into the next (cf. James et al, 2012). The research project therefore intersubjectively views all research participants (including the research team) in this project as hybrid, traversing across layers of the social through time (past and present) and space (Papunya, Alice Springs, Darwin and Melbourne).

Ethnographies hold the best potential for getting to the essence of cultural matters, if they acknowledge and represent the intersubjective reflexivities of the research situation. As well, scholars (e.g. Coram & Hallinan, 2013; Denzin, Lincoln & Tuhiwai Smith, 2008; Moreton-Robinson, 2000; Moreton-Robinson & Walter, 2009; Tuhiwai Smith, 1999) have brought necessary attention to how and why many of the standard prescriptive texts fall short with paradigmatic assumptions. Also, the acknowledgement of Indigenous methodologies still does not account for the particulars of various language group communities. For students and academics seeking to become better acquainted with ontological dispositions, the construction and rationale of our project involving Papunya may be of benefit.

Acknowledgements

We wish to acknowledge the Australian Research Council for supporting this research (ARC project number: IN150100017). We also would like to acknowledge Peter Fairbrother and Geoff Stokes for their critical reviews of materials that have contributed to the development of this research.

References

AIATSIS. (2012). *Guidelines for ethical research in Australian Indigenous studies.* Retrieved from http://aiatsis.gov.au/sites/default/files/docs/research-and-guides/ethics/gerais.pdf [last accessed 30 May 2015].

Attwood, B. (2005). *Telling the truth about Aboriginal history.* Sydney: Allen & Unwin.

Barton, R., & Cairns, G. (2013). De(constructed) and reconstructed images of the workplace: A case from the edge of Tasmania. In *Proceedings of the 27th Annual Australia New Zealand Academy of Management (ANZAM) Conference*. Hobart, Australia.

Bazeley, P. (2007). *Qualitative data analysis with NVivo* (2nd edition). London: Sage.

Besnier, N. (2012). The athlete's body and the global condition: Tongan rugby players in Japan. *American Ethnologist, 39*(3), 491–510.

Bhabha, H.K. (2004). *The location of culture*. London: Routledge.

Boje, D.M. (2001). *Narrative methods for organizational and communication research*. London: Sage.

Bonnett, A. (2009). The dilemmas of radical nostalgia in British psychogeography. *Theory, Culture & Society, 26*(1), 45–70.

Booth, D. (2006). *The field: Truth and fiction in sport history*. London: Routledge.

Bourdieu, P. (2005). *The logic of practice*. Cambridge: Polity Press.

Broome, R. (1980). Aboriginal boxers and social control in Australia 1930–1979. *Aboriginal History, 4*(1), 48–71.

Brown, A.D., & Humphreys, M. (2002). Nostalgia and the narrativization of identity: A Turkish case study. *British Journal of Management, 13*(2): 141–159.

Bruner, J. (1991). The narrative construction of reality. *Critical Inquiry, 18*(1), 1–21.

Butcher, T. (2013a). Longing to belong. *Qualitative Research in Organizations and Management: An International Journal, 8*(3), 242–257.

Butcher, T. (2013b). Coworking: Locating community at work. In *Proceedings of the 27th Annual Australia New Zealand Academy of Management (ANZAM) Conference*. Hobart, Australia.

Butcher, T., & Judd, B. (2015). Cultural encounters with sporting organisation: Ethico-politics at the interface of Indigenous culture and organisation. In C. Rhodes & A. Pullen (Eds.) *Handbook of ethics, politics and organizations*. London, UK: Routledge.

Clark, I.D. (1994). Sharing history: A sense for all Australians of a shared ownership of their history. *Key Issue Paper (Council for Aboriginal Reconciliation), No. 4*. Canberra: Australian Govt. Pub. Service.

Coram, S., & Hallinan, C. (2013). Resisting critical analyses? Gatekeeping issues with Aborigines and Torres Strait Islander 'subjects'. In C. Hallinan & B. Judd (Eds.), *Native games: Indigenous peoples and sports in the post-colonial world* (pp. 107–126). London: Emerald.

Cunliffe, A., & Coupland, C. (2012). From hero to villain to hero: Making experience sensible through embodied narrative sensemaking. *Human Relations, 65*(1), 63–88.

Curthoys, A., & McGrath, A. (2001). *Writing histories: Imagination and narration*. Melbourne: Monash University, School of Historical Studies.

Denzin, N., Lincoln, Y., & Tuhiwai Smith, L. (Eds.) (2008). *The handbook of critical Indigenous methodologies*. Thousand Oaks, CA: Sage.

Emerson, R.M, Fretz, R.I., & Shaw, L.L. (1995). *Writing ethnographic fieldnotes*. Chicago: University of Chicago Press.

Frenkel, M., & Shenhav, Y. (2006). From binarism back to hybridity: A postcolonial reading of management and organization studies. *Organization Studies, 27*(6), 855–876.

Gabriel, Y. (1993). Organizational nostalgia: Reflections on 'the golden age'. In S. Fineman (Ed.), *Emotion in organizations* (pp. 118–141). London: Sage.

Gardiner, G. (1993). Running for country: Australian print media representations of Indigenous athletes in the 27th Olympiad. *Journal of Sport and Social Issues, 27,* 233–260.

Godwell, D. (2000). Playing the game: Is sport as good for race relations as we'd like to think? *Australian Aboriginal Studies, 2,* 12–19.

Gorman, S. (2005). *Brother boys: The story of Jim and Phillip Krakoue.* Crows Nest, NSW: Allen & Unwin.

Hallinan, C., & Hughson, J. (Eds.) (2001). *Sporting tales: Ethnographic fieldwork experiences,* University of NSW: ASSH.

Hallinan, C., & Judd, B. (2007). 'Blackfellas' basketball: Aboriginal identity and AngloAustralian race relations in provincial basketball. *Sociology of Sport Journal, 24,* 421–436.

Hallinan, C., & Judd, B. (2010). Race relations, Indigenous Australia and the social impact of professional Australian football. In R. Spaaij (Ed.), *Social Impact of Sport* (pp. 1220–1235). London: Routledge.

Hallinan, C., & Judd, B. (2012a). Producing benevolence and expertise: Whitestreaming marn-grook and the other constraints of Australian football. *Journal of Australian Indigenous Studies, 15*(2), 5–13.

Hallinan, C., & Judd, B. (2012b). Indigenous studies and race relations in Australian sports. *Sport in Society, 15*(7), 915–921.

Hallinan, C., & Judd, B. (2014). Duelling paradigms: Australian Aborigines, marn-grook and football histories. In C. Hallinan & B. Judd (Eds.), *Indigenous people, race relations and Australian Sport* (pp. 61–72). London: Routledge.

Hallinan, C.J., Bruce, T., & Coram, S. (1999). Up front and beyond the centre line: Australian Aborigines in elite Australian rules football. *International Review for the Sociology of Sport, 34,* 369–383.

He, H., & Brown, A.D. (2013). Organizational identity and organizational identification a review of the literature and suggestions for future research. *Group & Organization Management 38*(1), 3–35.

Hearn Mackinnon, B., & Campbell, L. (2012). Warlpiri Warriors: Australian rules football in Central Australia. *Sport in Society, 15*(7): 965–974.

Hokowhitu, B. (2013). Foreword. In C. Hallinan & B. Judd (Eds.), *Native games: Indigenous peoples and sports in the post-colonial qorld* (pp. xv–xxi). London: Emerald.

Jack, G., Westwood, R., Srinivas, N., & Sardar, Z. (2011). Deepening, broadening and re-asserting a postcolonial interrogative space in organization studies. *Organization, 18*(3), 275–302.

James, P.L, Nadarajah, Y., Haive, K., & Stead, V. (2012). *Sustainable communities, sustainable development: Other paths for Papua New Guinea.* Honolulu: University of Hawai'i Press.

Judd, B. (2008). *On the boundary line: Colonial identity in football.* Melbourne: Australian Scholarly Publishing.

Judd, B. (2012). The question of Indigenous origins and the unlevel playing field: Outside the boundary of the dominant paradigm. *Sport in Society, 15*(7), 1026–1033.

Mangan, J.A. (2013). *The fames ethic and imperialism: Aspects of the diffusion of an ideal.* London: Routledge.

McCoy, B.F. (2012). Bridging the Indigenous health divide: Football and men engaging. *Sport in Society, 15*(7), 952–964.

Milligan, M.J. (2003). Displacement and identity discontinuity: The role of nostalgia in establishing new identity categories. *Symbolic Interaction, 26*(3), 381–403.

Mills, C.W. (1959). *The sociological imagination.* Oxford University Press.

Moreton-Robinson, A. (2000). *Talkin' up to the white woman: Indigenous women and feminism.* St Lucia, QLD: University of Queensland Press.

Moreton-Robinson, A., & Walter, M. (Eds.) (2009). *Social research methods.* London: Oxford University Press.

Moses, A.D. (2004). *Genocide and settler society: Frontier violence and stolen Indigenous children in Australian history.* New York: Berghahn Books.

Norman, H. (2012). A modern day Corroboree – the New South Wales annual Aboriginal rugby league knockout carnival. *Sport in Society, 15*(7), 997–1013.

Our Communities. (2014). MacDonnell Regional Council. Retrieved from macdonnell. nt.gov.au/communities [last accessed 30 May 2015].

Phillips, M. (2006). Introduction: Sport history and postmodernism. In M. Phillips (Ed.), *Sport history into the new millennium: A postmodern analysis* (pp. 1–24). Albany: State University of New York Press.

Pink, S. (2008). An urban tour the sensory sociality of ethnographic place-making. *Ethnography 9*(2): 175–196.

Povinelli, E.A. (2001). Radical worlds: The anthropology of incommensurability and inconceivability. *Annual Review of Anthropology, 30*, 319–334.

Pullen, A., & Rhodes, C. (2013). Corporeal ethics and the politics of resistance in organizations. *Organization,* May.

Reynolds, H. (1987). *Frontier: Aborigines, settlers, and land.* St. Leonards, NSW: Allen & Unwin.

Richards, L. (2009). *Handling qualitative data: A practical guide* (2nd Edition). London: Sage.

Robertson, R. (1990). After nostalgia? Wilful nostalgia and the phases of globalization. In B.S. Turner (Ed.), *Theories of modernity and postmodernity* (pp. 45–61). London: Sage.

Shellam, T. (2009). *Shaking hands on the fringe: Negotiating the Aboriginal world at King George's Sound.* Crawley, WA: UWA Press.

Silverstein, P.A. (2004). Of rooting and uprooting Kabyle habitus, domesticity, and structural nostalgia. *Ethnography, 5*(4), 553–578.

Skelton, R. (2010). *King Brown country: The betrayal of Papunya.* St Leonards, NSW: Allen & Unwin.

Stauth, G., & Turner, B.S. (1988). Nostalgia, postmodernism and the critique of mass culture. *Theory, Culture & Society 5*(2), 509–526.

Stokes, G. (2002). Australian democracy and Indigenous self-determination, 1901–2001. In G. Brennan & F. Castles (Eds.), *Australia reshaped: 200 years of institutional transformation* (pp. 181–219). Cambridge, UK: Cambridge University Press.

Strangleman, T. (2007). The nostalgia for permanence at work? The end of work and its commentators. *Sociological Review, 55*(1), 81–103.

Strangleman, T. (2012). Work identity in crisis? Rethinking the problem of attachment and loss at work. *Sociology, 46*(3), 411–425.

Sullivan, P. (2011). *Belonging together: Dealing with the politics of disenchantment in Australian Indigenous affairs policy.* Acton, ACT: Aboriginal Studies Press.

Tatz, C. (1995). *Obstacle race: Aborigines in sport.* Sydney: University of New South Wales Press.

Tatz, C. (2012). Aborigines, sport and suicide. *Sport in Society, 15*(7), 922–935.

Tengan, T.P. Kāwika. (2008). *Native men remade: Gender and nation in contemporary Hawai'i.* Durham, NC: Duke University Press.

Tuhiwai Smith, L. (1999). *Decolonizing methodologies: Research and Indigenous peoples.* London: Zed Books.

Wenitong, M. (2002). *Indigenous male health: A report for Indigenous males, their families and communities, and those committed to improving Indigenous male health.* Canberra, ACT: Commonwealth Department of Health and Ageing.

Westwood, R., & Jack, G. (2007). Manifesto for a post-colonial international business and management studies: A provocation. *Critical Perspectives on International Business, 3*(3), 246–265.

Ylijoki, O.H. (2005). Academic nostalgia: A narrative approach to academic work. *Human Relations, 58*(5), 555–576.

Yuval-Davis, N. (2011). *The politics of belonging: Intersectional contestations.* London: Sage.

Part III

Future considerations and directions

Chapter 13

Walking the streets

The flâneur and the sociology of sport

Alan Bairner

As Jonathan Meades (2012, p. xv) reminds us, "We are surrounded by the greatest of free shows. Places." For me, the best such entertainment is to be found in cities. It took me a long time to recognise what really interests me. Until that moment of realisation, I had been a dabbler (and probably still am). Although I have only intermittently lived in cities, I increasingly became aware that they have undeniably formed (and informed) a major part of my life. The aimless wandering around such diverse cities as Belfast, Seville and Tokyo that eventually led me to this self-awareness is apt since it is in many ways analogous to the walks taken by the *flâneur*, ostensibly lacking direction but punctuated by interesting sights, sounds and smells.

The potential overlap between *flânerie* and ethnographic social research, including psychogeography, has been increasingly recognised (Bairner, 2006a; Frisby, 1992; Jenks, 1995). But what is *flânerie*? The conceptualisation of *flânerie* originated in Paris in the first half of the nineteenth century as part of the commentary on an emerging leisure society (Burton, 1994). Despite the *flâneur's* status as a cultural icon, however, there has been considerable debate about his or her worth in terms of understanding the world around us and, particularly, urban life. The *flâneur's* principle activity consists of strolling and looking. Yet *flâneurs* are also curious about the life of cities. One suspects, however, that there remains considerable suspicion in conventional social scientific circles about the role of the *flâneur* and the validity of his or her activities.

The *flâneur's* 'discoveries' are undeniably impressionistic rather than realistic (whatever that might mean in a non-positivist world) but that is arguably their greatest strength. Impressionistic as they are, they represent cities in sociologically interesting ways. They offer alternative visions, not unlike those provided by those writers of fiction who are equally enthralled by the urban life. This chapter examines various ways in which *flânerie* can contribute to our understanding of the social significance of sport and its places. Whilst not as yet a common form of ethnographic research, its potential is identified. One can argue that it is a form of ethnography without the customary direct contact with individuals as opposed to society conceived of in more general terms. The chapter concludes with three vignettes that take us from Belfast to Seville to Tokyo and focus not only on the venues where certain activities take place but also, at least as significantly, on the surrounding streets, restaurants, bars and shops on days where nothing much appears to be happening in relation to sport except what the *flâneur* sees.

Flânerie and sociology of the city

The origins of urban sociology can be traced to the work of the Chicago School in the 1920s and 1930s, with Robert E. Park as the founder of an ecological approach which likened cities to biological organisms (Short, 1971). Many subsequent studies of cities have been influenced by this approach even though its emphasis on the natural development of the city tends to ignore the importance of economic and political decisions about planning.

The potential overlap between *flânerie* and ethnographic social research has been increasingly recognised (Bairner, 2006a, 2006b; Jenks, 1995). Polley (2010), for example, has commented on the value of this type of activity for the study and teaching of sport history. But what precisely is *flânerie*? According to Gluck (2003, p. 53), "the *flâneur* has become a generalized symbol of urban experience and cultural modernity in recent scholarly debates". As Tester (1994, p. 1) notes, "*flânerie*, the activity of strolling and looking which is carried out by the *flâneur*, is a recurring motif in the literature, sociology and art of urban, and most especially of the metropolitan existence". At one level, as Edmund White (2001, p. 16) claims, the *flâneur* is "that aimless stroller who loses himself in the crowd, who has no destination and goes wherever caprice or curiosity directs his or her steps". That said, the *flâneur's* curiosity about life in the modern city helps to explain why, as Tester (1994, p. 1) argues, "the figure and the activity appear regularly in the attempts of social commentators to get some grip on the nature and implications of the conditions of modernity and post-modernity". Key figures in the history of *flânerie* include such otherwise disparate individuals as Charles Baudelaire, Walt Whitman and Walter Benjamin.

It is the activity of seeing that is crucial, as Benjamin, Louis Wirth and also Georg Simmel recognised, if the city is to be understood. In his quest to understand, the *flâneur* "stands apart from the city even as he appears to 'fuse' with it; he interprets each of its component parts in isolation in order, subsequently, to attain intellectual understanding of the whole as a complex system of meaning" (Burton, 1994, p. 1). For this reason, the nineteenth-century *flâneur* might be described as an embryonic urban sociologist insofar as he (and, as is discussed below, the *flâneur* has customarily been male) is willing and able to take up the challenges set out by the likes of Wirth a century later (Reiss, 1964). Furthermore, despite evidence of scepticism, it continues to be argued that the *flâneur* reads the city as a text and "from a distance" (Ferguson, 1994, p. 31). As a consequence, Tester (1994, p. 18) finds it possible to argue that "the *flâneur* and *flânerie* become different and intriguing keys to understanding the social and cultural milieu". Mazlish (1994, p. 53) goes even further, arguing that "in the end, the *flâneur's* vision of life, based on his peripatetic observations, creates reality".

For Jenks (1995, p. 150), "there is a difficult and continuous moral problem facing the *flâneur* in relation to the issue of gender". Featherstone (1998) questions the assumption that the forms of activity normally associated with *flânerie* have been exclusively male. However, even in those contemporary societies that might be regarded as relatively enlightened in terms of gender relations, men continue to enjoy much easier access to a wider range of public spaces, and hence to the activity of *flânerie*, for a variety of reasons (Skeggs, 1999).

Edmund White (2001, p. 145) further postulates a close relationship between male homosexuality and *flânerie*, suggesting that "to be gay and cruise is perhaps an extension of the *flâneur's* very essence, or at least its most successful application". Whilst this argument appears to rely heavily on stereotypical images both of the *flâneur* and of the male homosexual, more convincing is the argument that the *flâneur* should certainly be a solitary figure. As Ferguson (1994, p. 27) argues, "companionship of any sort is undesirable". "*Flânerie*", Ferguson continues, "requires the city and its crowds, yet the *flâneur* remains aloof from both" (p. 27).

It is also important that the *flâneur* has sufficient free time to walk and read the city. As White (2001, p. 39) observes, "the *flâneur* is by definition endowed with enormous leisure, someone who can take off a morning or afternoon for undirected ambling, since a specific goal or a close rationing of time is antithetical to the true spirit of the *flâneur*". In addition, it is vitally important that the *flâneur* should walk or, if need be, use public transport. With alternative forms of transport in mind, Featherstone (1998) wonders what difference speed makes. The fact is that inside the bus, the train or the tram, people speak and act at normal speed. The city only appears to move faster.

The distinction between *flânerie* and certain unlawful activities such as voyeurism or stalking is certainly narrow. Furthermore, it is important that the *flâneur* is willing to enter the criminal or less salubrious recesses of society, to live "outside the bounds and bonds of bourgeois life" (Mazlish, 1994, p. 51). Yet, as Ferguson (1994, p. 28) notes, "the *flâneur* remains anonymous, devoid of personality, unremarkable in the crowd". The *flâneur*, as Tester (1994, p. 2) describes him, is "a man who is only at home existentially when he is not at home physically". It is the city that provides the ideal environment for such a man and, as Polley (2010, p. 141) argues, "being there gives us at the very least a sense of place, an appreciation". An additional benefit of this approach to research is that it can easily be adopted without prior ethical approval although risk assessment could be a more constraining factor.

Writing in 1995, Chris Jenks (1995, p. 145) noted that "sociology has long since evacuated methodological sites that claimed any correspondential relation with the 'seen' phenomenon". In response, Jenks (1995, p. 145) sought "to reconstitute the analytic force of the flâneur". The *flâneur* offer an alternative vision, one that is, according to Jenks (1995, p. 149), "more optimistic than that founded on 'power-knowledge'". Wearing and Wearing (1996, p. 241) argue that "the fleeting sights experienced by the 'flâneur' may well be shown... to be flat and unimaginative reflections of a one dimensional way of seeing the world". But much depends on the individual *flâneur*.

The radicalism of the streets

One of Britain's greatest observers of cities was Ian Nairn, most famous perhaps for his *Nairn's London* (1966). Whilst ostensibly describing the buildings of London and of other cities and towns, Nairn did much more besides. According to Meades (2012, p. 394),

> *Nairn's London* is questionably useful and it does not report. It creates *places* which did not previously exist. It's fiction without characters, or rather the décor of a fiction with just one character. The true subject of *Nairn's London*, the book's protagonist is Nairn and his sensibility, his visual, intellectual, emotional responses to what is around him – and his expression of those responses. It is authoritative precisely because it dispenses with all pretence of impersonal objectivity.

This is what the *flâneur* can achieve and, in so doing, add a creative dimension to the ways in which we understand the social life of cities. The agenda might also be political. As Gros (2014, p. 177) suggests, "the urban stroller is subversive. He subverts the crowd, the merchandise and the town, along with their values."

Virilio (2006, p. 30) poses the question, "Can asphalt be a political territory?" The answer is surely an unequivocal yes. From Paris at the end of the eighteenth century to Manchester in the nineteenth century, from Prague in 1968 to Bangkok in 2009, the record of people taking to the streets in protest is endless. It is no accident, therefore, that the famous architect and planner, Le Corbusier, regarded the street as a symbol of disorder and disharmony. According to Solnit (2002, p. 216), "public marches mingle the language of the pilgrimage, in which one walks to demonstrate one's commitment, with the strike's picket line, in which one demonstrates the strength of one's group and one's persistence by pacing back and forth, and the festival, in which the boundaries between strangers recede". As Virilio

(2006, p. 31) asserts, "all through history there has been an unspoken, unrecognized revolutionary wandering, the organization of a *first mass transportation* – which is nonetheless revolution itself".

At times, this revolution has been aimed specifically at winning access to space. Thus emerged "the great trespasses and walks that changed the face of the English countryside" (Solnit, 2002, p. 164). Arguably one of the best known of these was the ramblers' mass trespass on Kinder Scout in England's Peak District. As Hargreaves (1986, p. 92) relates, "set aside exclusively for the rich to shoot grouse, the area strongly symbolized the relationship between leisure, sport and privileged power". But here the location was rural and the central objective was to secure access to a particular place. According to Solnit (2002, p. 173), "rural walking has found a moral imperative in the love of nature that has allowed it to defend and open up the countryside". In keeping with the image of the *flâneur*, on the other hand, "urban walking has always been a shadier business, easily turning into soliciting, cruising, promenading, shopping, rioting, protesting, skulking, loitering, and other activities that, however enjoyable, hardly have the high moral tone of nature appreciation" (Solnit, 2002, pp. 173–4). That said, at least one of these activities – protesting – is also closely identified with higher goals. Indeed, urban protest inevitably combines a desire to access the street with the use of that access for numerous other political objectives.

Such a combination underpinned the arguments and actions of the French situationists, led, amongst others, by Guy Debord, who "deployed détournement, or hijacking, to monkey wrench accepted behaviour and meaning in bourgeois cities" (Merrifield, 2002, p. 98). The situationists' concept of *dérive* was essentially "the search for an encounter with otherness, spurred on in equal parts by the exploration of class, ethnic and racial difference in the post war city, and by frequent intoxication" (McDonagh, 2009, pp. 10–11). The lessons of the *dérive*, according to Debord, "permit the drawing up of the first surveys of the psycho-geographic articulation of the modern city" (cited in McDonagh, 2009, p. 84). In addition, for political or quasi-political movements, the street had to be taken over but primarily as a precursor to seizing society or, as in the case of Gay Pride marches and ethnic minority carnival parades, simply as a means of announcing, 'We are here.'

Walking the streets in protest is one way of engaging with strangers although the latter remain onlookers – supportive, perhaps, and enthused by the collective meaning embodied in the walk but also potentially hostile, both ideologically ('I disagree with their cause') and pragmatically ('What right do they have to stop the traffic?'). However, the street also demands more immediate, even intimate, association with strangers – with the 'otherness' that the situationists craved. As de Certeau (1988, p. 100) describes, "the walking of passers-by offers a series of turns (*tours*) and detours that can be compared to 'turns of phrase' or 'stylistic figures'".

Encounters with strangers

According to Jane Jacobs (1992, p. 56), "the trust of a city street is formed over time from many, many little public sidewalk contacts". It is on the city street that we are most likely to come into physical contact with strangers. As Erving Goffman (1966, p. 33) noted,

> when individuals come into one another's immediate presence in circumstances where no spoken communication is called for, they none the less inevitably engage one another in communication of a sort, for in all situations, significance is ascribed to certain matters that are not necessarily connected with particular verbal communications.

Furthermore, traffic relationships in cities, as Hannerz (1980, p. 106) comments, "are a pure form of meetings among strangers, a result of the crowding of large numbers of people in a limited space". Seldom is that more apparent than when we walk.

We brush up against another person and invariably apologise. We try to avoid walking into other people. We laugh when in so doing we move to the left as the oncoming stranger moves to the right and our subsequent movements are choreographed through uncertainty. Unlike roads, pavements or sidewalks have very few signs indicating where we should walk and at what speed. Instead we behave according to time-honoured custom. If we did not walk the streets, we would miss out on a valuable lesson about sharing – in this case, the sharing of public space. The implications of such a loss are serious inasmuch as they might lead to a preference for spaces which we do need not share with strangers, thereby strengthening the case for creating places of exclusion. As Sharon Zukin (2010, p. 142) describes the process, "Offering special events in pleasant surroundings, with a low risk of 'worrisome encounters', these places set up islands of calm in a turbulent world, re-creating urban life as a civilized ideal." It is a civilised ideal, however, that necessarily lessens contact with strangers, simply defined as 'people who are not like us', and as a result, ensures that valuable lessons that the streets can teach will be lost.

Although for the most part, there is little reason to fear physical aggression in street encounters with strangers, there is one specific potentially threatening feature of life on the streets that must be considered. Given that the *flâneur* is traditionally male and his behaviour has often been seen as shady at best and decadent at worst, the question of the 'male gaze' inevitably arises (Mulvey, 2009). This concept has often been used simply to describe the way in which heterosexual men look at and sexually objectify women and, as such, it has become a metaphor for power asymmetry and patriarchal domination. In reality, however, the street is a place where virtually everyone looks at everyone else. For example, the object of the male gaze need not be a heterosexual female. Consider for example the disruption caused by the appearance on many streets even today of a lipstick (or hyper-feminine) lesbian accompanied by her girlfriend (Probyn, 1995).

The street is also a site for the straight 'female gaze' which is directed both at men and at other women (Goddard, 2000). Think also of the indirect impact of the straight 'male gaze' on gay men's perceptions of their own bodies (Wood, 2004) and on the gaze that is exchanged between gay men themselves. According to one of the most celebrated modern *flâneurs*, Edmund White (2009, p. 210), "in New York people check each other out to find out who they are, whereas in other cities there's no reason to bother since no one is ever anyone". He makes this point in support of his claim that, in New York, everyone, not only gay men, 'cruises'. Whilst he is correct in his analysis of New York, he is wrong to deny that similar patterns of behaviour can be witnessed in other towns and cities. Fewer people may be famous in other locations but everyone becomes 'someone' precisely because of another's gaze.

According to Solnit (2002, p. 13), "exploring the world is one of the best ways of exploring the mind, and walking travels both terrains". She adds, "while walking, the body and the mind can work together, so that thinking becomes almost a physical, rhythmic act – so much for the Cartesian mind/ body divide" (p. xv). Cities and towns are particularly important locations in this regard. In the words of Macauley (2000, p. 3),

> perhaps even more than walking in the wilderness, sauntering and strolling in the city and its suburbs involves multiple, repeated and deeply imbricated border crossings, including nested neighbourhoods, traffic flows, ethnic enclaves, residential and commercial zones, subcultures, historical sites, sacred spaces and outcroppings of the wild in parks, cemeteries and abandoned lots.

Solnit (2002, p. 171) adds that "cities have always offered anonymity, variety, and conjunction, qualities best basked in by walking: one does not have to go into the bakery or the fortune-teller's, only to know that one might". For Sorkin (2009, p. 81), "walking is not simply an occasion for observation but an analytical instrument". This can manifest itself when walking and talking with others. Thus, we return to the educational benefits to be derived from the solitary stroll.

Psychogeography and the pedagogies of the streets

Debord's idea of psychogeography, which he himself did little to develop, offers a dimension to *flânerie* which is both intellectually stimulating but also frequently radical in its ambitions. According to Nicholson (2011, p. 48), "walking was, and remains, psychogeography's main mode of operation". There is, of course, a certain degree of cynicism about psychogeography not unlike that which was once directed at the *flâneur*. As Nicholson (2011, pp. 49–50) observes, "psychogeography often seems to be a way for clever young men to mooch around cities doing nothing much, claiming that they're *flâneurs* who are doing something, you know, significant, and often taking Iain Sinclair as their role model". As Nicholson admits, however, none of this is Sinclair's fault and, indeed, by using his feet, his ears, his eyes and his erudition, Sinclair is able to combine his experiences of walking "with various overlapping historical traditions; the literary, the bohemian, the criminal, the mystical, the alchemical..." (Nicholson, 2011, p. 47).

The learning experience takes two distinct forms. First, we learn about the city through which we are passing from its buildings, its smells, its sounds and from the snatches of conversation that we overhear if people are speaking a language we know. Our observations subsequently impact on how we behave, for as Goldbard (2010, p. 57) reminds us, "what we perceive and understand when we look at the world – the stories we tell ourselves to explain what we see – is what shapes our actions". Secondly (and here it can help if we cannot understand what others are saying), there is the opportunity to daydream or, less whimsically, simply to think. In the latter regard, it is worth bringing to mind Jean-Jacques Rousseau's (1979, p. 12) claim that his whole life had been "little else than a long reverie divided into chapters by my daily walks". Underlining the importance of urban walking in this respect, Gregory Dart (2010, p. 79) comments, "daydreaming is inescapable in the metropolis" – as, it can be argued, is thinking even when the walker is preoccupied by the various products of new technology courtesy of the special relationship between the eye, hands and feet that has been attributed to the practices of the mobile phone pedestrian (Richardson and Wilken, 2009). Morris and Hardman (1997, p. 328) end their important scientific argument about the physiological benefits of walking with a quote from G.M. Trevelyan (1913, p. 56) – "I have two doctors, my left leg and my right...". To this might be added the following – "I also have two educators, my right leg and my left". So what can we learn about sporting places through acts of *flânerie*?

Sport and the city (or what the flâneur saw)

Although I had already spent hours walking the streets of Edinburgh where I had studied in the early 1970s, I probably began to take *flânerie* seriously (without recognising it as such) in Belfast where I began working in 1978. As Bale and Vertinsky (2004, p. 1) have shown, "the significance of space and place as central dimensions of sport is well recognised by scholars who have addressed questions of sport from philosophical, sociological, geographical and historical perspectives" (Bale and Vertinsky, 2004, p. 1). The question is how best to study sporting places.

Being a *flâneur* in the vicinity of sporting venues is not simply a matter of attending games; it is also about visiting those venues at other times as well. It is then that one is able to fully appreciate the locations and their immediate surroundings and to gauge what tales the streets can tell about the sport that is played there and about the people who play that sport. The following vignettes offer a *flâneur's* insights into sport and its places in three cities – Belfast in Northern Ireland, Seville in Spain and Tokyo in Japan.

Belfast

Sport has been long recognised as a marker of identity in Northern Ireland. The sports that one plays and watches and the places where one chooses to do so testify, far more often than not, to communal loyalty centred on the relationship between national identity and social space. Even participation in physical activity more generally has been greatly influenced by feelings of fear and mistrust. Sports stadia such as Casement Park, home to the Gaelic Athletic Association (GAA) in County Antrim, and Irish league soccer grounds, including Windsor Park, the Oval, Seaview and Solitude, although unimpressive when set against the high standards of major stadia in other countries, are vitally important inscriptions on Belfast's cultural landscape. Even though the composition of the teams that play at these soccer grounds may evolve over time, most of the fans who attend their games remain constrained by the cultural myopia that has underpinned inter- and intra-communal conflict. Being present at sporting places is often a matter of affirming either explicitly or, at the very least implicitly, one's political allegiance.

In terms of physical space, Belfast is a relatively easy city in which to idly wander; most of the main sports venues are in walking distance of the City Hall. In the worst days of civil unrest, however, few people would have simply wandered from one sporting place to another or, indeed, from one neighbourhood to another. Rightly or wrongly, fear was a major constraint, and almost certainly remains so even in these times of relative peace. It is also worth noting that, even if a sense of fear has no rational foundation, it is always real for the person who feels it. It helps, of course, that there are clear indications – murals, painted kerbstones, flags – that one is in close proximity to an area which one might have some cause to fear. As an outsider (or incomer), I walked the city's streets far more than most.

The two largest football grounds in Belfast, Windsor Park and the Oval, are located at different ends of the city. Both, however, are situated in what have traditionally been regarded as Protestant working-class areas. Admittedly, the population around Windsor Park, home to Linfield Football Club and the Northern Ireland national team, is now less homogeneous than was once the case and this is also true of the east Belfast streets that surround The Oval, home to Glentoran Football Club. Nevertheless, the environs around both grounds are still characterised by loyalist iconography in the form of painted kerbstones, murals and flags. It comes as little surprise, therefore, that many Catholics are unwilling to visit either stadium. This is equally true of Protestants who show no desire to visit Casement Park in west Belfast, the major venue for Gaelic games in Northern Ireland. In this instance, the surrounding area is solidly nationalist and Catholic – hence, the topophobic response. In addition, the GAA, which governs Gaelic games throughout Ireland, has long been seen by many Ulster unionists as a republican organisation.

As one walks up the Falls Road towards Casement Park, black taxis speed past. They provide a mode of transport not unique to Belfast but one which has conferred its own particular character on the city. Cabs leave various sites close to the city centre and travel along a number of main roads leading to residential areas in the north and west of the city. The operation itself reflects the city's patterns of residential segregation. Drivers wait until six passengers (including one in the front passenger seat) have taken their places. The ultimate destination of the taxi that has just picked up two passengers is Twinbrook, a working-class estate on the outskirts of west Belfast, once home to Bobby Sands, the first of the republican hunger strikers to die in the Maze Prison in 1981. The walk to Casement is intermittently marked by republican iconography and suffused with memories of the troubles – an Irish Republican Army (IRA) memorial on the left and, on the right, a *Sinn Féin* information centre, the gable end of which is adorned with a large mural depicting Sands. Further on, to the left, is Milltown Cemetery with its republican burial plots. This was the scene of loyalist gunman Michael Stone's audacious attack on an IRA funeral in 1988. Soon Casement Park appears. As in most nationalist areas of the city, street names in the surrounding Andersonstown district are rendered in Irish Gaelic as well as in English. So this is *Páirc an Casement*, named after Sir Roger Casement, a nationalist hero but, in the eyes of unionists, a traitor to Britain. This is in keeping with a fairly widespread practice within the GAA to call stadia and clubs after prominent nationalist and republican figures.

The stadium itself is impressive in an old-fashioned way – a large oval-shaped bowl with a much bigger playing surface than at soccer grounds. Inside as well as outside the signs are in Gaelic. The location, the iconography, the use of the Irish language – nothing about Casement would seem welcoming to most Protestants although one suspects that overseas visitors to the city might feel more comfortable here than in the streets surrounding the major soccer grounds, particularly The Oval. The fact remains that this is an Irish nationalist place, not a stadium that could be in the forefront of a campaign to put Belfast on the global sporting map. Walking back toward the city centre, however, there is the Red Devil Bar, named in honour of Manchester United, one of the world's most successful sporting brands. In these terraced streets which have witnessed so much violence over the years, the idle wanderer observes the juxtaposition of global and local sporting reference points.

Seville

Even visitors to the city of Seville who are repelled by the whole idea of bullfighting must surely be impressed by the beauty of Plaza de Toros de la Real Maestranza, the city's bullring. It is unlikely, however, that they would spend long in the surrounding area or be equally impressed by the images of *toreros* at work and the heads of long dead bulls that adorn the neighbourhood bars of El Arenal, the district of which La Maestranza is the centrepiece. But it is here that the idle wanderer can acquire a sense of why this form of entertainment – sporting or cultural – survives in so many parts of Spain.

Even when the rain is heavy and the opening of the new season is almost certain to be abandoned, the excitement created by bullfighting is palpable. Once the event is called off, many *aficionados* make their way home to distant parts of the city, to other towns and villages in Andalusia and to other regions of Spain. Some decide to remain in the neighbourhood and enjoy the evening by drinking and eating tapas. In one small bar only a few short steps from La Maestranza, a group of old men sit in the corner drinking large glasses of red wine. As is customary, the wall behind the bar is covered with images of the Virgin Mother, a number of football related memorabilia (here associated with Real Betis, one of the city's two La Liga teams), and a group of signed photos of bullfighters, some of them with their arms around the shoulders of the bar owner who stands proudly in front of his personal gallery. The atmosphere is subdued. On such an unusual night as this, thoughts and words are preoccupied with what might have been rather than with what has actually taken place.

All of a sudden the mood changes. The door opens. A tall young woman with long blonde hair comes in followed by a handsome young man and what appears to be their bodyguard. I take a quick look at the programme produced for the now cancelled event and see at once that the young man is one of the *toreros* who had been scheduled to perform. The old men become animated as does the bar owner. For a moment, I feel like an intruder. The young bullfighter crosses to the table where the old men are sitting. He shakes hands with each of them and orders more wine. His girlfriend and their associate take their seat at a nearby table. The young man then approaches me, the silent, idle onlooker in the corner. Another handshake, and a beer ordered for a complete stranger. Everyone is smiling. It is as if we are now in the presence of a demi-God. This is not the excitement that the arrival of a famous footballer or a pop star would cause. There is a deeper reverence shown towards the new arrival – inspired perhaps by the recognition that only a few hours ago he had been preparing to enter the ring on two occasions and confront the prospect of death, almost certainly that of the bulls but possibly his own.

Anyone who wishes to understand bullfighting properly must witness bullfighting. It is undeniable, however, that one's understanding is also aided by simply walking close to the great, and not so great, arenas of Spain.

The in-house infirmaries are a constant reminder of the danger that *toreros* face, as is the statue of Alexander Fleming at the Plaza de Toros de Las Ventas in Madrid. The bemused *flâneur* may initially be surprised that a Scottish doctor should be celebrated at such a venue and in the street names of countless Spanish towns and cities. The explanation is, of course, quite simple. The discovery of penicillin saved the lives of many bullfighters who would previously have died as a result of the wounds inflicted by a *toro bravo*. Always the streets have stories to tell.

Tokyo

Ryoguko Kokugikan is the home of sumo wrestling in Tokyo. For an outsider to fully understand sumo is arguably a virtually impossible task achieved by only a few. Attending one of the three annual *basho* that take place at the stadium will certainly help. At least as instructive, however, is to wander around the surrounding area. Traditionally, many of the stables where the wrestlers live and train were situated nearby and it is still possible to catch a glimpse of a junior wrestler doing some shopping or even going to attend a practice session. As one leaves the nearby station, the first thing to notice is a small, squat statue of two wrestlers. Close by are stalls bearing a variety of sumo related souvenirs and a photo board similar to those seen at British seaside resorts but here allowing visitors to the neighbourhood to insert their heads above the body of a sumo wrestler and be captured for posterity. There are also restaurants where fans of sumo can eat the food that accounts for the bulk of the wrestlers. This is *chanko nabe*, a protein-packed stew with innumerable ingredients.

Only five minutes' walk from the station is a place where sumo is celebrated very differently. The Eko-in Temple is regarded as the spiritual home and original venue of sumo. Visiting it in the half light of a late January afternoon is a moving experience. Here is the Chikara-zuka or 'Mound of Strength' which was erected as a gift from the Sumo Association in 1937 and remains an object of veneration for new wrestlers.

Again there is so much to be learned from the streets although a visit to a *basho* is also important. First, there is the reception committee of fans waiting to cheer their favourite wrestlers and their attendants as they step from private cars or taxis and make their way to the stadium. Tickets are taken by a former wrestler now making his way up the retired sumo wrestlers' ladder within the organisation. Once inside, there is more *chanko* and also bento boxes with contents linked to the names of prominent wrestlers. Then there is the arena itself – full of strange sights and sounds. Invented or not, there is something which to the outsider is distinctively Japanese, with the exception, of course, of many of the wrestlers. The two star performers are both Mongolian. Other countries represented include Bulgaria, Estonia, and the Czech Republic. This causes the traditionalists considerable angst. Yet, the irony is that, during this particular visit to Tokyo, the death was announced of Taiho, considered to be the greatest sumo wrestler of the second half of the twentieth century and arguably the greatest of all time. He had been born Ivan Boryshko Karafuto on the Japanese half of the island now controlled by Russia and called Sakhalin. His father was Ukrainian, his mother Japanese. After the Red Army occupied the entire island at the end of World War Two, his father was arrested and he and his mother fled to Hokkaido, Japan's northernmost island. Not only did he go on to become a great wrestler, but he was also a popular celebrity especially in the eyes of Japanese children. After his retirement, however, he was never rewarded with high positions in the Sumo Association, a fact that some felt was attributable to his lack of pure Japanese blood. The small museum at the stadium is exhibiting a small collection of Taiho's memorabilia. Inside and outside the stadium, the symbolism of sumo is both beguiling and educational.

Conclusion

In this chapter, I have sought to advance the case, first proposed by Georg Simmel, for impressionism as a sociological method of investigation (Frisby, 1992; Wolff, 1950). If the social scientist is in truth a trained observer of social life, then he or she must be prepared to put that training to the test. The *flâneur* gathers data without recourse to such techniques as triangulation. He trusts his own powers of observation at least as much and perhaps more than the words of interviewees or the information provided in official documents. Because of his willingness and ability to move easily from one social setting to another, he is able to accumulate a massive amount of subjective, but nonetheless insightful, data.

It is undeniable that at present few ethnographers have turned to *flanerie* as their chosen research method. I believe that many more should consider doing so this. But they should note that it is never enough simply to wander idly. It is crucially important that the social scientists who wish to use *flanerie* successfully must complement their wandering with wide reading of both fictional and nonfictional accounts of the particular urban setting which is the focus of their study. Armed with the knowledge that such reading conveys and their own analytical skills, their strolls will thereupon cease to be purely idle.

References

Bairner, A. (2006a). The *flâneur* and the city: Reading Belfast's 'new' leisure spaces. *Space and Polity*, *10*, 121–134.

Bairner, A. (2006b). Titanic town: Sport, sporting space and the re-imag(in)ing of Belfast, *City and Society*, *18*(2), 159–179.

Bale, J., & Vertinsky, P. (2004). Introduction. In P. Vertinsky & J. Bale (Eds.), *Sites of sport. Space, place, experience* (pp. 1–7). Routledge: London.

Burton, R.D.E. (1994). *The flâneur and his city. Patterns of daily life in Paris 1815–1851*. Durham: University of Durham Press.

Dart, G. (2010). Daydreaming. In M. Beaumont & G. Dart (Eds.), *Restless cities* (pp. 79–97). London: Verso.

de Certeau, M. (1988). *The practice of everyday life*. Berkeley: University of California Press.

Featherstone, M. (1998). The *flâneur*, the city and virtual public life. *Urban Studies, 35*, 909–925.

Ferguson, P.P. (1994). The *flâneur* on and off the streets of Paris. In K. Tester (Ed.), *The flâneur* (pp. 22–42). London: Routledge.

Frisby, D. (1992). *Sociological impressionism: A reassessment of Georg Simmel's social theory*. London: Routledge.

Gluck, M. (2003). The *flâneur* and the aesthetic appropriation of urban culture in mid-19th-century Paris. *Theory, Culture and Society, 20*, 53–80.

Goddard, K. (2000). 'Looks Maketh the Man': the female gaze and the construction of Masculinity. *Journal of Men's Studies, 9*(1), 23–39.

Goffman, E. (1966). *Behavior in public places. Notes on the social organization of gatherings*. New York: The Free Press.

Goldbard, A. (2010). Nine ways of looking at ourselves (looking at cities). In S.A. Goldsmith & L. Elizabeth (Eds.), *What we see. Advancing the observations of Jane Jacobs* (pp. 57–67). Oakland, CA: New Village Press.

Gros, F. (2014) *The philosophy of walking*. London: Verso.

Hannerz, U. (1980). *Exploring the city. Inquiries toward an urban anthropology*. New York: Columbia University Press.

Hargreaves, J. (1986). *Sport, power and culture*. Cambridge: Polity Press.

Jacobs, J. (1992). *The death and life of great American cities*. New York: Vintage Books.

Jenks, C. (1995). Watching your step. The history and practice of the *flâneur*. In C. Jenks (Ed.), *Visual vulture* (pp. 142–160). London: Routledge.

Macauley, D. (2000). Walking the city: An essay on peripatetic practices and politics. *Capitalism Nature Socialism, 11*(4), 3–43.

Mazlish, B. (1994). The *flâneur*: from spectator to representation. In K. Tester (Ed.) *The flâneur* (pp. 43–60). London: Routledge.

McDonagh, T. (2009). *The situationists and the city*. London: Verso.

Meades, J. (2012). *Museum without walls*. London: Unbound.

Merrifield, A. (2002). *Metromarxism. A Marxist tale of the city*. New York: Routledge.

Morris, J.N., & Hardman, A.E. (1997). Walking to health. *Sports Medicine, 23*(5): 307–332.

Mulvey, L. (2009). *Visual and other pleasures*. London: Palgrave Macmillan.

Nairn, T. (1966). *Nairn's London*. Harmondsworth: Penguin.

Nicholson, G. (2011). *The lost art of walking. The history, science, philosophy, literature, theory and practice of pedestrianism*. Chelmsford, Essex: Harbour.

Polley, M. (2010). 'The archive of the feet': field walking in sports history. *Journal of Sport History, 37*, 139–153.

Probyn, E. (1995). Lesbians in space. Gender, sex and the structure of missing. *Gender, Place and Culture, 2*(1), 77–84.

Reiss, A.J., Jr. (Ed.) (1964). *Louis Wirth on cities and social life*. Chicago, IL: University of Chicago Press.

Richardson, I., & Wilken, R. (2009). Haptic vision, footwork, place making: A peripatetic phenomenology of the mobile phone. *Second Nature: International Journal of Creative Media, 1(2)*, 22–41.

Rousseau, J.J. (1979). *Reveries of the solitary walker*. New York: Penguin Books.

Short, J.F., Jr. (Ed.) (1971). *The social fabric of the metropolis: Contributions of the Chicago School of Urban Sociology*. Chicago, IL: University of Chicago Press.

Skeggs, B. (1999). Matter out of place: Visibility and sexualities in leisure spaces. *Leisure Studies, 18*, 213–232.

Solnit, R. (2002). *Wanderlust. A history of walking* (new edition). London: Verso.

Sorkin, M. (2009). *Twenty minutes in Manhattan*. London: Reaktion Books.

Tester, K. (1994). Introduction. In K. Tester (Ed.), *The flâneur* (pp. 1–21). London: Routledge.

Trevelyan, G.M. (1913). *Clio, a muse and other essays*. London: Longman, Green and Co.

Virilio, P. (2006). *Speed and politics*. Los Angeles: Semiotext(e).

Wearing, B., & Wearing, S. (1996). Refocussing the tourist experience: The *flâneur* and the chorister. *Leisure Studies, 15*, 229–243.

White, E. (2001). *The flâneur. A stroll through the paradoxes of Paris*. London: Bloomsbury.

White, E. (2009). *City boy. My life in New York during the 1960s and 1970s*. London: Bloomsbury.

Wolff, K.H. (Ed.) (1950). *The sociology of Georg Simmel*. New York: The Free Press.

Wood, M.J. (2004). The gay male gaze. *Journal of Gay and Lesbian Social Services, 17(2)*, 43–62.

Zukin, S. (2010). *Naked city. The death and life of authentic urban places*. New York: Oxford University Press.

Chapter 14

The marginal place of ethnographic research in sport management

John Harris

Whilst many different academic disciplines have embraced qualitative research methods for a number of years, the broad field of management has not universally utilised this approach (Edwards & Skinner, 2010). This is reflected in the area of sport management, when it is compared with related areas such as sport psychology or the sociology of sport, where there has been a relative paucity of research framed by an ethnographic approach. This, in part, might be attributed to the lack of what is sometimes termed the more critical analyses of sport management. Some sport management scholars have in the last ten years called for more critical work in the area (e.g. Frisby, 2005; Skinner & Edwards, 2005) and have also noted that qualitative research "is gradually evolving into a more accepted practice" (Edwards & Skinner, 2010, p. 263) in this field. It would be inaccurate to suggest that there is no critical sport management research, or more specifically as relates to the focus of this chapter, no qualitative or ethnographic research. Yet it would be fair to state that whilst this may be gradually evolving, there is still a long way to go until such work is firmly embedded within the field and assumes a central place in sport management scholarship.

In this chapter, I will first briefly outline the positioning of sport management as a field of study and then explore some of the reasons behind the lack of ethnographic research in this domain. I then go on to consider the place of the sociological imagination in developing ethnographic research in sport management. To do this I will then look at some selected studies that have used ethnographic research to show how this approach has contributed to the field and tease out some of the key issues shaping contemporary sport management. Finally, the chapter concludes by looking at the promise of a postmodern sport management discipline where ethnography assumes a more central role.

Sport management: shaping the field

Pitts and Stotlar (2007, p. 4) define sport management as "the study and practice of all people, activities, businesses, or organizations involved in producing, facilitating, promoting, or organizing any sport-related business or product". Most programmes in the USA are located within business, health or education schools (Mahony, 2008). Many, though not all, of these courses are housed in departments where traditional (positivist) research methodologies dominate and there continues to be an emphasis on reliability, validity and the testing of hypotheses. This of course is also the case for a number of the other subjects featured in this collection on sport and exercise research, and there will be similar stories of marginalisation and a struggle for approval in a variety of locales. It may well be though that this struggle is exasperated in sport management given that it might be conceived as a particularly narrow field. In their work on the social construction of knowledge in the field, Quatman and Chelladurai (2008, p. 663) note that "a large majority of the work in the field of sport management has been produced by a small minority of actors". Here then, as one would expect, there will be a noticeable dominance of particular methodological approaches and theories within the available literature (see also Ciomaga, 2013).

Within sport scholarship more broadly an increased focus on the subjective nature of what counts as knowledge, and viewing research as a way of telling tales, has now been an accepted and valued part of the area for some years (Sparkes, 2002). Edwards, Gilbert and Skinner (2002) pointed to the lack of engagement with postmodern theory within sport management and made a cogent argument for a much greater engagement with emerging methodologies in the discipline. More than ten years after this call, it is noticeable that there is still a relative dearth of work that does this. As a reflection of the points noted above, there is only a limited amount of published work in sport management that has utilised ethnographic research. Before returning to the specifics of sport management scholarship I will briefly first look at the ways in which boundaries limit our understanding of where work may fit in a broader perspective and outline the potential of the sociological imagination as a means to move beyond some of these.

Beyond the boundaries: the case for the sociological imagination

We each view the universe "from a centre lying within ourselves" (Polanyi, 1958, p. 3). The work of C.W. Mills (1959/1970) offers a useful point of departure from which to further explore this. For Mills (1970, p. 22) the sociological imagination "is a quality of mind that seems most dramatically to promise an understanding of the intimate realities of ourselves in connexion with larger social realities". In outlining his vision, Mills (1970, pp. 245–6) offered the following advice to researchers:

> Be a good craftsman: avoid any rigid set of procedures. Above all, seek to develop and use the sociological imagination. Avoid the fetishism of method and technique. Urge the rehabilitation of the unpretentious

intellectual craftsman, and try to become such a craftsman yourself. Let every man be his own methodologist; let every man be his own theorist; let theory and method again become part of the practice of a craft. Stand for the primacy of the individual scholar; stand against the ascendancy of research teams of technicians. Be one mind that is on its own confronting the problems of man and society.

Such an approach of course was viewed as a radical one within sociology at the time, and perhaps would have been conceived as even more so within domains such as sport management many years later. This reflects the ways in which different subject areas develop, evolve and adapt at divergent speeds. What counts as knowledge, and the boundary lines within and between academic subjects, is shaped by a range of factors including geography, history and methodological primacy. What we as individual scholars see, or more often do not see, is shaped by these boundaries.

The boundaries around certain academic subjects and groups, limit the development of particular approaches outwith the accepted status quo. Almost twenty years ago, Trevor Slack (1996) called for more sport management research beyond the confines of physical education administration and intercollegiate sport. All subjects take time to evolve. If we look at the newer, but closely related, area of event management here we see further evidence of the ways in which "a congratulatory idiom prevails" (Rojek, 2013, p. 22). Here there is a largely unsubstantiated narrative repeated that over-emphasises the perceived positive impacts of events and so "obscures the degree to which human problems reflect mesmerising inertia on structural questions of power, inequality and injustice" (Rojek, 2013, p. 23). As I have outlined elsewhere, with specific reference to the relationship between sport and tourism scholarship, we have often failed to combine disciplines in a truly integrated way (Harris, 2006). As one of the leading proponents of an area of research referred to as sport tourism, Heather Gibson (1998) noted that scholars have often failed to bridge "the artificial academic divide" between the disciplines of sport and tourism and highlighted that "there are two distinct communities of discourse" (p. 46). Weed (2003, 2005) has also contributed much to this particular area including work focusing on the policy level evidencing that it is not only in academia that these boundaries permeate the lack of connectivity between different areas.

Sport management and the sociology of sport are two seemingly closely related disciplines which would seem to have much in common. Attending conferences in both of these areas would probably have revealed a distinct difference in the literature sets referred to. Subjects such as globalisation and migration are examples here where there is not always any interplay between the knowledge bases in the sociology and management domains as applied to the sports world. Although her work focuses more broadly on the subject of migration, and does not consider sport, the words of Levitt (2012, p. 498) are worth noting here:

Our blind spots and miscommunications are also a function of our networks. If we're honest, that's in part due to a divide between those who can and like getting on airplanes and speaking other languages, and those who can't or don't. Who wants to leave the comfort of his or her own parochial national fan club or go beyond the few cherry-picked outsiders we invite into it? The incentive structures of the academy mitigate against interdisciplinary work at the edges because rewards and visibility are still organized along disciplinary lines.

The academy then in some ways acts against the sharing of ideas and good practice. This is not a specific criticism of the sport management community, for it is something that could be applied to any number of academic disciplines and groups. Levitt's (2012) observation clearly shows the ways in which cliques may be formed and how dominant ideologies and methodologies can easily become *de rigueur*. Zeigler (2007) notes the importance of keeping a healthy balance between the theoretical and the practical in sport management's ongoing scholarship and research. He recalls the case of the Philosophic Society for the Study of Sport (IPAS), of which he was the third president, as an organisation who did not embrace this and now "has very few members and they speak to no one except each other" (Zeigler, 2007, p. 301). They are not alone. Look at the most recent conference schedule for a chosen organisation and, if it is available, look back ten years at the same organisation's conference. At times it is difficult to distinguish between the two. As different disciplines develop, other new and niche areas emerge, and we often see repeated and extended calls for papers as conference organisers struggle to get enough people interested to make the conference viable. An extension on an already extended call for abstracts and panel proposals does not look good. Sport management though remains in relatively good health and the North American Society for Sport Management (NASSM), for example, has a fairly modest acceptance rate of abstracts submitted for its annual conference (of course this is not to ignore the fact that some of the abstracts rejected could be those based on ethnographic research, but that is a discussion for another day!).

It is important to note here that I am not suggesting that all sport management research should be guided by a sociological approach or that ethnographic methods are the only way of undertaking research in this area. Rather, good ethnographic research will complement the existing body of knowledge and contribute to advancing and extending the boundaries that shapes this area. A vibrant academic field is one that looks at the subject from a variety of perspectives and is open to work from a range of other disciplines and perspectives. Tribe's (1997) work on the indiscipline of tourism is a good example here of work that maps the terrain of a particular field and poses key questions as to how it has evolved as an academic subject. The struggle for status and legitimacy is a challenge for many emerging fields of study, and within any given field there may then also be further struggles to present alternative ontological, epistemological and methodological approaches.

Research perspectives and sport management

Hammersley and Atkinson (1995) suggest that the prime goal of research is the production of knowledge. I have long preferred to view data as something that is 'produced' rather than 'collected' as this acknowledges the role of the researcher within the research process. When I was an undergraduate student, the suggested research text for those studying courses broadly relating to sport management was something such as Thomas and Nelson's (2001) *Research Methods in Physical Activity*. The prime focus of early editions of this text, as still evident in later editions, was very much on the quantitative aspects of research. This is not a criticism of this comprehensive and informative account for it is clearly a text written primarily for sport and exercise scientists. It is used here as an example to illustrate the marginal place of qualitative research within the confines of sport scholarship more broadly. Ethnography, in this context, may have warranted a small mention under a broader chapter title of qualitative research but always seemed something of an annex to the main purpose of such texts. Yet often overlooked in many traditional research methods texts is that research must be creative and imaginative in order for this base to be extended. This, for me, was the point best articulated by Mills (1970) when he urged researchers to avoid the temptation of merely labelling work and standing for the primacy of the individual scholar. Sport management, in a global perspective, has historically been dominated by texts where qualitative research has been given minimal attention.

Kuhn (1962/1970), in *The Structure of Scientific Revolutions*, stated that generations of researchers adopt a particular paradigm, and engage in their scientific work, until enough conflicting data force a 'paradigm shift'. Work looking at critical research approaches in sport management reflects this dominant discourse and makes reference to research paradigms (e.g. Amis & Silk, 2005; Frisby, 2005). I prefer to use the word perspective as these are less well-developed systems and can be more easily moved between (Harris, 2006). It is sometimes overlooked that Kuhn himself did not see the concept of paradigms as strictly applicable to the social sciences, since he saw the latter as being made up of a number of different views, in which none were dominant. Anderson, Hughes and Sharrock (1985, p. 3) offer a sound argument as to why perspective rather than paradigm seems a better descriptor:

> There is however, an important ambiguity involved in the idea of perspectives. The expression itself, taken from painting, suggests 'points of view' taken with respect to the same subject-matter. In other words, the relationship between 'points of view' is a complimentary one, each linked to others by the fact that they are about the same subject.

Diverse perspectives bring varied aspects of an object into view and provide different angles on the same thing. Theoretical approaches to the study of sport management then should not be seen as disconnected by the boundaries between them, but viewed as being characterised by considerable overlap.

In his book, *Research Methods for Leisure and Tourism*, which for many years was perhaps the key text for undergraduate sport management students beyond the more traditional sport science texts described above, Tony Veal (1997) highlighted how the interpretive model places more reliance on the people being studied to provide their own explanation of their situation or behaviour. By attempting to see the world from the participant's point of view, the aim is to try and understand how individuals construct social reality (Berger & Luckman, 1966). This perspective is characterised by the adoption of an idealist-internalist stance where the knower and the process of knowing cannot be separated from what is known. This may be viewed as hermeneutical, in that the researcher constructs reality, and what is presented as research findings are just an interpretation of the data (Gadamer, 2006). Hermeneutic theory highlights how an individual can only interpret the meaning of something from someone's perspective. Such work can be described as heuristic, in that personal experiences assume a central place in any study. Patton (1990, p. 73) points out that "heuristic research emphasises the phenomenological emphasis on meanings and knowledge through personal experience". Here the researcher assumes, and wrestles with, multiple identities within the research process. Such an approach challenges traditional 'scientific' concerns relating to objectivity and detachment and continues to be a concern for many sport management scholars as they try to publish their work in journals that may remain resistant to such an approach.

It is noticeable that with a few exceptions (e.g. Andrew, Pedersen & McEvoy, 2011; Downward, 2005; Edwards & Skinner, 2010; Weed, 2005), there has been somewhat limited consideration of the ontological and epistemological issues framing sport management research. Weed (2005, p. 239) has noted how "methodological and epistemological considerations tend to be glossed over in many refereed journal articles". Yet it must also be acknowledged at this point that we now have a much better availability of research methods texts to help prepare sport management students for undertaking research (e.g. Andrew, Pedersen & McEvoy, 2011; Andrews, Mason and Silk, 2005; Edwards and Skinner, 2010; Gratton & Jones, 2004). These provide undergraduate students with a much wider range of texts to go to for an introduction to research methods in sport management and related disciplines.

It is important to state that I am not suggesting that sport management researchers have completely failed to engage with many of the issues touched upon in this chapter. Yet a look through the table of contents of the main journals in the subject area will clearly show that these are still very much in the minority. Good ethnographies are harder to find not only because of the reasons identified above, but also because of the challenges in gaining access to sporting organisations (see Trujillo, 2013).

Show me the money: the challenges of 'doing' ethnography

Jerry Maguire is a 1996 film about a sports agent, played by the Hollywood star Tom Cruise, nominated for a number of Academy awards. Given its visibility and widespread success it is perhaps one of the first things that people think of when asked what sport management might entail. Slack's (1996) call to move beyond researching the areas of physical education and collegiate sport has been answered and "the field is increasingly focused on themes that resonate with a commercial logic" (Ciomaga, 2013, p. 570). Whilst a certain degree of artistic licence is used when making films about professional sport, like *Jerry Maguire*, what cannot be disputed is that the increased commercialisation and commodification of sport has (re)shaped the field of sport management as we now know it.

Researchers using ethnographic methods each have their own tale to tell. As Atkinson (1990, p. 106) has noted, "thought of initially as a type of story, the journey of discovery and self-discovery/revelation constitutes an account of personal development". One of the strengths of ethnography is its potential to capture the finer details underlying the cultural context in which the research is located. It offers an opportunity to move beyond generalisations and focus on the specifics of time and place. The 'restrictive' shackles of some dominant theoretical approaches constrain, rather than cultivate a 'release' of, the sociological imagination (see Mills, 1970). Van Maanen (1988) argues the case for confessional tales in telling stories of the research experience. Such work develops the views of Mills (1970) who argued against adherence to any particular theoretical 'model' and urged researchers to work from, and reflect upon, their own role in the research process.

Ethnographers all share with each other the common problem of 'getting in' – gaining access to a particular setting or group of people. As Janesick (1994, p. 211) has noted "access and entry are sensitive components in qualitative research, and the researcher must establish trust, rapport, and authentic communication patterns with participants". The challenge of gaining access to a sports world that is increasingly commercialised and commodified represents a significant barrier to ethnographic research. Trujillo (2013) wrote about the challenges of gaining access to sporting organisations. Sporting organisations can be very insular so outsiders are treated with a mixture of suspicion and distrust. Some of the best work that has examined aspects of football management, for example, has been undertaken by individuals who have played the game at the professional level and are recognised and accepted as insiders in this notoriously closed subculture (e.g. Kelly, 2008).

Sands (2002) authored the first book to focus specifically on sport ethnography. In this work he noted the importance of sport as enormous business, part of the global economy, and an area ripe for employing ethnographic techniques. He also highlighted the importance of discarding the shackles of particular theoretical approaches and that in the business world (including the business of sport) the focus is all about results (Sands, 2002). I now briefly turn to the subject of reflexivity before outlining the promise of postmodern sport management.

Reflexivity and ethnographic research

Usher (1996) notes that "we all have an individual trajectory which shapes the research we do, the questions we ask and the way we do it" (p. 32). This directs the kind of reflexive questions that need to be asked but rarely are. Reflexivity is a form of intellectual autobiography whereby the researcher reflects in-depth on the whole research process, her/his own place within it, and critically analyses aspects of it. Given the acknowledged subjectivity of interpretive accounts, the authenticity of the research may be ascertained by readings of the autobiographical account of the research process (Humberstone, 1997).

Usher (1996) suggested that interpretations are always circular. This determination of meaning in the interaction of part and whole is called the hermeneutic circle of interpretation which, according to Usher (1996, p. 19), means that "knowledge formation is therefore conceived as circular, iterative, spiral" and not linear as portrayed within a positivist/empiricist epistemology. Gadamer (1975) characterised research within the hermeneutic circle as a "fusion of horizons". Horizon here refers to the standpoint or situatedness (in time, place, and culture). This fusion results from seeking knowledge while grounded in a perspective arising from one's positioning, a perspective that cannot be bracketed during the process of enquiry. The resulting fusion can be conceptualised as an enlargement of one's own horizons. This of course echoes the call for a greater recognition of the relationship between biography and history that Mills (1970) argued convincingly for many years ago.

Merlau-Ponty (1962, p. 356) noted that:

> I am not the outcome or the meeting point of numerous causal agencies which determine my bodily or psychological makeup. I cannot shut myself up in the realm of science. All my knowledge of the world, even my scientific knowledge, is gained from my own particular point of view.

Research is often an expression of personal interests and values and can be delineated as a 'creation' through representation. Hereby, what personal reflexivity draws attention to is that researchers have an autobiography, yet we are not always given an insight into that autobiography. What we can be sure of, for sport management is no different to other similar disciplines, is that many of the published studies will be based on convenience sampling and following an established protocol of data collection as established within disciplinary boundaries. Usher (1996, p. 38) argues that these are "socio-cultural products" which are part of the practice of writing and which have effects on both the form and outcome of research. What is also important is the way that we write of these experiences. Increasingly, work is now read in narrative terms, as 'tales of the field' (Van Maanen, 1988), and our ways of writing about the sports world have also changed considerably (Sparkes, 2002).

Some of the most interesting and insightful research into the governance of sport has applied ethnographic methods. The work of sociologists John Sugden and Alan Tomlinson (1998) is a good example here. Their research has been important in uncovering and explaining issues of corruption within the governance of elite sport. Numerato and Baglioni's (2012) work on sport governance in Italy and the Czech Republic offers an interesting insight into the 'dark side' of sport governance. The authors note that they were not always welcomed by the sporting organisations and that "we were occasionally referred to as spies, inspectors, controllers, or allies" (Numerato & Baglioni, 2012, p. 598). This evidences some of the challenges of undertaking such research within sporting organisations. It is also worth noting here that neither of the works I refer to above appeared in sport management journals so may not be as well known to researchers in this area. Some evidence of the more critical approach called for by scholars (e.g. Amis & Silk, 2005; Frisby, 2005) is evident within the edited collection of Nauright and Pope (2009) and shows how the field continues to develop and evolve. Ethnography offers fantastic potential to uncover more about areas of sport management that have up until now remained under-explored and outside of the core focus of the field.

Towards a postmodern sport management discipline

Richardson (1994, p. 516) highlights that it is important that we do not simply view writing as a "mopping up activity at the end" but acknowledge that writing is itself a way of knowing. Our findings are inscribed in the way we write about things and are not detached from the presentation of observations, reflections and interpretations (Atkinson, 1990). Van Maanen (1988) argued that we need more not fewer ways to tell of culture but there are still instances where scholars receive reviews of work submitted to management journals that question the absence of a hypothesis or the limited generalisability of the data. Good ethnography, of course, emerges through an inductive process and does not follow a 'traditional' deductive model as is the norm in work shaped by a more positivistic research philosophy. Richardson (1994) encouraged researchers to explore their own processes and preferences through writing and called for individual voices to be more fully present in the work. Eisner (1988, p. 18) noted how "we talk of our findings, implying that we discover the world rather than construct it". Such writing loses the personal self behind the voices and 'the author', 'the subject', or 'the researcher' is inscribed upon the text. These linguistic conventions are "rhetorical devices designed to persuade the reader that we, as individuals, have no signature to assign our work" (Eisner, 1988, p. 18).

A construction of the text, in this sense, gives the impression of a researcher who is concerned only with 'managing the data' and the reader is faced with what seems to be an 'author-evacuated text', where the author is everywhere, but nowhere (Geertz, 1988). Here the researcher should remain distant from his/her work – a translated teller of the tale, who remains away from the object of study (Woolgar, 1988). Realist tales are said to "swallow up the fieldworker" (Van Maanen, 2011, p. 47). This supposedly increases the 'objectivity' and 'validity' of accounts, demonstrating the perceived neutrality of both the researcher and the final text (Van Maanen, 1988, 2011). Realist tales are characterised by their claim to put over the point of view of the researched. Often this is attempted through closely edited quotations, whereby the aim is to convince the reader that the views put forward are those of the researched, not of the author.

Confessional tales would seem to have an important part to play in allowing the subjective experiences of the researcher into the sport management literature. In this sense, as I understand it, such accounts have a clear fit with postmodern approaches to research. Denzin (1994, p. 504) suggested that "the postmodern sensibility encourages writers to put themselves into their texts, to engage writing as a creative act of discovery and inquiry". Such an approach resonates with what Edwards, Gilbert and Skinner (2002) called for when arguing the case for developing theoretical frameworks in sport management (see also, Skinner & Edwards, 2005). Confessional tales are characterised by their highly personalised styles and their self-absorbed mandates. The writing of such tales is also useful to show how particular works come into being. Confessional tales differ most markedly from realist tales in the respect that an intimacy is established, and the development of a personal character is inscribed within the text. Confessional tales do not replace realist tales and more often than not they stand alongside them. Early career sport management researchers are more likely to be steered away from such an approach and encouraged to stay on safer ground. There is still a strong resistance in places to first person narratives and/or moving away from the dominant narratives that shape this particular field.

Postmodern thinking highlights that all studies take place within a particular social, historical and cultural framework (Real, 1998). Postmodernism in the wider sport literature has been utilised to highlight the place of multiple perspectives on contemporary issues (e.g. Fernandez-Balboa, 1997; Rail, 1998). Despite the contested nature and use of the term, this invisibility of the postmodern within sport management and marketing seems strange as marketing and consumption are positioned as central to the postmodern condition. Skinner and Edwards (2005) made a robust case for sport management researchers to engage with critical and postmodern approaches to examine their theoretical accomplishments, epistemological assumptions, and methodological procedures. Calls to engage with such questions have also been central to discussions of related subjects such as tourism and event management (e.g. Rojek, 2013; Tribe, 1997).

Concluding remarks

Ethnographic research in sport management can develop and extend the knowledge base within this field and challenge some of the dominant ideologies that have been in situ for some time now. Mills (1970) highlighted the primacy of the individual scholar but within all types of organisations the honours boards and executive positions are often implicitly linked to particular schools of social thought. Challenging established practices and hierarchies is no easy task and the gatekeepers that police these boundary lines may need some convincing that there are alternative ways of doing research.

Even when looking at seemingly closely related areas such as sport management and the sociology of sport, it is clear that there is only limited engagement between the two (Love & Andrew, 2012). In their application of social network analysis, the authors point to the importance of institutional affiliation as a factor in explaining some of the collaborations and publications across the disciplinary boundaries (Love & Andrew, 2012). Shilbury and Rentschler (2007) have commented on the exclusion of most sport management journals from the majority of rating systems and attribute this both to factors of youth and 'fit'. Sport management "does not fit neatly within the areas of management, marketing, sociology, economics or law" (Shilbury & Rentschler, 2007, p. 31) so this works against the development of the field. Yet in other ways we may also view the above as an opportunity and a chance to develop new boundaries and horizons.

Sport is now a large business and a key component of globalisation in a range of spheres. The continued growth of sport in a global perspective is evidenced by the number of academic texts focusing on the ways in which different sports and sports leagues are changing (e.g. Giulianotti & Robertson, 2009; Harris, 2010; Klein, 2006). In the core sport management literature we also see scholars in North America focusing more on the international profile of sport and the ways in which the sport business is a truly global industry. Some of the more recent sport management anthologies offer wide-ranging insights into the continued development of sport management as an area of academic study (e.g. Li, MacIntosh & Bravo, 2012; Nauright & Pope, 2009;

Pedersen & Thibault, 2014). As Skinner and Edwards (2005) have noted, sport management scholars occupy an excellent vantage point from which to engage with a range of people from different walks of life and are in a very good position to take up many of the challenges of postmodern critique. Further ethnographic research will surely help to uncover new and varied aspects of this rapidly changing landscape and allow us to better explore the many domains of sport management.

References

Amis, J., & Silk, M. (2005). Rupture: Promoting critical and innovative approaches to the study of sport management. *Journal of Sport Management, 19*(4), 355–366.

Anderson, R., Hughes, J., & Sharrock, W. (1985). *The sociology game.* Harlow: Longman.

Andrew, D., Pedersen, P., & McEvoy, C. (2011). *Research methods and design in sport management.* Champaign, IL: Human Kinetics.

Andrews, D., Mason, D., & Silk, M. (Eds.) (2005). *Qualitative methods in sports studies.* Oxford: Berg.

Atkinson, P. (1990). *The ethnographic imagination: Textual constructions of reality.* London: Routledge.

Berger, P., & Luckman, T. (1966). *The social construction of reality.* London: Penguin.

Ciomaga, B. (2013). Sport management: A bibliometric study on central themes and trends. *European Sport Management Quarterly, 13*(5), 557–578.

Denzin, N. (1994). The art and politics of interpretation. In N. Denzin & Y. Lincoln (Eds.), *Handbook of qualitative research* (pp. 500–515). Newbury Park, CA: Sage.

Downward, P. (2005). Critical (realist) reflections on policy and management research in sport, tourism and sports tourism. *European Sport Management Quarterly, 5*(3), 305–322.

Edwards, A., & Skinner, J. (2010). *Qualitative research in sport management.* Oxford: Butterworth Heinemann.

Edwards, A., Gilbert, K., & Skinner, J. (2002). *Extending the boundaries: Theoretical frameworks for research in sports management.* Altona: Common Ground Publishing.

Eisner, E. (1988). The primacy of experience and the politics of method. *Educational Researcher, 17*(5), 15–20.

Fernandez-Balboa, J.-M. (Ed.) (1997). *Critical postmodernism in human movement, physical education, and sport.* Albany, NY: State University of New York Press.

Frisby, W. (2005). The good, the bad, and the ugly: Critical sport management research. *Journal of Sport Management, 19*(1), 1–12.

Gadamer, H. (1975). *Truth and method.* London: Sheed and Ward.

Gadamer, H. (2006). Classical and philosophical hermeneutics. *Theory, Culture & Society, 23*(1), 29–56.

Geertz, C. (1988) *Works and lives: The anthropologist as author.* Cambridge: Polity.

Gibson, H. (1998). Sport tourism: A critical analysis of research. *Sport Management Review, 1*(1), 45–76.

Giulianotti, R., & Robertson, R. (2009). *Globalization and football.* London: Sage.

Gratton, C., & Jones, I. (2004). *Research methods for sport studies.* London: Routledge.

Hammersley, M., & Atkinson, P. (1995). *Ethnography: Principles in practice* (2nd edition). London: Routledge.

Harris, J. (2006). The science of research in sport and tourism: Some reflections on the promise of the sociological imagination. *Journal of Sport & Tourism, 11*(2), 153–171.

Harris, J. (2010). *Rugby Union and globalization: An odd-shaped world*. Basingstoke: Palgrave Macmillan.

Humberstone, B. (1997). Challenging dominant ideologies in the research process. In G. Clarke & B. Humberstone (Eds.), *Researching women and sport* (pp. 199–213). Basingstoke: Macmillan.

Janesick, V. (1994) The dance of qualitative research design: Metaphor, methodolatry and meaning. In N. Denzin & Y. Lincoln (Eds.), *Handbook of qualitative research* (pp. 209–219). Newbury Park, CA: Sage.

Kelly, S. (2008). Understanding the role of the football manager in Britain and Ireland: A Weberian approach. *European Sport Management Quarterly, 8*(4), 399–419.

Klein, A. (2006). *Growing the game: The globalization of Major League Baseball*. New Haven, CT: Yale University Press.

Kuhn, T. (1970). *The structure of scientific revolutions* (2nd edition). Chicago: University of Chicago Press. (First published in 1962.)

Levitt, P. (2012). What's wrong with migration scholarship? A critique and a way forward. *Identities: Global Studies in Culture and Power, 19*(4), 493–500.

Li, M., MacIntosh, E., & Bravo, G. (Eds.) (2012). *International sport management*. Champaign, IL: Human Kinetics.

Love, A., & Andrew, D. (2012). The intersection of sport management and sociology of sport research: A social network perspective. *Sport Management Review, 15,* 244–256.

Mahony, D. (2008). No one can whistle a symphony: Working together for sport management's future. *Journal of Sport Management, 22*(1), 1–10.

Merlau-Ponty, M. (1962). *The phenomenology of perception*. New York: Humanities Press.

Mills, C.W. (1970). *The sociological imagination*. Harmondsworth: Penguin Books. (First published in 1959.)

Nauright, J., & Pope, S. (Eds.) (2009). *The new sport management reader*. Morgantown, WV: Fitness Information Technology.

Numerato, D., & Baglioni, S. (2012). The dark side of social capital: An ethnography of sport governance. *International Review for the Sociology of Sport, 47*(5), 594–611.

Patton, M.Q. (1990). *Qualitative evaluation and research methods*. Newbury Park, CA: Sage.

Pedersen, P., & Thibault, L. (Eds.) (2014). *Contemporary sport management* (5th edition). Champaign, IL: Human Kinetics.

Pitts, B., & Stotlar, D. (2007). *Fundamentals of sport marketing* (3rd edition). Morgantown, WV: Fitness Information Technology.

Polanyi, M. (1958). *Personal knowledge: Toward a post-critical philosophy*. Chicago, IL: University of Chicago Press.

Quatman, C., & Chelladurai, P. (2008). The social construction of knowledge in the field of sport management: A social network perspective. *Journal of Sport Management, 22*(6), 651–676.

Rail, G. (Ed.) (1998). *Sport and postmodern times*. Albany, NY: State University of New York Press.

Real, M. (1998). MediaSport: Technology and the commodification of postmodern sport. In L. Wenner (Ed.), *MediaSport*. London: Routledge.

Richardson, L. (1994). Writing: A method of enquiry. In N. Denzin & Y. Lincoln (Eds.), *Handbook of qualitative research* (pp. 516–529). Newbury Park, CA: Sage.

Rojek, C. (2013). *Event power: How global events manage and manipulate*. London: Sage.

Sands, R. (2002). *Sport ethnography*. Champaign, IL: Human Kinetics.

Shilbury, D., & Rentschler, R. (2007). Assessing sport management journals: A multi-dimensional examination. *Sport Management Review, 10*, 31–44.

Skinner, J., & Edwards, A. (2005). Inventive pathways: Fresh visions of sport management research. *Journal of Sport Management, 19*(4), 404–421.

Slack, T. (1996). From the locker room to the board room: Changing the domain of sport management. *Journal of Sport Management, 10*(1), 97–105.

Sparkes, A. (2002). *Telling tales in sport and physical activity: A qualitative journey*. Champaign, IL: Human Kinetics.

Sugden, J., & Tomlinson, A. (1998). *FIFA and the contest for world football: Who rules the people's game?* Cambridge: Polity.

Thomas, J., & Nelson, J. (2001). *Research methods in physical activity* (4th edition). Champaign, IL: Human Kinetics.

Tribe, J. (1997). The indiscipline of tourism. *Annals of Tourism Research, 24*(3), 638–657.

Trujillo, N. (2013). Reflections on communication and sport: On ethnography and organizations. *Communication & Sport, 1*(1–2), 68–75.

Usher, R. (1996). Textuality and reflexivity in educational research. In D. Scott & R. Usher (Eds.), *Understanding educational research* (pp. 33–51). London: Routledge.

Van Maanen, J. (1988). *Tales of the field: On writing ethnography*. Chicago: University of Chicago Press.

Van Maanen, J. (2011). *Tales of the field: On writing ethnography* (2nd edition). Chicago: University of Chicago Press.

Veal, T. (1997). *Research methods for leisure and tourism* (2nd edition). London: Pitman.

Weed, M. (2003). Why the two won't tango: Explaining the lack of integrated policies for sport and tourism in the UK. *Journal of Sport Management, 17*(3), 258–283.

Weed, M. (2005). Sports tourism theory and method – Concepts, issues and epistemologies. *European Sport Management Quarterly, 5*(3), 229–242.

Woolgar, S. (1988). Reflexivity is the ethnographer of the text. In S. Woolgar (Ed.), *Knowledge and reflexivity: New frontiers in the sociology of knowledge* (pp. 14–34) London: Sage.

Zeigler, E. (2007). Sport management must show social concern as it develops tenable theory. *Journal of Sport Management, 21*(3), 297–318.

Index

Endnotes are indicated with 'n'. For example, 42n1 indicates endnote 1 on page 42.

Lightning Source UK Ltd.
Milton Keynes UK
UKHW02f1943220118
316640UK00002B/157/P